"The Higher Christian Life"

Sources for the Study of the Holiness, Pentecostal, and Keswick Movements

*A forty-eight-volume facsimile
series reprinting extremely
rare documents for the study of
nineteenth-century religious
and social history, the rise
of feminism, and the
history of the Pentecostal and
Charismatic movements*

Edited by

Donald W. Dayton
Northern Baptist Theological Seminary

Advisory Editors

D. William Faupel, *Asbury Theological Seminary*
Cecil M. Robeck, Jr., *Fuller Theological Seminary*
Gerald T. Sheppard, *Union Theological Seminary*

A GARLAND SERIES

ADONIRAM JUDSON GORDON
A BIOGRAPHY

Ernest B. Gordon

Garland Publishing, Inc.
New York & London
1984

For a complete list of the titles in this series
see the final pages of this volume.

Library of Congress Cataloging in Publication Data

Gordon, Ernest B.
ADONIRAM JUDSON GORDON.

("The Higher Christian life")
Reprint. Originally published: New York :
F.H. Revell, c1896.
1. Gordon, A. J. (Adoniram Judson), 1836–1895.
2. Baptists—United States—Clergy—Biography.
I. Title.   II. Series.
BX6495.G65G6   1984   286'.1'0924 [B]   84-18857
ISBN 0-8240-6421-6 (alk. paper)

The volumes in this series are printed on
acid-free, 250-year-life paper.

Printed in the United States of America

A. J. Gordon

ADONIRAM JUDSON GORDON

A Biography

WITH LETTERS AND ILLUSTRATIVE EXTRACTS
DRAWN FROM UNPUBLISHED OR UNCOL-
LECTED SERMONS AND ADDRESSES

BY HIS SON
ERNEST B. GORDON

FLEMING H. REVELL COMPANY
NEW YORK   CHICAGO   TORONTO
Publishers of Evangelical Literature

CONTENTS

ILLUSTRATIONS

But thou wouldst not alone
Be saved, my father, alone
Conquer and come to thy goal,
Leaving the rest in the wild.
We were weary, and we
Fearful, and we in our march
Fain to drop down and to die.
Still thou turnedst, and still
Gavest the weary thy hand.
If, in the paths of the world,
Stones may have wounded thy feet,
Toil or dejection have tried
Thy spirit, of that we saw
Nothing: to us thou wast still
Cheerful and helpful and firm.
Therefore to thee it was given
Many to save with thyself,
O faithful shepherd, to come
Bringing thy sheep in thy hand.

M. ARNOLD, *Rugby Chapel.*

CHAPTER I

A STUDY IN ORIGINS

New England, past and present—Dr. Gordon's ancestry—Early days—
Conversion—School life in New London

THE central portion of New Hampshire is a land of far
distances and blue outlines, of winding roads, upland
pastures, and sun-crowned hills. Dozens of lakes, small and
great, stretch their bared breasts to the July sun. Great tracts
of maple and birch blaze with a fire of scarlet, of orange, of
crimson, of yellow, in the shortening afternoons of October.
Threading its way like a stream of quicksilver from the high-
lands in the north through the smiling hill-country, the Pemigewasset carries seaward the contributions of unnumbered
mountain brooks. It is a land of idyllic beauty, with a charm
of its own, half indefinable—perhaps the result of the endlessly
new combinations of the simple elements of its landscape,
which no one who rides over its rough roads can fail to make.

A quiet country withal, quite unlike the rest of our great,
busy, commercial land. Life here is to the fevered and strenuous life of the cities below as the peaceful mountain pool is to
the mill-race' which drives ten thousand spindles. For great
changes indeed have come over the face of the land in the
course of a third of a century. Those subtle but omnipotent
economic forces which, apparently from sheer arbitrariness, destroy the patiently constructed foundations of generations of
industry, while rearing with superhuman energy new creations
elsewhere, have made themselves felt here. New England

farm life has gone down before the inordinate competition of the great West. Farms have become pasture, pasture has grown into wilderness, homesteads have disappeared. Those monuments of untiring energy, the endless stone walls, are themselves tumbling apart. Back roads are closed; the strange faces of Canadian habitants are more and more common. The old order is passing away. The most encouraging indications of a future in the general decadence are the attractive villas of Boston and New York, which are rising here and there in coigns of vantage wherever the outlook is unusually striking and beautiful.

And where are the old occupants of these farms? What has become of the children of these lovely hillsides? Not a city in the land but has representatives from their large families, not a State in the Union but has benefited by the reserve of granite energy which they have carried with them into the exacting life of the day. Grappling with other problems now, —of finance, of justice, of legislation,—they show the same indomitable spirit which solved the humbler though equally knotty problem of wringing sustenance for a dozen little ones from these boulder-strewn fields. Fifteen miles from the spot where this is written was born that imperial man with the mighty brow, under which glowed two coals for eyes—the great commoner, the expounder of the Constitution, Daniel Webster. Fifty-three miles away as the crow flies stands the little school-house on one of whose benches the name Horace Greeley, cut with school-boy's knife, is still to be seen. Looking off from my window, I can see on a distant hill the old white homestead of the Magouns, name distinguished in pulpit, in counting-house, in college chair. The remembrance of venerable Parson Morton, with his unfailing black gloves, is still fresh in the minds of the old people of the adjoining town. His son, whom they recall as a barefoot lad, has become a leading banker at the metropolis, a vice-president of the

United States, and much else.   At Hillsborough Bridge below was born the Nestor of American journalism, Charles A. Dana. Somewhat to the west is the old home of Austin Corbin, the wizard of speculative finance.   At a distance farther south stands the town where John P. Hale first saw daylight.   Of the others—the Miners, the Brewsters, the Wentworths, the Pillsburys, the Colbys—it is not necessary to speak.   They have been worthy children of the New Hampshire soil—strong, shrewd, hard-hitting, much-enduring men, very like the Scotch, also bred in rugged hills under a Calvinist régime, and vitalizing the British empire, world over, as these New Englanders have vitalized the great Republic.

The thoughtful American cannot but question whether, in the new homes of Kansas and Dakota, where the black loam of river-bottoms furnishes an easy livelihood, but where there can be two elements only, sky and prairie, in the background of his mental pictures, the transplanted New Englander will not lose something of the idealism and poetic sensitiveness which have been so finely blended with the more masterful elements of his character.   Still greater will be his misgivings as to the future of this people in the luxurious homes which they have made for themselves in every American city.   Plain living was the necessary condition of existence on these rocky hillsides.   High thinking was an almost equally necessary consequence of life in such lovely natural surroundings.   Can the stock retain its noble characteristics under the new conditions?

Concerning the more remote ancestry of the subject of this sketch little is known.   That the blood of the saint of Leyden, John Robinson, coursed in his veins is fairly well authenticated.   The Gordons themselves were perhaps the flotsam drifting to the American coast from the great wreck of their clan at Culloden.   Yet wheresoever they came from, they were a sturdy race with "the thews of Anakim," performing great feats with ax and plow.   The Puritan, steel before, was now thrice hardened by the pioneer experiences of wilderness life. Pushing up from Massachusetts, he cut his roads far up the mountain-sides, as if in scorn of rich intervales, cleared away the primeval forests, built his churches and schools, and took his properly accredited place on the map of the world like a straightforward, matter-of-fact man.

Old Levi Robinson, Dr. Gordon's great-grandfather, was a man of this rugged type. When hostilities with the mother-country became imminent, he shouldered his flint-lock, and tramped through wood and over stream, one hundred miles to Boston. Arriving too late to take part in the engagement at Bunker Hill, he served through the remainder of the campaign with Washington. A stout-hearted man who believed what he believed, he first in the region saw the cogency of the Baptist position, and on sight accepted it, spite of the opposition of standing order, spite of the odor of fanaticism popularly supposed to cling about Anabaptist notions. Some there are even now in his native town who remember the old man, in his powdered wig and with a huge silver-topped stick, walking Sunday mornings seven miles or more to the distant church of his persuasion.

What traditions of piety there were in this Puritan family! We recall especially one old grandmother, hid away on a back farm with but two books, the Bible and Bunyan, who tended and nurtured a spiritual life fairly efflorescent in its devotion, its sweetness, its humility. In extreme age interest in the Lord's work never dimmed. Often did her grandson, coming back to the old home in the summer-time, marvel at the depth, the richness, the fulness of this hidden saint life. Often did he wonder that, in her obscurity, she should show such an intelligent perception of the truth. A prayerful life is as a corn of wheat in the ground—sure to bring forth fruit in the years to come. Who shall say how much the flower of a later noble and saintly career owed to this hidden, unobserved, unobtrusive life, rooted and grounded in God?

John Calvin Gordon, the father, was a man in whose character our own easy-going age would doubtless find much
amusement.   To the average jellyfish, convinced of the perfection and completeness of the invertebrate state, a back-
boned creature must seem little short of a freak.   A man to
whom the doctrine of God's sovereignty was even more important than a five-per-cent. change in the newest tariff, would
be equally curious and unaccountable nowadays.   Yet this
was such a one, cast in the mould of earlier days, whose whole
life was bound up in the " five points " of the Genevan system,
whom the fire-cry of "dogma" never alarmed, whose little
property was spent in building churches and providing for the
religious instruction of his generation.   It was a period of doctrinal agitation on a subject somewhat obsolete in these days
of exegesis—a subject which, as Froude says, has ever divided
men who tamper with it, and will to the end.   The problems
of "fixed fate, free will, foreknowledge absolute," were then
the standards round which battles were waged.   The disagreement resulting from these discussions led to division and the
formation from the parent organization of a new body, the
Free Baptists.

  Deacon Gordon went with the hyper-Calvinists.   To him
the very principle and foundation of things was involved.   He
often declared humorously that he could tell an Arminian
farmer by a glance at his woodpile, so disorderly and so irregular were the adherents of a disorderly and irregular system apt
to be.   Yet we would not give the impression that here was a
wrangling, disputatious schoolman to whom controversy was
the breath of the nostril and doctrinal disagreement meat and
drink.   On the contrary, few men have left behind them such
traditions of piety and devotion.   The morning exercises of
the family were held in a corner room of the old homestead,
close to the cross-roads, where the villagers were constantly
passing.   The recollection of Deacon Gordon's prayers, wafted

out of the open windows into the June air, are still present in the minds of the older people, as the aroma of long-preserved sandalwood. Nor did insistence on tenet interfere with the weightier matters of practical Christianity. Rectitude, charity, self-denying effort for the advancement of the kingdom, won for the rigid Calvinist the affection of the whole region. Strength and sweetness were here blended as in the greatest of New England Calvinists, Jonathan Edwards. And the sweetness was as different from the sweetness of our modern saccharine, humanitarian theology, as the honey of Hybla is from the candy of the little corner store.

And of the mother how shall we adequately speak? Genius for goodness, as pronounced in Dr. Gordon's character as ever the genius for music or mechanics in any, presupposes a good mother. Here was a woman like Susannah Wesley, self-effacing in her unselfishness, quaintly unconscious of her own surpassing goodness, and endowed with minor excellences, discernible daily in the son's life. Those who were present at her funeral will not soon forget the tribute which he paid to the still face wrapped in its death-sleep. How full of love, of gratitude, of longing reminiscence! What references to her laborious life, to the unrecorded sacrifices, to the solicitous care with which she brought up her twelve children, to the constant ministry among the sick and needy of her village; for if there was want of watcher or nurse she was ever ready, spite of her large family, to spend the night away from home, ever back at her work in the early morning. At the risk of anticipating, we cannot refrain from reproducing here a letter written immediately after the son, in anguish of spirit, had laid the mother away. It is a breath from the flood-tide of blessed memories which death alone awakes, revives, gathers up. He walks back from the grave dug in a hillside white with February drifts to the old home. One hope alone can in any degree assuage the sorrow; and so he takes up the New Testament, and for two days reads and ponders on every passage referring to the resurrection.

"I have spent two days here," so the letter goes, "much of the time alone in the dear home where mother spent her last years. So far from seeming lonely, I should be glad to spend days there where everything reminds us of the beloved one. I have many times gone into her vacant bedroom and knelt where she so often bowed and prayed for her children. Her family was her parish; to them she ministered, and for them she ceased not to pray until the end. 'Father, I pray for those that thou hast given me, that they may be with me where I am, and behold my glory.' All my sorrow for her has been turned into unspeakable joy in view of the rest into which she has entered."

It was into this home with its long heritage of Christian living that a son was born on the 19th of April, 1836. A new era was opening for American Christianity, a new impulse was throbbing with springtime energy in its veins. The greatest of modern missionaries had gone forth, in the spirit of Boniface, to grapple with the forces of heathenism in their very stronghold. And now the story of the heroic career in Burmah had reached the homes of America. In city, in hamlet, in distant farm, wherever devout hearts were praying for the spread of Christ's kingdom, the history of hardship and suffering and faithful testimony was being rehearsed. The tale of the agony of Oung-Pen-La wrung the heart of the New Hampshire villager, and in his admiration he determined to name his child after the apostle, Adoniram Judson. The interval of keynote 'twixt the name of John Calvin Gordon and that of his little son marks in a significant way the transition in American Christianity from its speculative to its practical and missionary phase. To the new generation Christianity was to be not so much a bunch of theories for debate and discussion as a universal economy, a régime whose sway was to extend over all peoples. Few men entered more earnestly, though in a humble way, into the robust life of Calvinistic Christianity than the father. Few men have, under God, been more active and helpful in emphasizing the new purposes and revived mission of the Christian church of our century than the son.

Calvin Gordon was the owner of a woolen-mill. Nowadays, in the era of capitalism, such a statement would imply the possession of at least considerable wealth. Not so then. Mills were small, and run usually by the owner himself with the help of his family. The type is now obsolete. The all-absorbing system of centralized production, with its proletariat work-people, its immeasurable capital, its dreary history of strike and lockout, has crushed the little mill as completely as the Dakota wheat-field has crowded out the New England farm. The stream which supplied power to the Gordon mill and to five others now runs untroubled through the alders. It has become the sole property of a wealthy manufacturer, who uses it for trout much as the patricians of old Rome used the lakes of Campania for carp and barbel. The plain, brave life of New England has vanished; the old economy, with its relatively meager productivity, but its incomparably better distribution of wealth, is a thing of the past. The coming socialistic synthesis, if it be no mirage, is at best far, far distant. And, meantime, suffering, want, class hatred, economic chaos!

We can easily imagine what life in such a diminutive factory would be. Duties were of course multifarious. To bargain with the farmer at the door, who came to exchange his year's shearing for substantial, long-wearing cloth; to follow the shuttle back and forth in its magical course; to attend to any stoppage in the water-wheels; to repair breaks in machinery; to keep the accounts in the little closet office—doubtless the days were full enough. Commission-agent, machinist, accountant, mill-hand—all functions were centralized in one man. Work then was an education; it is now a form of slavery. Then the diversity of labor developed an ingenuity which has made the New England name proverbial; now the machine-like task, pursued ten hours daily throughout a lifetime, of throwing a hand this way or bending the body the other, ends usually in mental stupefaction and moral inertia. Work in the fields, too, was in the spring season often substituted for the labors of the mill. Doubtless the lad eagerly left his ordinary task of washing greasy wools in the big iron kettle—a vessel that in after-years was the treasured receptacle for flowers on the lawn of his summer home—for the more welcome labor of following the plow through the fresh-turned sod under the skies of May. It was in these years too, doubtless, so healthfully varied, so full of opportunity for the observant mind, that the gift of comparison and illustration from the common things of life was developed—a gift which made the discourses of later years as instinct with naturalness and vitality as the parables of the synoptists themselves.

So passed the early years in a quiet village lying in the trough of the billowy New Hampshire hills, in a home of exceptional piety, amid such surroundings as could hardly fail to nurture a wholesome, high-souled, nature-loving character. When the boy reached his fifteenth year a great change passed across his inner life. Hitherto a thoughtless, somewhat indifferent, unresponsive lad, he now became intent on new things. New vistas opened out; a new seriousness sobered him; a new thoughtfulness was turning his attention to a larger life than that which had to do with fuller's tub and farmer's team. The weightier interests of the spiritual life began to absorb his thoughts. First came the struggle, the wrestling as at Peniel till the gray dawn. The conviction of sin was intense, unendurable. A realization of the corruption of the human heart, a vision of the perfect God, high and lifted up—to what conclusion could these lead save that of unqualified unworthiness, of utter helplessness? The conflict of soul darkened and

intensified.   A whole night was finally spent in such anguish
of spirit that the father was obliged to sit with him till day-
break.   Sorrow endureth for the night, but joy cometh in the
morning.   Calm as the sunshine which flooded the hills the
next day was that boy spirit which had found peace with God
through our Lord Jesus Christ.

On a lovely Sabbath in June he witnessed, with his two
sisters, a good confession, going down with them in mystic
death into the waters of the old mill-stream, which enlarges
itself into a bit of a lake above his home.   His conversion was
a new impulse in all directions.   Books had been an aversion,
study an almost penal discipline.   With what avidity did he
now go back to these distasteful tasks !   For did they not constitute the necessary preparation for a future, the anticipation
and hope of which he was now treasuring in his heart?

This hope and purpose he did not long keep to himself.
Shortly after his sixteenth year had opened he confessed before
the church hi ; determination to enter the ministry.   One who
was present has described the scene to the writer.   A warm
evening in late spring; the sounds of the wakeful world of the
lower creation coming in the open doors and windows; a shy,
awkward boy, yet with a light on his face, announcing, with
much difficulty and stumbling, his purpose to devote his life
and best powers to his Saviour's work.   " Judson is a good
boy, and would make a good minister if only he had *energy*,"
remarked one old deacon to the writer's informant.   Not the
first person, forsooth, to mistake noisiness for force, and, conversely, to disregard the latent power which lies hid in the
quietest mill-pond.

This decision made, the first step to be taken was preparation for college.   There was a fitting-school in the village, but
its connection was with the new and lax seceding party.   The
boy was sent, therefore, by his stanchly Calvinist father to a
trustworthy denominational school at New London, N. H.   In

a suit of clothes made by his mother's hands from cloth spun in the old mill, (how reverently in after-years did he speak of these ministrations!) he started from home. A long walk truly, thirty-four miles, when one is baggage train as well as infantry. Yet doubtless the bag in which he carried his effects was not heavily freighted—a change of clothing, a Virgil, and an algebra constituting a not unsupposable inventory of its contents. The country, too, through which he trudged is peculiarly beautiful, past Cardigan and Ragged mountains, round the base of Kearsarge and by Sunapee Lake, into the plain in which the school town is situated.

Of his life in New London there is very slight record. Foundations, though more essential than finials, are usually hid in the earth and forgotten. Up to this time there had been little preliminary instruction. The classes, therefore, were much in advance of the new-comer. But, though the cabbage outstrips the oak in the first months of spring, final results are never uncertain. The difficulties were further complicated by that problem of self-support which so often meets and vexes students in American schools. Odd moments, the small change of leisure, were all carefully economized against the day when term-bills should come due. On one occasion young Gordon took the contract of painting the exterior of the main school building, a structure four stories in height. The whole spring recess was spent in work on corner boards and cases and window-sashes. His room-mate, a young man with better financial backing, generously assisted in the task without pecuniary return. This copartnership, begun on high ladders with paint-pots and brushes, was resumed in a very different sphere later on. The two painters became respectively executive chairman and corresponding secretary of the missionary society of the Baptist denomination in America, and shoulder to shoulder labored for the evangelization of the world.

We have before us a small bundle of themes or essays in

fine, copperplate handwriting, much faded now, which were written in these school-boy days. Among them is the text of an address before the literary association of the school, which bore the pretentiously classical name of "The Euphemian Society." It is full of references to the duties of the hour in the moral-political crisis which the slavery agitation had brought on. There is much attempt at *bravura*, and a turgid style which contrasts strangely with the calm, unruffled, lake-like lucidity of later years. On the other hand, we find in these years the stagings going up which were to support the delicate, aërial, and yet geometrically accurate exegesis which constituted so great a charm in Dr. Gordon's writings and addresses. In anticipation of future needs and interests, Greek became immediately the subject of special study. His old teacher writes:

"Greek he began with me. He liked the language, and pursued it with a genuine zest. He seemed to realize that it was the tongue specially prepared by God as the depository of his highest spiritual revelations. With this language he was specially to deal in all his future study and work. Hence, thoughtful and high-purposed as he was, he sought to know it. He studied his long and tedious lessons in the Greek paradigms as though in pursuit of game which he was bound to round up. In later years, when I have noted in his writings specially fine and discriminating renderings of difficult texts in the New Testament, I have thought I could detect an apt and skilful use of the principles of the Greek language first learned in New London."

CHAPTER II

At Brown University—Conditions of college life in 1860—Incidents

IN the summer of '56 the last term of preparatory-school life closed, and in the fall of the same year Gordon was matriculated at Brown University. At one time he had been drawn to Dartmouth College, the noble and richly historic university of his native State; but various considerations led him to decide finally for the denominational school at Providence. Not the least important of these was the prestige of the great president, the Arnold of America, Francis Wayland, who had just closed his career as an educationalist, but whose fame and the immediate influence of whose multifarious labors were still strongly felt in the Christian circles of New England. With consummate ability and sagacity he had anticipated the whole course of university reform which is fast making of American colleges the most elastic, effective, comprehensive, and widely influential educational agencies in the world. In his own sensible and independent way he had opened evening lectures in practical subjects for the artisan class. Long before the days of university extension hundreds of Providence jewelers entered these courses in metallurgy, chemistry, and kindred subjects. It was he too who first emancipated the American college from the immemorial trivium of Greek, Latin, and mathematics. True, the curriculum was meager enough, even after the enrichment in courses which he brought about, if one compares it with the vast *à la carte* for '96 of Johns Hopkins or of the University of Chicago. Yet there were compensations which amply made up for any apparent poverty in instruction. Emphasis was laid on training and discipline. Power of assimilation rather than amount and variety of acquisition constituted the end of education. The claims of character, too, were considered, as well as those of scholarship.

The output of the New England college before the present era of expansion and specialization was, therefore, wonderfully true, tempered, and substantial. It was hand-made, of selected raw material, with the personal touch of such masters as Wayland, Mark Hopkins, and Timothy Dwight ineffaceably inwrought. These distinctive qualities, this peculiar timbre, which can be imparted only by human contacts, is more rare as universities become assimilated to the wholesale, factory tone of our civilization. The successful president now is the one who secures the most numerous legacies, the most sumptuous dormitories for his college. He no longer draws and moulds and shapes young men. He no longer visits and counsels and, if need be, prays with them. He has not the sense of accountability which made the great president of Brown say, quoting Arnold, that if he could ever receive a fresh boy from his father without emotion he would think it high time to be off. He is now a mere executive.

And just as at that time there was no middle wall of partition 'twixt student and authorities, so there had not then arisen the minor distinctions of caste based upon wealth which now divide student from student. The children of Midas had not then built unto themselves stately and luxurious dwellings in the precincts of intellectualism. Beck Hall and Vanderbilt were undreamed of. Iron weighed more than gold. The youths in tennis flannels who gather and smoke hookahs in these gorgeous dormitories would have received little recognition among the sturdy, self-supporting, hard-battling fellows from the back farms. Poverty was the rule, affluence was the exception—a condition of things largely reversed in our Eastern universities. At Brown the catalogue summary of necessary expenses for 1856 foots up to the amusingly insignificant sum of sixty-seven dollars. This covered tuition, room-rent, lights, fuel, and minor expenses. The entire charges for a collegiate year, therefore, amounted to somewhat less than one fifth the present-day room-rent of a single student in one of the gilded *fin-de-siècle* palaces of Yale or Harvard. Board, of course, was not included in this estimate. It averaged for the poorer student something under two dollars a week. Students frequently boarded themselves, living, as did a contemporary of Gordon's at college who became distinguished later, upon the extremely meager sum of seventy-five cents weekly. As with Scotch students, oatmeal was in this instance a staple in the dietary. This inconsiderable pecuniary outlay enabled hundreds of young men who became afterward exceedingly useful in all walks of life to gain an education from which nowadays they would be debarred as by an impassable wall.

At best, even with these favoring circumstances, it was a hard struggle for one student in the late fifties. Assistance from home he could hardly look for. Church friends in Providence helped much; yet at times the exchequer verged perilously upon bankruptcy. On one occasion, when it seemed hardly possible to continue for want of money, Gordon started down Westminster Street in an aimless state of dejection. A sudden shower drove him into a porch. Somewhat later a ragged and wayworn negro hurried under the same cover, and, seeing the kindly student face, thought it an opportune time to beg. He laid his whole pitiable case, with its undoubted fringe of exaggeration and extended commentary, before his fellow-refugee. The latter, at the time as impecunious as Walter the Penniless himself, was of course unable to respond.

He explained his own plight, answering the other's fiction with a detailed recital of his own difficulties. The new acquaintance listened with interest, and finally drew from his pocket a nickel, which he handed his anticipated benefactor with the remark that, after all, he thought himself better off than a struggling student.

Gordon was twenty years old when he entered upon his college course. As the average age was several years less, there was much that was boyish in the character of the lower classmen. The traditions of practical joking, now happily almost wholly faded out of university life, traditions surviving, perhaps, from the wandering student life of the middle ages with the tenacity of nursery rhymes, flourished with vigor. There were night-gown parades on hot summer evenings. There were burials of hated text-books in the blue waters of the Narragansett, when brass bands played solemn dirges and orators delivered Latin valedictories. There was much obnoxious hazing of freshmen. Boys in the full consciousness of second-year rank are apt to take special delight in humiliating those below them; it seems in some way to accentuate their recent promotion. In the present case their ardor was doubly inflamed by the fact that the subject to be treated was a student for the ministry, and possessed, therefore, presumably, with a wholesome aversion to rowdyism and nicotine.

When a freshman of but a few weeks' standing, Gordon was visited in his room, "smoked out," and imperiously ordered by his visitors to mount the table and preach a sermon. The new-comer's resources in this line had not been suspected. With admirable appositeness he chose as his text, "A certain man went down from Jerusalem to Jericho, and fell among thieves." Never was more pointed discourse delivered. Never was application of subject-matter to immediate circumstances made more mercilessly. The listeners, taking umbrage, rushed like beasts of Ephesus at the speaker, upset the table, and would have treated him hardly indeed if his Christianity had not passed forthwith from its didactic to its muscular phase, with excellent results. He sprang at the ring-leader, tore his coat in halves, and, with the efficient coöperation of John Hay,* who just then appeared on the scene, routed the intruders from the premises.

The years in Brown were years of diligent application, of recognizable progress. In pure scholarship Gordon took but medium rank. The inadequacy of his "fit" was as ball and chain to the runner's ankle. Yet his native gifts were acknowledged by all. His reading at this time was extensive and within certain limits multifarious in character. We have before us a copy of Todd's "Index Rerum" close packed with quotations, indicating, as by graduated scale, the quantity of illustration and reference which was gathering for use in later years like water in a mountain pool. Carlyle, as was fitting in those days, occupies a prominent place in its pages. Byron, Coleridge, Mrs. Browning, Ruskin, Archbishop Leighton, Bunsen, Edward Irving, Pascal, Richter, St. Augustine, John Foster, and Tholuck are names that recur again and again. A love for devotional reading was early developed. Thomas Fuller's writings and the quaint "Religio Medici" of Sir Thomas Browne were favorites with the meditative young student. In his regular work, special aptitude in composition was noticeable. A warm interest in the classics, too, could not be wanting in those fortunate enough to read the Greek tragedies with Professor Harkness, and the Satires and Epodes of Horace with John L. Lincoln. The accurate scholarship, the delicate humor, the fine, discriminating literary sense of the latter made him for two generations the especial favorite of young men. To hear his " Bene," " Optime," after an unusually felicitous translation was suffi-

* Later known as the private secretary and biographer of President Lincoln.

cient reward for hours of night study. Here was no "gerund-grinder," but one to whom Latin was literature and the classics "humanities." To please "Johnny Link," as he was endearingly called, was an indirect way, therefore, of obtaining recognition for one's own scholarship and taste, inasmuch as that alone gratified him which was refined, subtle, delicately flavored. During Gordon's second year a prize was offered for the best Latin essay. One of his classmates, who had unjustly, though good-naturedly, animadverted upon his diligence as a student, announced with boyish loquacity and with much confidence his determination to capture the prize. Gordon with characteristic reticence, coupled with a humorous resolve to defeat his confident friend, went to work, wrote out his theme, and passed it in to the committee. In due time it was returned with the announcement of his success. He had appealed to Professor Lincoln's inordinate love of Horace by importing into his paper as many Horatian expressions and turns of thought as he could. The flavor of the Odes, as of old Chianti, pleased the professor's palate. His vote was cast decisively for the essayist who shared his appreciation for the *vers de société* of old Rome.

The severest test of character is that which considers the every-day life, which scrutinizes those close personal relations involved in the occupancy of a common room and the daily use of the same student-lamp. How well Gordon stood this test the following communication will show. The copartners on the long ladders at New London had entered Brown the same year. Throughout the college course they lived together in the third story of old University Hall, the windows of which look out over the elms of the campus upon the city and bay and westering sun below. So long an association is fruitful in incident. Many are the stories of those days which have come down to us illustrating the humor, the geniality, the bonhomie of Gordon's character. These traits were in later years, at least to outsiders, obscured by the gravity and preoccupation which the stress of great responsibilities occasioned. In younger days they had full rein. In company he was the first called upon to sing. The dialogues and comedies which he collaborated with his room-mate became a tradition of the preparatory school. There is one amusing story of these days—a story we should hardly venture to introduce if we had not heard it from the victim of its point himself— which reminds one of a well-known incident connected with the Methodist leaders of the last century. On one occasion, when Wesley and Whitefield were on their evangelistic circuits together, they retired for the night to a single room. Whitefield, being very weary, tumbled into bed with scarce a prayer. Wesley, equally tired, insisted on longer devotions, but fell asleep on his knees, much to the amusement of Whitefield, whom he had chided for negligence. The latter made haste to relieve as far as possible Wesley's mortification by summarily waking him.

In the present instance no such mercy was shown. Gordon's room-mate, impulsive and full of enthusiasm for the Lord's work, was somewhat apt to question the interest of his undemonstrative friend along these lines. Being at one time greatly impressed with the need of a religious awakening in college, he went around inviting students to his room for concerted prayer. On the evening assigned for the meeting a dozen or more students met together. All were bent in earnest supplication. Some eight or nine had taken part, and the time had come for the organizer of the meeting himself to pray. After a long pause, it was perceived, to the great enjoyment of all, that he had dropped asleep. As if by one impulse, the rest arose and filed out of the room. Gordon himself remained, put out the lights, went to bed, and slept soundly until, several hours later, the chill morning air had brought his room-mate to a full consciousness of the situation.

It is in these terms, then, that this companion of the long student years characterizes his old friend:

"I wish to bear testimony to the majestic character and exalted worth and influence of my classmate and lifelong friend, Dr. Gordon. For six years in academy and college— a portion of that time as room-mates—we lived in relations of tenderest intimacy. The same serenity of disposition, the same fine equipoise that has marked his riper years was characteristic of his youth. I cannot recall, during all this period of uninterrupted intercourse, a single instance of petulance or irritation. I cannot remember a single utterance from his lips that he might have wished unspoken. His religious life was steadfast, cheerful, and uniform, free from short-lived raptures on the one hand, and seasons of lukewarmness on the other. The unfaltering purpose of declaring the gospel of the grace of God, with which his own life had been enriched, dominated him completely, and from this he never, amid the ambitions and temptations of college life, for one instant swerved. He was a moral and spiritual leader in college, apparently without the slightest thought of being such, and without any special effort on his part, just as he has since been in the broader sphere of life. He realized more perfectly than any man I now recall the high ideal of a deep, genuine, uncompromising piety, without the least trace of austerity or sanctimoniousness or asceticism. There was in him a delightful vein of humor, always, however, so graciously tempered that it never descended, as is frequently the case, to the level of coarseness or levity, and was never suffered to become an occasion of wounding the feelings of the most sensitive. He was withal so natural, so consistent, so magnanimous, so charitable, that he won the love and admiration of all; yes, even of those who were utterly ignorant of or indifferent to the heavenly grace that dwelt so richly in him."

It was in these years that a new and important tributary entered Gordon's life. We begin to find a greater volume of correspondence—letters, too, which reveal more precisely the interior man. It is as if, after a long, blank interim, a number of photographs had been taken in rapid succession, portraying all the finer lines of the heart's expression. Acquaintance had been formed with the young woman who became in later years his wife and the efficient helpmate in all his enterprises. A quarter-century after his happy college years had closed, he returned to Providence, a trustee now of the university, and went up into the old room which he had occupied in the fifties. Sitting there with all the memories of the past flooding his mind, he wrote back to Boston this noble letter to her whom he always called the most valued treasure which he carried away from the university town:

> " No. 44 University Hall,
> " Brown University, Providence, R. I.,
> " June 21, 1860.
> [Actual date, June, 1882.]

" *Miss Maria T. Hale.*

" DEAR FRIEND: I am sitting in my room for a few moments after the commencement dinner meditating. I just saw you come down Prospect Street and turn down College Street, and I almost thought you cast a glance upward to my window, as if to say, . . . 'I would not object to your joining me in a walk.' Excuse my presumption in suggesting such an idea, but you know that I have now and then run down to join you, and you never were greatly opposed to my doing so. Well, I have just finished my studies in this honored university, and from my lofty lookout in this old ante-Revolutionary building I am gazing into the future and dreaming of what it shall be. I know you will pardon me for repeating my dream, since it is only a dream. It seemed to me that twenty-two years had passed, and the pale-faced, slender student had become a portly man of forty-six. He had become, moreover, a minister of a large city parish with a wide field and great responsibilities. Through the dim mists of futurity I see his house and his family. I count his children—five ruddy and splendid children; and a shadow in which the outlines of two others are faintly descried sleeping as though they were and yet were not. And there is the fair vision of the wife; I cannot name her here, but she looks strangely like one whom I just saw passing. I dream that people say of her that she is wonderfully efficient, and that a large share of her husband's success is due to her; that she has inspired him, who used to be rather slow and backward, with much of her energy and enthusiasm. They say, indeed, that, between his hold and her push, the result is a pretty strong team; that they are the center of no mean circle of activities. And I dream that she sometimes interprets his natural reserve and stolidity and abstractedness as indifference, and she says that he doesn't appreciate her. Then his heart opens, and he says, 'Nay; never man had such a helpmeet, and if she bears many burdens and does much hard work for him, he thanks her in his heart, and prays that the Lord may spare her for many years to walk by his side.' And the thought became so emphatic and the emotions so strong that he repeated the last words aloud—*walk by his side*—and that woke him up. Yes; here I am in the window of 44, looking down College Street, and you are just coming back with a book in your hand, from the Athenæum, I suppose. And so I have written it all out. When will you take another of those moonlight walks out toward the Red Bridge and round by the Friends' College? Excuse my boldness; for I remember that, though you are not shy, you are often a little offish—well, no matter; when shall we have the walk? And do so arrange it, if we go, that your venerable father shall not stand at the door to welcome you in and to wave me off with that sweeping gesture. But then I do not mean anything or much; that is, I don't mean to mean more than you would have me mean, since you have said that we must be no more than friends. So good-by from

"Your esteemed friend,

"A. J. GORDON."

CHAPTER III

THE YOUNG MINISTER

Seminary life at Newton — Influence of Dr. Hackett — Pastor of the
    Jamaica Plain Church — Letters — Called to Clarendon Street —
    Criticism of Robertson on baptism — The Church Unity Society
    examined

THE time for special preparation for life-work had now
    arrived. In 1860 Gordon entered the theological school
at Newton. Located on a commanding hilltop, the institution
buildings afforded one a view of real beauty. An undulating
country of meadow and pasture, not yet built over with the
suburban villas of Boston merchants, stretched in all directions. The faint blue top of Monadnock could be descried in
the north, while the flashing dome of the state-house sent its
reflection into the west of summer afternoons.

Contiguity to Boston brought the new-comer into new
climates of opinion. Speculation and the standing discussions
of New England were in the sixties, however, brushed aside
by portentous public events. The nation was entering into
the valley of darkness. The remission of sin which it had
hoped to find in interminable compromises was to come now
in the blood of a thousand battles. Walking into Boston
to browse among the old book-stores of Cornhill, Gordon is
attracted by a vast crowd about the entrances to Tremont
Temple. He asks the cause of the gathering, and is told that
they are mobbing Phillips within. At another time he goes
in to see the immense night parade organized during the first

Lincoln campaign. As he stands at the gates of the Common, an unending stream of torches pours past him over the historic slopes. He can think only of the vast musterings in Milton. We find him eagerly reading Gasparin's new book, " The Struggle of Christianity with Slavery," and later, with every one else in the North, the second series of the " Bigelow Papers." The martyrdom of John Brown sets his correspondence fairly ablaze. This, after all, is not strange ; for he had been bred in the strictest sect of the abolitionists, his father of the woolen-mill being an antislavery debater and lecturer in the local lyceums of New Hampshire ; while the Providence home, whither most of his letters are directed, had from early days been visited by Garrison and his confrères. As the gloomy tragedy deepened, he was led to consider personal accountability in the crisis. Almost all of his male relatives were at the front, and he himself seriously meditated joining a New Hampshire regiment. But the family investment had been placed in his education, and the family verdict decided finally against the project.

Of the new surroundings, with their somewhat subdued atmosphere, he speaks half jocularly as follows :

" Newton is such a contrast to college. I am almost lost when I go into recitations and find such stillness and decorum. I have never in my life longed so much for some genuine outburst of fun, and I am really afraid that in an unguarded moment I shall break over all the proprieties and disturb the still air with the tones of some jolly college psalm. Yet I cannot but rejoice in the quiet of the place and in the advantages for study which it affords."

The special advantages to which he refers were larger liberty in the use of time, enabling him to rummage about in libraries, and the companionship and direction of the great master, Dr. Hackett, in his favorite study, New Testament exegesis. We find him more deeply immersed than ever in

hymnology, devotional literature, and the Fathers. Krumma-
cher, "The Hymns of the Ages," and À Kempis fed his spiritual
life.   Patristic literature he searched to find, not buttresses for
ecclesiastical pretension, but fellowship in a common love
and service.

"I have been reading," he says, "with a delight which is
to me of the very highest kind, the writings of the old Fathers.
Their quaintness is only equaled by their sweetness.   I have
perhaps a peculiar taste in this respect, and were I to buy all
my favorite books, I am sure my library would be of quite
an antique cast.   St. Augustine's ' Confessions ' afford delinea-
tions of almost seraphic raptures.   They give one an idea of
what Christianity is able to impart to him who is willing to
bear its sternest self-denials. . . . I feel, with him, what we
most of all need is the power to commune with God.   I know
of no greater attainment than the ability to hold unbroken
communion with the Saviour, closing up those avenues through
which sinful thoughts and vain desires steal in, and, as À
Kempis says, making of the soul a tabernacle with but one
window, and that for Christ."

Of those other Fathers, the Fathers of Reformed Christianity,
he made fast friends.   Rutherford's " Letters " were discovered
in an old issue of 1826, uncut and thick with dust.   Its jewels of meditation and ecstasy were gathered with eager hands.
This volume held him throughout life with the charm of an
abiding fascination.   Reference is made again and again, in
his Newton letters, to "sweet Rutherford."   And with these
references, in a contrast which is almost grotesque in its extreme remove, are coupled appreciative allusions to contemporary humorists :

"I wish Artemus Ward would bring out something new.
What should we do without those benefactors of the human
race, the humorists?   Wouldn't society stagnate?   Wouldn't
sanctimoniousness become soon the presiding genius where

now only a decent gravity and a moderate decorum reign? I see an advantage in trying to weave a little of this element into the texture of my clerical web that is now making."

The influence of the great teacher, Hackett, that extraordinarily erudite rabbi, with his little, shrunk frame, mobile face, and spectacled eyes, was the most important of those years. With him were made those laboratory studies in Greek, as exacting and as scientific as if the two were scrutinizing a tissue or a cell with the most powerful Zeiss microscope. It was said of Hackett that "he never went into his class, during the whole forty years of his career as a teacher, without a new investigation and revision of the lesson for the hour," and "that no man has lived, in America at least, who has been able to impress the most minute and recondite indications of the Greek original upon the minds of New Testament students." From him Gordon learned that "every phrase of the New Testament has a meaning definite and single—a meaning that can be accurately ascertained and clearly expressed according to fixed and settled laws of human speech." From him he got "that reverent regard for divine revelation which, on the one hand, brooks no mystical importation of human fancies into the sacred text, and, on the other, does not permit the smallest Greek article or conjunction to be treated as an idle or ambiguous thing in that Word, which holy men of old wrote as they were moved by the Holy Ghost." *

The years at Newton passed smoothly. Gordon writes frequently of visits to Providence—"visits," as he said, "which form pleasant little inns for hope and anticipation to rest themselves in as they journey out into the future." The letters which he sent to the same home, like faded rose-leaves long kept, full of suggestions of life and color, exhale an aroma of contentment and gratitude.

* Memorial Address by Dr. A. H. Strong on Horatio Balch Hackett, D.D.

Health was returning. " I am better than for a long time,"
he writes. " Trials are good, but I sometimes think happiness
makes me more religious even than grief. I know I never felt
more devoutly thankful for blessings which seem clearly to
have come from God." And again: " I have concluded to
avoid brooding over any anxieties. I have learned to believe
it wrong. It is gathering and pressing together into an intolerable burden the troubles which God has mercifully scattered
over years of time. I confess I cannot see so far and so distinctly the path of my future life as I was confident I could in
boyhood, before I thought of the possibility of such a thing
as adversity or disappointment. Still when I have taken one
step I have always had light enough to see where to take the
next. So I try quietly to adopt the words of Christ, ' Take
no thought for the morrow.' ' Do the duty that lies nearest
to thee ' has become quite a motto for me. We need to be
patient above all things. I am anxious, too, that you as well
as myself may learn that generous and self-denying labors for
others bring the sweetest and richest rewards. The smallest
action may thus be made noble, and the very drudgery of life
become divine. I sometimes hope that it is one of the lessons
which experience is gradually teaching me, that if I am to be
anything that is truly good and noble, it must be by conquering those narrow and sordid ambitions by which the world is
so much controlled. Still I am aware I have enough of them."

To those three too frequent intruders into the contemporary
pulpit, a metaphysical jargon, a shallow Pelagianism, and a
uniformed officialism, he makes references in different letters.
Going into Boston, he strays into church, and listens to the
philosophical essay of a distinguished pulpiteer. He remarks
that it is " too full of scholastic terms and metaphysical tech-
nicalities, which are even more objectionable than cant and
slang; for ordinary people can comprehend the latter, but
very rarely the former "; adding confidentially to the pro-

spective minister's wife, "which would you rather have me use ? "

On the receipt of a hand-wrought sermon-case from the same intimate correspondent, he says, mingling theology and love-making in a way not necessary to divulge here :

" I will try to do as you request, and write some good sermons for it, practical because spiritual. *There is nothing practical in religion but the spiritual.* I feel that I must not disguise the fact that men are sinners, though that may seem to be an antiquated idea and an exploded theory of Jonathan Edwards. If they are as much so as I am, I am quite safe in making the statement."

The next extract repels the bantering imputation of clericalism with some heat :

" There is one thing about which I am going to remonstrate with you. I don't wish you to use the term ' white cravat' in any way to me. It is no more a symbol of the ministry than a bald head or a sore finger. It is worn, I know, but generally by the men who need something to bring them up to the standard of a decent debility."

The seminarist was now beginning to preach in small country and suburban churches—entering upon a sort of pastoral clinic introductory to his coming career. He had preached occasionally in the church of his own village. Often in later years did he describe that first placid morning when with fluttering heart he stood up before a full congregation of critically curious neighbors and relatives. His own two grandmothers, impartial and rigid as two Norns stepped out of an Icelandic saga, occupied the front seat, to pass judgment upon his orthodoxy. When asked after service as to their opinion, the one kept ominous silence ; the other retorted that she " had known it all before." But such unresponsiveness must, after all, have been the child of an honest family pride that refused to betray itself from very self-consciousness ; for everywhere else he was received with kindly appreciation, though with popular expressions of surprise at his apparently extreme youth. "The people, D—— tells me, were quite astonished to see such a boy in the pulpit, and made various conjectures about his age, none of them going above seventeen or eighteen. In passing down the middle aisle to-day after meeting, I was accosted by an estimable, near-sighted lady, who was apparently considering the current opinion as to my age, with the somewhat confusing question, 'Do you suppose that that young man really wrote the sermon himself?'"

The Sundays were spent in this way among the various churches of eastern Massachusetts. Now and again he felt disheartened. "There seems to be so little real appreciation of what has cost so much toil of brain, and so little apparent good from the words spoken." At other times he was greatly encouraged. One day, just previous to his graduation, a letter was received from the Baptist society in Jamaica Plain, asking the young minister to "supply" the pulpit there. The gentle, open face and thoughtful sermon won the hearts of all; at the month's end he was "called."

On the evening of the 12th of June, 1863, the little church was hung with greenery, and the people were assembled for the ordination service. We have before us the faded printed "Program for the Installation of Mr. Adoniram Judson Gordon as Pastor of the Jamaica Plain Church, West Roxbury." There was the usual formal sermon, the charge, the blessing by the older ministers present. Then all united in the familiar, fervent hymn:

> "Gird thou his heart with strength divine;
> Let Christ through all his conduct shine;
> Faithful in all things may he be,
> Dead to the world, alive to thee,"

and the simple exercises were over.

The village of Jamaica Plain was at that time perhaps the

most delightful spot in the outskirts of Boston. It was a suburb of close-shaven lawns, well besprinkled, across which querulous robins ran, and over whose walks spirea, flaming rhododendrons, and gorgeous, golden forsythia hung in profusion. Bending elms and thick-foliaged chestnut-trees lined the roads. Pleasant homes, deep bedded in shrubbery, and filled with books and all the comforts of an ample, affluent life, welcomed the new pastor in his round of calls. His own house stood just at the edge of a sedate little pond, not far from the place where the heroic Parkman, battling with disease, raised incomparable roses and wrote incomparable histories. The church where Theodore Parker preached lay off a mile or two in West Roxbury, and in the same direction the undulating meadows of Brook Farm, long since deserted of its idealist and book-writing tenantry, stretched their grassy slopes under the sun. Altogether the new surroundings were well suited to a man of quiet tastes. His marriage, which occurred soon after his settlement at the Plain, heightened the joy of the new home. And with all these circumstances contributing to his happiness, there went along a deep gratitude to God for his mercies—a gratitude reflected in the letters written to his wife when he was called away from his own church to speak. In the note from which the following is taken, after dwelling on his recent marriage he says:

"But I look back on the time when I first realized that we were one in Christ, and a higher gratitude fills my heart for that. Dear wife, I wonder now, when the thought of our life in Christ so fills my soul, that we do not talk more about it. Oh, what is it to be joined together in the Lord, to be the privileged guests of the constant bridal of the Lamb? My heart is filled with love to Jesus while I write. 'Whom have I in heaven but him, and there is none on the earth that I desire beside him.' I want to go everywhere trying to persuade men to be reconciled to God through him."

And again:

"I sometimes fear that my perfect happiness and content-ment in my home, and my complete earthly bliss with my wife, may lead me to forget God. Let us make it a special subject of prayer that God may keep us from forgetting him or neglecting our duty to him. And when you come back to me, may I find you with a heart not only glowing with a love for me, but kindled with a more intense devotion to our dear Lord and Master Jesus Christ. How I thank God that you love him with me! and I do believe that even in heaven I shall rejoice that these hands were permitted to bury you in death with him by baptism, and raise you up in the likeness of his resurrection. Bless the Lord."

We get an idea of the young minister's personal appearance from a portrait painted about this time. It shows us a wealth of chestnut hair brushed across a high forehead, grave though kindly eyes of an indeterminate blue-gray shade, spare cheeks, a full under lip suggestive of meditative moods, and a mouth mobile and genial, ready at any moment for harmless pleasan-try, with jaws behind it locked in the decision of strongly held convictions. His height was above the medium. The years of study, however, had left him with a frame somewhat scant-ily clothed upon, which contrasted markedly with the massive mould of after-years. His voice was full, rich, flexible, yet a little roughened, they said, as a Cremona violin before it at-tains the mellow timbre of maturity. The old sexton of the Jamaica Plain Church still recalls him walking to and fro in the church vestry week-days persistently working to overcome this defect. In manner he was shy and reserved, though de-lightfully genial when once the restraints of new acquaintance were well melted. The social duties of a pastor—calling, giv-ing in marriage, and the like—demanded an expenditure of real effort, and were the source of much misgiving. We get a glimpse of this in the following letter:

"I have just been interrupted by another couple to be married. One of the parties was Miss R——. It is painful to stand in the presence of such a modest, shrinking couple with no possibility of getting up a conversation. I greatly wished you had been here to speak your piece beginning, 'I trust you may be as happy in your married life as I,' etc. I really missed it, and was so embarrassed after I got through the service in thinking to myself, 'Well, there is something I have forgotten; I am sure it does not seem quite complete.' I couldn't for the life of me think what it was till they had gone; then it flashed upon my mind, 'Why, it's my wife's speech!'"

If timid in the parlor, he was certainly not so in the pulpit. In an address given at this time, he reproaches "those ministers who start with ghostly horror at the thought of taking weapons against the iniquities which infest our land, who refuse to speak out against such sins as slavery and corruption in high places, but, with wonderful dexterity of conscience, dodge behind the shadow of what they call the dignity of the pulpit, and spend their days writing metaphysical disquisitions on long-forgotten theological jangles." He did not hesitate then more than in later life to "preach politics" when "politics" was but the synonym for righteousness. In the dark days of '63 his voice rang out constantly and unequivocally in behalf of freedom and the Union, much to the disgust of many of his lukewarm parishioners. On a certain occasion, during the climax of one of these appeals, a "leading member" rose up in the body of the house, drew forth, with utmost deliberation, hymn-book, Psalter, and Testament from the rack in his pew, placed them resolutely under both armpits, and marched slowly down the main aisle and out of the church. Thus did he shake the dust from off his feet as a witness against this infamous commingling of the sacred with the secular, of the things of the Bible with those of the newspaper.

Never afterward was he seen in the church. Years passed; Gordon had long since left the scene of his early ministry, and was settled over his Boston charge; the solitary secession of that Sabbath morning was completely forgotten. One day he received a note asking him to attend a funeral in the suburbs. Street and number alone were given. On entering the house he was surprised to learn that the dead man was the stiff dissenter of war times. He had insisted on his death-bed that none other should conduct his funeral exercises than the young pastor of former days, "who never feared to preach what he believed."

As a pastor, Gordon's relations with his people were most familiar, tender, *intime*. Formality had here no place. He was wont to gather his little flock around him in the Friday evening prayer-meetings, conferring, instructing, opening the Word, encouraging all in "the practice of the presence of God," and in the conflict with the temptations incident to the daily walk. The second year he preached a series of sermons on the development of the higher life, which indicated thus early the trend of his opinions and of his aspirations. Of one of these he writes:

"I find it is so hard to preach as I desire, so many little ambitions thrusting themselves in to influence and shape my sermons. A right heart has, I believe, as much to do with the matter as anything. I think yesterday's sermon was well received. I only hope the doctrine was according to the mind of the Spirit, and that God was not displeased with it. I feel more and more the worthlessness of man's applause, and I have a deepening desire to please Christ in all such works. I send you a little notice of it (very flattering). It is only for you, dearest, not for myself."

Six years flew by—years of study, of faithful pastoral work, of continuous growth. The little church developed in numbers and power. Pastor and people were bound together in the bonds of a heart-deep affection. Three children were born into the home by the pond. We get a peep into that home life now and then through the aperture of the father's correspondence.

"You will naturally ask," he writes on one occasion, " with your jealous disposition, if I have paid attention to any lady in your absence. I answer solemnly, none! Only your old dress fell at my feet as I was brushing through the closet, and in picking it up I involuntarily embraced it, and even clutched a kiss from the eloquent emptiness that protruded from the neck. I gazed this morning, I confess lovingly for a married man in his wife's absence, on one sweet face that crossed my path; but it was in gilt and hung, and therefore I plead no guilt for myself, or at least a suspension of judgment. I will make a clean breast of it. I have stopped several times a day before a certain window, and gazed perhaps too admiringly on a beautiful maiden face that has looked out therefrom. But you will forgive me. It's only 'Wosa,' seated just as Haley left her in the little rocking-chair at the parlor window. What touching reminders of the loved ones these little things are! 'Wosa' sitting so demurely, waiting for the return of her little mistress, and your winter dress pendent from the nail in the closet—these can hold enough of the subtle element to impart a strong shock to one who comes *en rapport*.

"P. S.—I send you the money, thereby showing my fidelity to my marriage vow, to love, honor, and buy things for you."

But the cloud that was to overcast his sky had now appeared above the horizon. Seated alone in his study one evening in the fall of '67, writing on his Sunday sermon, and rocking now and then the cradle of his last baby, who slept placidly beside him, he was suddenly startled by a sharp pull at his door-bell. That ring was to resound in his ears for the next two years, keeping him in a distress of doubt and hesitation. For it was the first summons to a new field of labor. The servant was even then ushering into his diminutive parlor the accredited delegates from an important pastorless Boston church, who came to tender him a call "hearty and unanimous." Should he accept? Impossible! No man was ever more loved by his people. No home was ever dearer to father and husband than the one where he was sitting. No field of usefulness could offer more opportunities for a measured, yet none the less vital, religious activity. His declination was given out of hand, and was soon followed by a more formal and decisive refusal. But the end was not yet. A year passed, and still the city church was without a head, and still the delegations continued to call at the suburban manse. "Why will they not let me alone," he writes, "and not press their suit? I wish I were out of it. If you will go to them and get me off in my absence, and agree that they shall never trouble me again, I will give you half of my kingdom. I am well-nigh insane over the matter. Tell all my flock how I love them, and how I loathe the pastures of Boston and the bulls of State Street, which are worse than those of Bashan. Thank God, their call cannot divide me from you, though it may thrust me forth from my Paradise. What a comfort it must have been to Adam that, though expelled from Eden, Eve went with him!"

At the expiration of the first year he yielded, and wrote out a letter of acceptance. But this step was followed by a revulsion of feeling. The letter was torn to pieces with many expressions of self-recrimination for his disloyalty to the church of his first love. Finally, however, the pressure became too strong, and, after two years of waiting, he agreed to become pastor of the Clarendon Street Church. In the month of December, 1869, amid the universal mourning of the flock, he left Jamaica Plain to take up the work the completion of which was to constitute the capital achievement of his life.

His Meisterjahre had now begun!

Two long-buried and long-forgotten essays, contributed to the "Baptist Quarterly" in these years, give one a glimpse into the things which then occupied his mind. In his after ministry he distinctly abandoned all that would suggest polemics, aiming to be, not a champion, but a proclaimer of the gospel. That he could reason closely and hit strongly—that he had a keen appreciation of his opponent's weak points, and of the opportunities which these offered—is seen in the subjoined extracts. To lay aside the tempting weapon of wit and of aggressive discussion, so easily and so admirably used, must indeed have cost much self-restraint. It evidences, too, a clearly changed conviction as to the duty of a Christian: to endure reproach, to disregard opposition, and to preach the simple gospel without turning to right or left—this was to be the program of the maturer years.

In the first of these articles he outlines and criticizes the position which F. W. Robertson had taken on the question of baptismal regeneration. He follows the anise-seed bag of Robertson's reasonings in its whole tortuous career, doubling with it when it doubled, running down upon it on every straight course of honest logic, detecting the scent where it seems least perceptible, and where a less close reasoner would be surely confounded. He breaks the ice, and beneath the shining rhetoric shows us the black, chill current of sophistry. We take from this paper the following suggestive extracts:

"It was a favorite theory of Robertson's that truth is a union of two contradictories. Rejecting that method in theology which seeks to go between two opposite views, and to find the truth in a kind of middle region, or temperate zone, removed alike from either extreme, he regarded all great truths as having such a latitude that they can embrace within themselves every zone and every temperature of belief. He would tell the Calvinist and the Arminian, the Romanist and the Protestant, that, however widely they may be separated from each other, their separation is, after all, only geographical; and that the belief of each is, in a certain sense, necessary for the equipoise and completeness of Christian doctrine. One is constantly discerning the influence of this pernicious maxim in his aversion to sharp discriminations and radical separations between the true and the false; in his fondness for seeking the soul of goodness in things evil; in his tendency to locate error on the extreme confines of truth rather than within another and totally different kingdom, and to look upon human depravity as rather a misconception by the soul of its true position, than an actual perversion from the right. In his discussions of the subject of baptism, this fault is everywhere apparent, and, though there is a great and admirably stated truth running through them all, it is always seen writhing, Laocoön-like, in the folds of the two 'contradictories,' and is therefore so disfigured and contorted that it presents no very engaging aspect. . . .

"Robertson reduces regeneration to an exceedingly small matter. It is with him simply the giving of full credence to a piece of information. Baptism is the bearer of that information. It comes to a man who is stupidly sleeping in sin, and before he has ever asked for the portion of goods that falleth to him, or ever thought whether he has any portion, it puts its hand upon his head and says, 'You are hereby informed that you are a child of God and have a right to all the privileges and emoluments of sonship.' If perchance the person thus addressed is incredulous, and refuses to believe, the message immediately becomes practically reversed, and announces to him that he is a child of wrath; that is, the 'eternal fact,' which was to be transmitted in the 'baptismal dew,' by coming in contact with the chilling unbelief of the candidate is precipitated into a practical fiction. . . .

"'*Baptism does not create the fact; it reveals it.*' It is the divine philosopher's stone, whose touch transmutes a *de jure* condition into a *de facto* one. The pure gold of grace was present, however, just as really before as after the subtle process of spiritual alchemy, but undiscerned by its fortunate possessor and unrecognized by God. Now it is discovered, assayed, and stamped with God's image and superscription, and put into circulation.

"All this is beautiful and satisfactory enough till some person brings back one of these rare coins to this ecclesiastical mint, and, displaying it all rusted and corroded with the pomps and vanities of this world, protests that it is spurious. In such a case it would seem that our author would be driven to the admission that some of his *de jure* material was not genuine, and that the stamp upon it was the symbol of an unreal value. Not at all. The whole difficulty lies in a want of confidence in it, and in a failure by the owner to recognize God's mark upon it. Let him believe that it is genuine, and it is genuine; or, in Robertson's language, 'to believe the fact (declared in baptism), and to live it, is to be regenerate.'

"Here is the same confusion of ideas introduced into the doctrine of baptism which the transubstantiator has introduced into the Lord's Supper. The thing demanded by the church in each case is the bringing in of the real presence into that which was designed simply for a sign and symbol. But in this instance both priest and people revolt from the materialism which an open, literal introduction of it involves, and attempt, therefore, to bring it in by a metaphysical sleight of hand, the belief in a practical falsehood being the *sine qua non* condition to the realization of the truth.

"'Believe that you eat the body of Christ in the eucharist,' said Sir Thomas More, in his discussion with Erasmus, 'and you eat it.'

"'Believe that you are regenerated in your baptism,' says Robertson, 'and you are regenerated.' The divergence here

from Scripture may be stated very briefly. The Bible represents men as 'believing a lie, that they might be damned.'
Robertson would have them believe a lie, that they might be
saved. . . .

"There is a saying of an old divine that a 'ceremony duly
instituted is a chain of gold around the neck of faith; but if,
in the wish to make it coessential and cosubstantial, you draw
it closer and closer, it may strangle the faith it was meant to
deck and designate.' This, we believe, is exactly what Robertson's argument does. He did not wish to make baptism
coessential and cosubstantial with regeneration, but his creed
required it. And so, while attempting to take off the coarse
and cumbersome chain which Rome has forged upon the neck
of regeneration, he has substituted another, wrought of finer
substance, and forged into an almost invisible tenuity; whose
delicate links of sophistry and error, while they bind in a less
oppressive bondage, suffocate with no less certain death.

"The doctrine of a radical renewal by the Holy Ghost, of
a thorough revolution and reconstruction of the moral nature
by the sovereign agency of the Spirit of God—a change
wrought in time, and made recognizable to the consciousness
—has no place in this theology. . . .

"The strict Episcopal view makes baptism, when it has been
performed, stand ever after for regeneration, as the currency
represents the coin in the vault; but, at the same time, the
church is so strongly convinced that her issue vastly exceeds
the piety which she can show for it, that she asks the 'judgment of charity,' and so virtually goes into ecclesiastic insol-
vency, though meanwhile still continuing to send forth her
bonds.

"The Pedobaptist who denies baptismal regeneration usually puts the rite for a hoped-for renewal, thus making it simply
promissory, with no security but the unmortgageable piety of
others. Those who carry out Robertson's definition to its

legitimate results make baptism stand for regeneration, vouched for by the best possible evidence in an inward experience and in the external life. At the same time, they stand ready to recall the act when they are convinced that, through a mistake of judgment, it has been wrongly applied. So that, while, according to each view, the ordinance professes to represent the same thing, we believe that the last has every advantage for representing it most fairly, and hence is least open to the stigma of being a hollow form. . . . The view which is most scriptural, however, regards the act as proceeding not from God, but from the candidate himself. It is not God's call or annunciation to him, but his *sacramentum*, or oath of allegiance, to Christ. If, through hypocrisy or self-deception, it is unworthily assumed, it is simply a false oath, and hence a totally invalid act; and that is all that need be said concerning it. No elaborate device of logic is demanded for releasing God from a seeming breach of his covenant; nor, on the other hand, any subtle mystification of words for endowing a baptized man with a character which is out of harmony with both his life and his consciousness.

" Baptism being, in our view, simply a divine symbolic language, given us for expressing certain spiritual ideas, can be truthful only as it is idiomatic—the vernacular, so to speak, of the new life. If strangers and foreigners use it, their expression is to be taken as the expression of those who know not what they say. If deceivers employ it, it is simply wrested to the uses of perjury. . . ."

The other article has in it just a trace of severity, which is not unnatural if one remembers the complacent assumption which characterizes the periodical summons to an Episcopal Canossa. In later years, when the subject of " church unity " was mentioned, Dr. Gordon was quite likely to tell good-humoredly the story of a quaint relative, a Congregational preacher, who defended " the validity of his ordination " by the contention that he was the best blacksmith who could make the best horseshoe, whether or no he could trace his descent from Tubal Cain. The hauteur of churchmen who "desire to be Catholic as well as Protestant, like those churchmen of evil memory who would be neither hot nor cold," ceases to irritate when one estimates it properly. No Christian experiences any difficulty in realizing the most vital unity if only he has grace and honesty enough to treat his fellow-Christians as common followers of a common Lord, and if his sense is sufficiently acute to comprehend that money is money whether it be broken into silver bits or dressed in the pretentious garb of the greenback. That the young pastor, in his study and among his periodicals, was, perhaps, unduly incensed by "the eddy of purposeless dust" which the advocates of "unity" were raising, is evident from the extracts which follow. That he valued, however, to the utmost, the communion and coöperation of the saints in the μεγάλη ἐκκλησία—that unity of the Spirit so far removed from a factitious uniformity, "icily regular, splendidly null "—is clear from his whole subsequent career.

This article was called out by the appeal of a recently formed "Christian Unity Society "; of the appeal he says :

"The spirit of the address is kind and conciliatory, as of course it could well afford to be. It denies in words that the unity sought requires 'absolute absorption and conversion into identity' with the church—conformity and uniformity in all things—but clearly proves the same in its arguments. In words it pays an appreciative tribute to the zeal and efficiency and usefulness of various Christian denominations, but in argument declares their existence to be an evil. In words it seems to have an enthusiasm for the work proposed that is totally disinterested and magnanimous ; in argument it proves that its zeal is for its own church and for the welfare of its own dearest cause. All this is natural enough. It does not offend. Only the whole subject suggests certain difficulties to our mind that the writer has failed to solve. These we propose at this time to consider.

"The fundamental idea of the association is this: that non-conformity in religion is the great evil of the church, and that the highest success of the gospel can be attained only in ecclesiastical uniformity. We believe, on the contrary, that there is much that is good, and much that calls for profound gratitude, in the present economy of an externally divided church. It undoubtedly gives free scope to her varied and otherwise conflicting activities, brings harmony out of her antagonisms, and economizes forces by separating them, which must else be wasted by their own friction. How much, too, does the church owe to the existence of sects for clearness and compactness in the statement of her doctrines; how many crude and unphilosophical symbols have been ground down and polished by the attrition of controversy; how much of error and misconception have been sifted out of the creeds by polemical winnowings and threshings; how repeatedly have the accretions of falsehood, which in the course of time gather about religious truth, been removed by the sharp antagonisms of sectarian strife; how many ideas, in fine, the most vital and precious to the church, have, humanly speaking, been kept alive by the jealous circumspections of the denominations! The evils which result from monopoly of the gospel, perversions of it in the interest of a single church, biased interpretations and one-sided expositions, have unquestionably been very largely prevented by the presence and watchfulness of differing religious orders.

"'Christianity,' says Bunsen, 'proves itself to be the religion of the world by its power of surviving the inherent crises of development through which it has had to pass.' Yes, and, we add, by its power of fully meeting those crises out of its own resources; of fitting itself into all the convolutions of history; of pushing itself out into the ever-varying want and woe of humanity.   And how has it been able to do this?   By the diversity of its outward organizations; by its ability to assume manifold forms of operation, and work successfully through them.

"Methodism is an exact illustration of what we mean.   It is perfectly clear that, at the time when it arose, the establishment had become so unwieldy, so hampered with civil and ecclesiastical rules, that it was utterly unable to meet the prevailing demand for a free and missionary gospel.   If, here and there, a preacher was to be found who had true evangelical zeal, his jurisdiction was so prescribed by the fences of the church that his zeal profited him nothing.   When John Berridge undertook to carry salvation to the poor and unprivileged about him, on the ground that his conscience impelled him to seek to preach the gospel to every creature, he was summoned before the bishop with the rebuke, 'As to your conscience, you know that preaching out of your parish is contrary to the canons of the church.'

"But Providence met the exigency.   Out of the church, and in spite of her opposition, came forth that noble system of itinerancy which has carried salvation to thousands and tens of thousands, and has continued until this day one of the most potent agencies for reclaiming lost men.

"But the churchman sees nothing in the origin of this society to rejoice over.   'All must feel,' says our author, 'how needless and how fearfully mixed with wrong on both sides was the Wesleyan separation.'   Needless, forsooth!   No power on earth can forever check a living stream in its course.   From the very dams that have restrained it, it will every day gain strength for the inevitable rupture.   Similarly, no device of priest or bishop can so choke the life of Christianity in the church as completely to shut it off from those who are panting for its blessings.   It must break out somewhere, and if it becomes irregular in its course, the fault lies with those who attempted to repress it. It is not a wrong on both sides. If the blood cannot flow in the arteries of the church because of the pressure of some human obstructions, then there must be an anastomosis. Vitality must be supplied to all the members of Christ's body.

"There are evils of which this address makes no mention, and for which it proposes no remedy—the dull immobility, the stagnation of religious thought and of religious life, which have been invariable accompaniments of ecclesiastical uniformity. Against these, sectarianism has been in constant antagonism. And if it had performed no other office, this were enough to secure it from the imputation of being an unmitigated evil.

"When the question comes between a dead uniformity and a living diversity, it would seem as if there could be very little difficulty in choosing. And yet we believe that the first of these conditions is the alternative offered us by this society.

"As though the illustration which Romanism has given of a Christianity completely paralyzed by the clamps and constraints of ritualism were not sufficient, it is now proposed to repeat the experiment: to take the faith of Christendom as it is held in solution by the various sects, and crystallize it about the Thirty-nine Articles or the Nicene Creed; to constrain its varied devotion into exact and rigidly defined channels; to put all its worship into regulation dress; to compress its free and plastic life into concerted formulas and modes; to sacrifice a variety which fully accords with a true unity to a unity that has no variety; and to call back all the 'children of the dispersion' from their widely different yet spiritually accordant labors, and bid them all march to the music and measure of the 'historic church.' Theoretically the proposition is untenable enough, but practically it is even more so.

' To ask Methodism, with its splendid record of fidelity to the claims of a missionary gospel, with its noble history of self-sacrificing and evangelic labor, to come back and be absorbed again into the church from which it sprang, abandoning that organism which, however faulty it may be in some respects, has penetrated a stratum of society that the cumbersome machinery of the Anglican Church never did, and never could, effectually reach; to ask Congregationalism, after having stamped its polity upon our rising institutions, and done more than anything else to mould and determine that noble republicanism which we now enjoy, to return into a church whose whole genius and history has been so manifestly on the side of monarchy—is to ask simply that Romulus and Remus, after having grown to manhood, should go back and be suckled on that creed which nourished them kindly enough in their infancy, but which was never designed to feed them in maturer life.

" And this suggests another grave objection to the theory of the address; namely, that it presupposes the possibility of a harmless return from spirituality to ritualism. That symbols have done much to develop ideas, that types have had a blessed mission in helping to bring forth spiritual conceptions, and to lead them through adolescence into maturity, is a fact too obvious to be denied. But to suppose that ideas that have once sloughed off their skins can be made to crawl back into them and still maintain a healthy life is quite another matter. It is to imagine that manhood can return to the swaddling-bands of infancy—that the church can leave the more ' stately mansions ' into which, by discipline and training, by reformations and revolutions, Providence has brought her, and crouch down again into her ' low-vaulted past.' . . .

" Since episcopalism professes to regard the Romish Church as corrupt and degenerate, the inference is that they hold it to be only a medium of communication, and not in any sense a vital part of the succession. So that, within its decay and

corruption, the germ of the true organic unity has been preserved, wrapped up, like the Egyptian wheat, in the swathes
of the mummy, waiting for Providence to bring about the
necessary conditions for its growth and development. This
theory seems certainly to be philosophical, perfectly consistent
with the analogies of history.

"But the hypothesis being once admitted, why cannot
those denominations which have sprung from the Episcopal
Church, and which charge that church with being a perversion,
rise up and claim that they have been derived from the true
germ—the germ of which episcopacy was the repository—and
hence that they have the only true succession? What then
becomes of the claims of the churchman? If, by a legitimate
process of exogenous growth, they who once constituted the
heart of Christianity find themselves pushed outward to its exterior, into the bark and tegument of mere formalism, surely
they cannot complain that there is anything anomalous in the
position of those who have supplanted them. Least of all can
they with good grace press their own claim of still constituting
the pith and marrow of the church.

"And the Scripture argument for any such succession of the
priesthood is still more unsatisfactory. It impresses one as
almost unparalleled in the annals of forced interpretation, two
or three texts being made to bear up the whole superstructure
of argument against hundreds whose genius is most obviously
opposed to it. Nine parts of conclusion are found to every
one part of premise, reminding us most forcibly of Coleridge's
description of such interpretations as 'smoke-like wreaths of inference,' or an 'ever-widening spiral *ergo* from the narrow aperture of perhaps a single text.'

"The boon, therefore, which is offered us in organic unity
as here defined has, we are constrained to say, no special value
to us, because we cannot appreciate our need of it.

"We see no necessity of drawing the life which we receive from Christ through a channel so long and tortuous that to explore it is an impossible task, or of tracing our descent from his apostles through a lineage so obscure that we cannot tell whether we are sons or bastards.   We believe in a Christ as the Head of the church, who lives and reigns forever, who not only holds his mysterious union with his church still unbroken, but constantly energizes and reinforces that church by fresh infusions of his life; so that the vitality of the children does not depend upon the vitality of their ancestors. We believe his union with his church is direct, not mediate— a union of incorporation, not of remote connection.   And hence it matters little whether we are connected with the original branches of the True Vine, so long as that Vine is capable of thrusting out fresh shoots alike for the church and for its ministry.

"For any one of the coördinate branches of the church, therefore, to attempt to bring about unity by setting forth its own pattern and polity as the one to be conformed to, exactly or approximately, by all, will necessarily be of little use.   No sectarian plea against sectarianism, no partizan tirade against religious partizanship, will avail.   But whatever brings the church into nearer accordance with the spirit of Christ and his gospel, whatever exalts the central and centralizing truths of our common faith, will do most toward promoting that unity for which we all hope and pray.   In the beautiful words of the author of ' The Patience of Hope,' ' The bosom of Christ is the grave, the only grave, of religious acrimony; we learn secrets there which render it possible for us to be of one heart, if we may not yet be of one mind, with all who lean upon it with us.   For, slightly as we may think to heal long-festering hurts, there is no cure for religious dissension except that of spiritual acquaintance with God, as revealed to us in the mind and spirit of Christ Jesus.   To acquaint ourselves thus with

God is to be at peace, for it is to learn how far more strong than all which separates is that which unites us in him. So long as the external is more to us than the vital, the accidental dearer than the essential, so long as we are more church-men, more Protestants, more anything than Christians, religious acerbity will continue.' "

CHAPTER IV

Difficulties of the Boston field—The periodic season of unbelief—
Unitarian-transcendentalism—Sluggish religious life of the Clarendon Street Church.

THREE things combined to give the field of work upon
which Gordon had now entered a character of exceptional difficulty: the general current of doubt at that time prevailing in educated circles here and abroad, the local Unitarian-
transcendental movement, then at the height of its prosperity,
and the somewhat contracted spiritual life of the church to
which he was now to minister.

I

The epoch was Sadducean. Men were passing into that
prison-house of which, for a whole generation, Mr. Herbert
Spencer has held the keys. The Ancient of Days had been
deposed in favor of the Unknowable. In matter the promise
and potency of all things were to be sought and found.
"Science," an o'ershadowing swash-buckler, defied all the
opinions and generalizations which had until its day been
maintained. Then were rung the changes on

> " Geology, ethnology, those little passing-bells
> That signify some faith's about to die."

How seductively the chimes did peal—not in violent clangor,
but with a charming melancholy as the old, beautiful, much-
regretted, but hopelessly obsolete, beliefs were laid away to
their long rest! A new anti-religious classification had arisen.

Men called themselves agnostics—a name of gentlemanly note, a pledge of culture, without the anarchic suggestions of unveiled atheism. Those were the days when the educated mob ridiculed the belief in a purposing, sovereign Maker. Teleology, that ancient prop of faith, was, they thought, being undermined and destroyed completely and for all time by the great Darwin, as he studied his earthworms and rock-pigeons. We know now that he was digging, though unconsciously, but to lay the foundations deeper; for Darwinism, which was to be the very escarpment of Doubting Castle, has proved in the end a buttress to the house of the Lord God. The evolution theory had its foundations in eternal verities. The deductions and misapplications and perverse generalizations which it fathered are alone false and frivolous.

II

Quite the contrary, however, was it with the local unbelief. Unitarian-transcendentalism was based upon a false psychology and upon a wholly non-ethical conception of history. The attitude of Unitarianism was and is distinctively negative. Denial has been its tradition from the days of Priestley down to the present hour. In earlier years it was busy in controverting bald statements concerning the nature of the Godhead. It was profoundly convinced that three could never be one, and was content to do battle with this alleged superstition. In the present era of paradoxical marvels, of matter-penetrating rays, and of mysterious fourth dimensions, its peculiar contention has not the support in antecedent improbability which it once might have seemed to have. The old watch-cry, accordingly, attracts little interest or attention.

Its negative positions have been modified to a great extent by the positive theory of "transcendentalism" which has flowed along, in greater or less confusion and intermixture, beside and within it. This revival of Gnosticism found its coryphæus in Emerson, whose influence in New England was due primarily to the fact that he first introduced to his countrymen, cut off from the intellectual life of Europe, and shut up to a rather dry and formal type of religion, the fermenting systems, the neologies and ideologies of Germany. He was the first to travel in the realms of gold, a naïve Marco Polo, first to break from the provincial life of old Massachusetts. His ship before all others brought over the strange fruits which now come daily and by steamer-load. We of the present forget that ship and its burden of novelties. No longer does the "seer" fill the whole sky like a new angel standing in the sun. He seems, on the contrary, a gentle mystagogue with a somewhat superficial culture, who unduly exaggerated the importance of the systems of Fichte and Jacobi, and who had not, alas! even the shadow of an idea of the evil that ravages this earth.

Amiel says that "the best measure of the profundity of any religious doctrine is given by its conception of sin and of the cure of sin." Judged by this test, Emersonian "transcendentalism" would be hardly important enough to command serious consideration. Yet, if it has no philosophical significance, it has had a place too baleful in the life of New England to be passed over.

"Transcendentalism," a modification and perverted expression of the theory of subjective idealism, makes of man a creator.* Of course, therefore, it cannot concede him to be a rascal. The logic of idealism is indeed undeniable; yet, after all, it remains as unbelievable as it is irrefutable. The "transcendentalist" induction from it as to man's moral make-up, however, is, when brought to the touchstone of history and of daily experience, both unbelievable and refutable. "It as-

* O. B. Frothingham, "Transcendentalism in New England," pp. 202, 119, *et passim.*

serts," to quote the word of its historian, "the inalienable worth of man." "It claims for all men what Christianity claims for its own elect." "It regards the inner light which Quakerism attributes to the supernatural illumination of the Holy Spirit as the natural endowment of the human mind." In short, it inverts the order of the Christian revelation in its estimate of humanity and of Christianity, making of the latter an illustrious example and fruit of the greatness of man instead of a resource for the repair of human shortcoming, and finding in Jesus a notable type of human nature, of which type we all partake by birthright without reference to repentance or to divine renewal. It teaches the essential goodness of man, and the indefinite perfectibility of society.

This unwillingness to acknowledge the corruption of the human heart was the essential feature of "transcendental" ethics. "Never wrong people with your contritions, nor with dismal views of society," Emerson used to say. Like his own humble-bee, he was capable of

> " Seeing only what is fair,
> Sipping only what is sweet,"

and the result was a serenity of mind hardly bought at the expense of a complete ignorance of the bitter, wisdom-bringing tragedies of life. "That horrid burden and impediment on the soul which the churches call sin," as well as "the courses of nature and the prodigious injustices of man in society, affected him with neither horror nor awe." * To him as to his fellows, the minor prophets of unbelief—the Alcotts, the Ripleys, the Parkers—the world was one rose-garden, the monotone of whose loveliness is disturbed by neither thorn nor hidden snake. They ignored "that sin which circulates in our bodies as blood." They forgot that "savage, brigand, and madman each of us harbors, in repose or manacled, but

* "Emerson," by Mr. John Morley.

always living, in the recesses of his own heart." * And as the natural and inevitable corollary of this superficial and false estimate of the place of evil in man's economy, there followed a low and inadequate conception of holiness.

Of course such views attained great popularity with those tired of two hundred years of honest Puritanism. Theodore Parker, after recounting the many theories to which the men of his day attributed his success, said, " The real thing they did not seem to hit was that I preached an idea of God, of man, and of religion which commended itself to the nature of mankind." † Sure enough. It is indeed cheering to " the natural man " to be told, for instance, that " sin has no more existence than the phlogiston which was premised to explain combustion," ‡ and to hear all reference to it branded as " damaged phraseology, tainted with infamous notions of God and man." ‡ And if, perchance, mention must be made of the petty errors, the venial omissions, the occasional peccadillos, which now and then force themselves on our attention, what more soothing and reassuring than to be told that such slips " are but the incidents of our attempt to get command over our faculties "; § that, " just as children in learning to write mistake letters, miscall words, and miswrite phrases," so we, by " these experiments which fail, learn self-command."

Such was the lavender-water theology preached for a whole generation by this priest of " transcendentalism." It was a theology, too, which was as full of opposition to Christianity as it was weak and irrational. What can be said of a man who could speak of the communion-table in this way:

" On what terms shall a person be allowed once a month in

* Taine, " Ancien Régime." Cf. the whole destructively critical treatment of the kindred views of J. J. Rousseau.

† Quoted in Frothingham's " Transcendentalism," p. 312.

‡ " Theodore Parker's Life and Letters," vol. i., pp. 151, 152.

§ Ibid., vol. i., pp. 400, 401, 149, 150.

a meeting-house on Sunday to eat a crumb of baker's bread and drink a sip of grocer's wine, which the deacon has bought at a shop the day before? The Lord's Supper as now administered is a heathenish rite, and means very little." *

Does not "liberalism" reach in such utterances its nadir? Does it not become the bare synonym for an indecent folly and hatred, comparable only to the bitterest, most raucous, hate-inspired antichristianity of Büchner or of Anacharsis Clootz? Yet this fanatic is even now spoken of currently by Unitarians as St. Theodore.

The refusal to recognize realities, and especially the most terrible of all realities, has been punished in our day by a comic mania for follies, which is a distinguishing feature of present-day Boston life.† This tendency is directly traceable to the early "transcendentalists." Any one who turns over the files of the "Dial" will find there the seed-corn of almost all the intellectual hallucinations which have here flourished. He will find there that headlong and unsophisticated enthusiasm, that undiscriminating, open-armed acceptance of new things, and that contemptuous rejection of what had been the milk of life, the source of vigor and of pristine strength. He can there run up and down the whole gamut of the now familiar "liberal slang," the wearisome phrases about ethnic religions, salvation by character, the bigotry of creeds, narrow literalism, and those peculiarly Emersonian classifications in which Jesus,

---

* "Theodore Parker's Life and Letters," vol. i., p. 322. He recommends as a substitute, we believe, the coming together in a parlor and eating, if one likes, curds and cream and baked apples.

† One recalls Heine's quatrain (the unquestioned sovereignty of dreamland seems to have passed from German to New England hands):

> " Franzosen und Russen gehört das Land,
>   Das Meer gehört den Britten;
> Wir aber führen im Luftreich des Traums
>   Die Herrschaft unbestritten."

Socrates, and Buddha are coupled in a patronizing impartiality. He will find the mystically meaningless utterances of Bronson Alcott, those Orphic sayings about " the poles of things which are not integrated," " the intertwining of the divine Gemini," and " the love which globes and the wisdom which orbs all things."

The manifestations of this spirit of eccentric novelty-hunting have been endless in number and variety. For years it found its most acute exhibition in the summer meetings of wayward " philosophers " at Concord. It has broken out in manifold scrofulous vagaries, such as spiritualism, Christian Science, theosophy, and esotericism. Indeed, as Pascal said, " it is the incredulous who are most credulous, the skeptical who are most surely and easily duped." A French epicure contended that the discoverer of a new dish is a greater benefactor than he who announces a new planet swimming within his ken. In like manner does this community estimate spiritual things. Any new fantastic religious importation from Asia precedes in popular interest the weightier matters of the law and of judgment.

We can trace this strange malady, this restless mania for the unusual, to that tendency in the " transcendentalist " teaching which destroys clean-cut distinctions, which, from its alleged absolute point of view, finds all religions good, and obscures in every sphere of life all that most men would call evil. We are able, on the other hand, to trace that icily critical temper which characterizes Cambridge and Boston—that unresponsiveness, that insensitive, stony, unsympathetic spirit which no man who stops overnight in the intellectual hostelries of Massachusetts fails to perceive or succeeds in forgetting— to the Unitarianism which was born struggling against its mother, Puritan orthodoxy, and which has spent its mature years as a permanent party of opposition.

As Emerson represents the first tendency, so Dr. Holmes, in

his religious phase, might, in spite of his sunny geniality, stand for the second. Here we have full culture, the kindly spirit, the enlightened humanism. But there is also a tartrate of acrimony in his mental reaction, which the slightest suggestion of Calvinism immediately precipitates. One drop, and the limpid soul is discolored as a hogshead of water into which falls one ten-thousandth of a grain of cochineal. To the New England Unitarian, Calvinism is as an August thunder-storm. It sours in his breast the milk of human kindness. We confess it is black, foreboding; that its locks threaten, that its shafts are terrible in their majesty. Yet it waters the thirsty fields, and has (history will bear us out) blessed every land which has lain across its track, even though it has turned the cream in the dairies of unbelief.

The attempts made by those of this connection to engage in work which is usually considered religious have been, on the whole, unimportant. Slight, too, have been the efforts put forth by them to reach the destitute, ignorant, helpless masses of the American cities. No missionaries have gone from their midst to preach even the " ethics " of Jesus to the gloomy heathenism of Asia and Africa. Their whole propaganda has been one of disintegration among evangelical Christians, and their favorite occupation has been that of lashing the dead lion of Calvinism. Parker, Holmes, Higginson, F. E. Abbott, Bartol, Clarke, and the whole Unitarian pulpit have busied themselves in conjuring up a nightmare, in which Edwards has played the part of chief ogre, and in which Norton, Cotton Mather, and the fathers of New England Puritanism have been made to act as the terrible and ghastly supernumeraries; predestination, hell-fire, and original sin being their gruesome stage properties.

Ah, well! we may be forgiven when we hear this outcry against that sweet soul, that massive intellect, that Doctor Angelicus, Jonathan Edwards, if we recall a remark of Heine's anent the romanticist detractors of Luther. "The ape on the giant's shoulders sees farther than the man on the ground," he says. We may, from the height of two later centuries, have wider outlooks and a clearer vision, but let us not dare to measure ourselves against the men below.

We have traced cursorily the influence and tendency of the Unitarian-transcendental movement. This influence was deepened and strengthened by the brilliant place which the leaders in these opinions attained in the contemporary literature. It was a season of unparalleled efflorescence in the intellectual life of New England. The prestige of this flowering time, of this season of admirable productivity in poetry and pure literature, naturally accrued, in a greater or less degree, to the party of religious revolt and of philosophical vagary.

Their authority was strengthened, too, by the noble part which as a body they played in the antislavery movement. One can hardly doubt that the devouring indignation against the slavocracy which possessed the soul of Theodore Parker did more to commend to serious people the interpretation of Christianity set forth by him each Sunday in Music Hall than a critical and sympathetic study of the New Testament possibly could. Yet the historian of that period and of the ideas then current will not be likely to fall into the mistake of supposing that the activity in reform noticeable in the careers of Parker, of Lowell, of Samuel May, and of other New England Unitarians, had its spring in the negations of Unitarianism, much less in the essentially unmoral and confused ethics of "transcendentalism." This would be to suppose that the lily blooming in the midst of a tangled mass of weeds grows actually upon one of the weed stalks. No reasonable man will forget that these were the children of the Puritanism which they assaulted, that Emerson, for example, was by birth the eighth in a series of Puritan ministers. That their moral courage and piety were largely exotic, we now know who com-

pare the work of Unitarianism, in the purely humanitarian lines
which it preaches, with that of such strange, bizarre, yet essentially evangelical agencies as the Salvation Army. We are
not unfaithful to the truth in asserting that the advantage lies
altogether with those who are without the social prestige, the
wealth, the great traditions, but who are empowered by the
very Spirit of God.

A community dominated by a party of this sort, full of pride
in its career of unbelief, full of bitterness against its opponents, ever assaulting and aspersing and pelting with catchwords
those who still preached the gospel in its fullness, was not by
any means an easy place in which to undertake religious work.
The infiltration from above of this weak rationalism, of this
insipid humanity-worship, among the thoughtless newspaper-
reading elements in the community popularized, while dilut-
ing, the current opinions. A pastor visiting among people
would find everywhere the objections to the revelation of God
in Christ which Cambridge and Boston made, only stripped
of the glitter, the garnish, the attractiveness with which the
educated had clothed them. Thus among all classes the tendencies were, to a great extent, away from evangelical Christianity. The tide was running out fast. Only strong men
could stand on their feet and resist its flow.

III

The church which Gordon was entering for a quarter-century's incessant work was, from some points of view, the most
important of the denomination in Boston. It was a "family"
church of an approved type, somewhat exclusive, with a generous sprinkling of rich men in its pews. It was a church in
which the line of separation between the Haves and the Have-
nots, so fatal to the best type of church development, was
defined with more or less conscientiousness. The *optimates*,

the "nice" people, the "best" people, were distinctly in evidence. A line of substantial merchants and bankers ran up and down the ends of the most desirable pews. If you had gone in any Sunday morning, you would have seen well-dressed ladies and gentlemen, singly or in groups, passing down the center aisles to their seats. The more common folk in the fringe of gallery and rear seats were, as befits the outer edge of a parterre, in more subdued dress. Numerous carriages at the doors lent a pleasant suggestion of capitalism to the exterior of the church.

The choir-loft was "a nest of singing-birds." One of the foremost American organists sat at the keyboard of the great new instrument. The music was faultless and severely classical. The preludes of Baptiste, the offertories of Barnby, the rapturous anthems of Stainer and of Berthold Tours, seem indissolubly connected with those old, cold, correct, formal days of fashionable Clarendon Street.

It was indeed a church of a well-defined and easily recognized type—a church which has its counterpart in every city of Protestant Christendom. It summarized, as all of its class, the admirable traits of Protestantism—comfort, order, intelligence, affluence, reserve, a not too aggressive religiousness. A church of this sort may be called the Church of the Disciples, the Church of the Covenanters, the Church of the Pilgrims. A more nearly correct and more modernized sobriquet would be, perhaps, the Church of the Bank Presidents. And why not? Do we Americans not believe that Montecucculi's three conditions for the prosecution of successful warfare—first, money; second, money; third, money—are alone indispensable in every other form of activity, social, commercial, religious?

This was the apprehension, evidently, of many who attended the church in Clarendon Street during the early seventies. The feeling of exclusiveness congealed finally into a condition

of things akin in some degree to that prevailing in close cor-
porations with elected membership. An officer of the church
was rebuked by one of the deacons for attaching the words
"strangers welcome" to some circulars for public distribution.
The theory which prevailed, apparently, was that which, in
the field of economics, goes under the name of Gresham's
Law. Base metal will drive out better currency; people of
humble social status will scare away the more "desirable"
families. The result may easily be imagined.

The severely facetious title of "The Saints' Everlasting
Rest," commonly applied to the church by outsiders, was
perhaps not altogether undeserved.

Years after, the young man who was now entering on his
pastorate here wrote of just such churches: "Ecclesiastical
corpses lie all about us. The caskets in which they repose
are lined with satin; they are decorated with solid silver
handles and with abundant flowers, and, like other caskets,
they are just large enough for their occupants, with no room
for strangers. These churches have died of respectability
and are embalmed in complacency." His own church was
not, however, beyond resuscitation. For years he worked on
it, turned it over and over, smote it mercifully severe blows,
rubbed it back and forth, refused to listen to its protests, to
its demand that it might be left to die in peace. And his
reward was to see it, in his own closing days, the ruddiest,
healthiest church in the city, bending all its strength for the
salvation of others.

In 1890, reviewing his twenty years' pastorate, Dr. Gordon
remarked:

"We believe we have learned much, through divine teaching, as to the true method of conducting the affairs of God's
church; have proved by experience the practicability of what
we have learned; and have largely united the church in the
practice thereof. *Innovations* have from the beginning been

strongly urged. 'Innovations'? No! that word implies new-
ness; and God is our witness that in theology, in worship, and
in church administration it is not the new to which we have
been inclined, but the old. *Renovation*, rather, is what we
have sought. With a deep feeling that many of the usages
which have been fastened upon our churches by long tradition
constitute a serious barrier to spiritual success, it has been my
steady aim to remove these. In general, we may say, it is our
strong conviction that true success in the church of Christ is
to be attained by spiritual, not by secular, methods; by a worship which promotes self-denial in God's people, and not by
that which ministers to self-gratification; by a cultivation of
the heart through diligent use of the Word and of prayer, and
not by a cultivation of art through music and architecture and
ritual. And with the most deliberate emphasis we can say
that every step in our return to simpler and more scriptural
methods of church service has proved an onward step toward
spiritual efficiency and success."

His whole ministry, then, faced backward—away from the
pitiable modern devices and schemes and substitutes, to "that
higher, holier, earlier, purer church," from which we are ever
departing, and to which we must ever return if we are to live.

CHAPTER V

The true aim of a church—Congregational singing—" The Service of Song "—Extracts from sermons on the worship of the church—The consummation of this reform

AS the reforms which reclaimed this church extended over many years, we shall be obliged to treat them in order as they were suggested and consummated. The idea of a church which must be first developed is that of a hospital. It is properly, to use the old English phrase, a " cure " for souls. This conception, so alien to the early life of Clarendon Street, was one of the best fruits of the Moody meetings of '77, held in the immediate vicinity. The entrance of reformed drunkards, and of all types of publicans and sinners, into membership opened the way for a progressive democratization culminating in the free-church system. Again, with the agitation for world-wide missions the next most important function of a local church began to be emphasized; namely, that of entrepôt and recruiting-station for the collection of munition and the enlistment of recruits for foreign service. How well the duties along this line came to be fulfilled we shall see further on. The reform which claimed the earliest attention of the new pastor, however, was in the worship of the church. For these changes he prayed and worked incessantly. During fifteen years preconceived opinions and prejudices stood out against his patient efforts; then they gave way, to his great joy and to the general satisfaction.

For long years Dr. Gordon's unwavering advocacy of congregational music seemed to his people an unaccountable eccentricity, the one hobby from which he never would dismount.
" Is it not necessary," they used to say, "for the success of
any well-ordered church that the choir should be of the most
select and well-trained sort ? " The outside world, so ran
their theory, must be drawn inside the church walls by the
sound of voluntary and anthem. When within, the preacher
has his opportunity. Why should a sportsman throw away
his decoy-ducks? Why should a pastor attempt to operate
without the aids which his people furnish freely for the further-
ance of his work?

Such was the argument, with all the collateral pleas for
high musical standards in a church of its rank. It was forgotten that the only condition which the new minister had
made in accepting this charge was the disuse of what he
called the ice-chest, i.e., the quartet gallery, and the substitution of hearty singing by the whole congregation for the dele-
gated worship there carried on.

In these days of substantial hymnaries, not to speak of the
endlessly issued gospel hymns—hymns which in the morning
spring up and flourish, and in the evening are cut down and
wither — congregational singing seems a perfectly natural
institution. A generation ago, however, the prevailing hymn-
books were of such a dry, jejune, characterless description
that the wonder is men and women ever sang at all. It was
an era of lugubrious tunes, of which " China," " Devizes," and
" Kentucky " are fairly representative. Lowell Mason still
ruled with autocratic sway over church collections. The
obvious thing, accordingly, for any one who wanted to encourage general participation in worship was, first of all, to furnish
an acceptable, thoroughly modern collection of hymns and
tunes. This Gordon attempted to do. The " Service of
Song," which he edited with much labor and evident taste,

became for many years a standard hymnal for Baptist churches, and was the text-book from which he first taught his own people to sing.

The next thing was to instruct his people in their plain duties in the worship of the church. This was done admirably in a series of sermons. The whole subject in all its features —singing, responsive reading, giving, and "the ministry of silence"—was discussed with acuteness and fervid scripturalness. To give an idea of his purpose, and of his conception of what a service should be in a church with the New Testament motive, the following extracts from these sermons are introduced:

"We are of the conviction that we have been tending entirely in the direction of ritualism (in its essential error of substituting priest for people) in allowing our praise to be rendered vicariously by quartet choirs, and our praying to be done largely for us by the minister instead of joining in it ourselves. . . .

"There are two classes of offenders in this matter of the worship of song: those who, having a good voice, do not sing with the heart, and those who, having a good heart, do not sing with the voice; and the latter is not the least culpable. For one who loves God and adores Jesus Christ to sit silent when their praises are sung, keeping time to the melody only with the muffled beating of the heart, ought to be considered almost an affront to the Most High. . . .

"How the expression, 'sacrifice of praise,' strikes at the idea of mere self-indulgence in the service of song! How it stamps with the brand of sacrilege our modern habit of regaling our ears with choice dainties of musical performance, and calling it worship! To whom was the sacrifice offered of old, to the people or to God? I need not answer the question. To whom is the sacrifice of praise presented in many of our modern sanctuaries? To the people, if the truth is told. It is fitted up to satisfy their taste, the incense of its melody wafted toward their ears. It finds its end in ministering to their pleasure. They sit down and listen to it exactly as though its whole aim were their delectation. . . .

"God would not have been pleased if the Israelite had gone to his neighbor's flock for a lamb because, forsooth, he might find one there that was whiter and more comely. And neither will Christ be pleased now if we borrow another's voice to utter our praises for his redeeming love, however exquisite and beautiful that voice may be. The offering must be taken out of the flock which he purchased with his own blood. Let us offer the sacrifice of praise; that is, the fruit of our lips. . . .

"You have noticed the fountains on the Common, with the water running so noiselessly through iron lips, which can neither taste its sweetness nor be refreshed by its coolness. And every Lord's day, in some of our churches, the most limpid strains of melody flow through lips that are just as oblivious to their import and just as unaffected by their sentiment as those lips of iron. How many times are the words, 'Come, Holy Spirit,' sung with no sense of longing for the blessed Comforter, with no apprehension of his holy mission, with no belief, indeed, in his divine personality! And what more direct and obvious method of violating the commandment, 'Grieve not the Holy Spirit,' is possible than this? . . .

"Men, like coals, kindle best in the mass. Each serves as a radiator to throw heat upon his neighbor, and so the zeal of the whole is quickly raised. But let each worshiper be only a dull absorbent of the warmth that is thrown upon him from Scripture, sermon, prayer, and hymn, and the preacher will find it a very onerous task to get the people into a devotional frame. Now singing is a means of spiritual radiation; truth and love and fervor are easily contagious when it is the medium of intercourse. What minister cannot feel the difference

in the touch of a congregation that has risen just before the
sermon and poured itself out in an inspiring and hearty hymn
of praise, from that of a religious audience that has been quietly
sitting and listening to a musical performance?   There is a
kind of spiritual elasticity in the former case which gives the
preacher's words back to him in a responsive echo very different from that dull thud which comes from dropping a sermon
into a listless and silent company of hearers. . . .

"To know by subtle intuition when you pray that faithful
souls are pressing round you, to second your desires and swell
the volume of your intercessions, is a blessed thing; but to
be assured of this by the audible response of a multitude of
voices is wonderfully strengthening.   Yet from the unhappy
custom—a custom that bears the stamp of an easy undevout-
ness—into which worshipers have so largely fallen, of listening to the public supplications instead of joining in them, how
often is the minister compelled to say to himself, after struggling in the pangs of unattended prayer, 'I have trodden the
wine-press alone; and of the people there was none with
me'! . . .

"Hear the summons to prayer which is given in the Epistle
to the Hebrews: 'Brethren, let *us* draw near.' . . . It is not,
'Let me draw near in your behalf, as your minister and mouth-
piece;' but, 'Let *us* draw near.'   Of course the summons
ought to be the same to-day, since the priesthood of believers
in Christ is an unchangeable priesthood.   Now, if the people
simply sit still in their places during this exercise, without a
single change of attitude, without a gesture of reverence,
without an utterance of the voice, without a single according
'Amen' at the end, do they not look more like Jews waiting
without than like purged Christian worshipers entering in
before the throne of grace?   And when the pastor stands up
alone without a sound or token of attendance with him on
the part of the flock, and shuts his eyes and so draws the cur-

tain between himself and the congregation, and enters into solitude while he pleads with God—the first salutation that greets him on his return being the subdued strains of the organ—does he not look too much like the high priest entering within the veil, and ministering by himself till the tinkling of the sacred bells announces his return to the waiting congregation? . . .

" Whether it be true or not physically, as has been asserted, that the striking and collision of sounds in the atmosphere can generate electricity, the spiritual fact is unquestionable. There is a marvelous magnetism in the blending and colliding of a multitude of voices in a great congregation. Nothing can compare with it as an incitement to religious enthusiasm; nothing can take its place as a means of stirring and maintaining a universal interest in public services. Now concerted reading is the simplest form of vocal worship. Some may complain that they have not the voice for singing, and others that they have not the training to follow the simplest melody of music; but none but the dumb or utterly unlettered can say that they cannot join in the audible reading of the Psalms. Here, then, is an exercise, scriptural and primitive in its character, that can enlist every worshiper, that can draw in every voice in the assembly to swell and deepen the current of devotion. . . .

" I know all that can be said of the danger of formality in our Lord's day worship; but formality belongs no more to thoughtless utterance than to thoughtless repression, to vain repetition than to vain silence. Indeed, the constant peril of non-participation in religious worship is that indecorous inattention, that worst kind of formalism, may become habitual. . . .

" We have never been more sensibly impressed than by a half-hour's still meditation around the table of the Lord. There are not only thoughts in us too deep for utterance, but

·thoughts which are repressed and drowned by another's utterance. 'To everything there is a season,' says the Preacher,
'and a time to every purpose under heaven'—'a time to keep
silence, and a time to speak.' So then, while we are seeking
for ministers who have a great gift for speaking, commend
us also to those of whom it can be said, as of a famous
Frenchman, that they have a great talent for silence. Even
in the ordinance of worship, which is especially for preaching
and prayer, we have often wished that we could make greater
use of the ministry of silence. But the organ and choir are
great, and they have prevailed. We have no sooner uttered
our 'Amen' than there comes a response; it may be from the
organ, or from the quartet, but we confess it always seems in-
trusive and distracting. It takes the thoughts away from
what has been said, appeals to our musical taste, if we have
any, setting us either to admiring or criticizing, or, if we have
no music in our souls, makes us impatient. 'A response'?
Yes; but we were praying to God, and wanted a moment of
stillness to see if we could not hear a response from the
throne. We had been shutting our eyes that we might thereby
the more completely shut ourselves in with God; we had been
turning our ears away from earth's distracting noises that we
might open them to the Lord, and were saying, 'Speak, Lord;
for thy servant heareth;' and before we have had time to
hear the divine voice in our soul, the vox humana stop has
broken in upon us, and music, with its voluptuous swell, has
rushed into the place where we were carrying on the sacrifice
of praise.

"A full minute of silence after prayer, of absolute congregational stillness—we have enjoyed it in one or two churches
where we have worshiped, and have never forgotten the impression. 'Be still, and know that I am God.' When shall
we learn that God is not in the wind of an organ-bellows, or
in the fire of exciting halleluiahs, but in the still, small voice?

And then, after the sermon, is apt to come another burst of violence against the kingdom of silence. If perchance the Spirit has helped us to make a serious impression upon our hearers, we wish so much that we could send them away with nothing to disturb that impression. But alas! who has not heard it? The organ with all its stops breaks out, like many bulls of Bashan. The seed of the Word has been sown, but cannot be let alone. A wild flock of quavers burst their cage in the organ-loft, and, like birds of the air, alight upon the hearers to catch away that which was sown in the heart. Who that has been present does not remember the gracious silence with which the sermon in Mr. Spurgeon's tabernacle closes? The people go away with the word of warning and exhortation and hope as the last sound that fell upon their hearts. They march out to the muffled beatings of a conscience accusing or else excusing, not to the tripping music of an organ. Oh, the power of silence!"

The fruits of this teaching were not yet. The preacher had turned the dry turf over, and thrown the seed of better things into the furrow. But years of instruction and of waiting passed before the important change in church worship which he sought was consummated. For years music committees met and jangled and voted money and received meekly the gratuitous criticisms of the church community. Quartet succeeded quartet like the passing birds of passing seasons. Gradually, however, opinions changed, and the pastor's plan became the people's policy. If one who had known the church in the seventies should enter it in the nineties, what a transformation in its worship he would observe! What a volume of sound in the singing! How it fills the nooks and corners of the church, as the full, swollen tide fills with its back-water the creeks and inlets of the coast! All are singing now, heartily, as unto the Lord, with an interested, worshipful spontaneity, very different from the lassitude of the old time, when to sit still on. the cushions and listen to trios from Mendelssohn or to the performance of fugues and contrapuntal études on the organ was the ideal of worship. God is not praised by the stagnant pool. But here the floods have lifted up their voice, and the languid congregational singing, with its omission of half the stanzas of the hymn, is now a thing of the past. To hear the counterpart of such singing you must go to the Lutheran churches of Prussia or Saxony, and listen to the common people as they sing the chorals of Paul Gerhardt.

CHAPTER VI

"In Christ" published—Private conferences for Bible study—Books
which had a formative influence on Dr. Gordon's ministry—Contact
with Brethrenism—The mission of this sect—In Europe, 1877—Estimate of preachers heard abroad

SOON after coming to Boston, Gordon published a remarkable study in the identities of Christ and the believer. "In
Christ" was the fruit of much deep meditation, the distillation
of many late hours in the Jamaica Plain manse. It is, perhaps, the most nearly perfect in form and content of any of
his works, quintessential in its compression, rich, finished, and
imbued with mysticism, the mysticism of the New Testament.
Such pages as these À Kempis or the Friends of God might
have written. How refreshing this profoundly penetrating
interpretation after the shallow syncretisms and nonchalant
denials of New England Unitarianism! It stands out to one,
working through the arid mass of the local religious literature
of its day, like a green spot, with feathery palms and tinkling
springs, in a choking expanse of unfruitful, limitless sand.

The Pauline phrases, "created in Christ," "crucified with
Christ," "risen with Christ," "baptized into Christ," "sanctified in Christ," "the dead in Christ," are taken as melodic
themes upon which to work out the variations of a sober,
fruitful exposition. Unitarianism made of Christ a mere pattern. This volume exhibits him as an indwelling principle,
incorporating itself in the believer and eradicating the old will,

the old personality. Through its action the former life is doomed to drop off and disappear as a scab, beneath which the new, wholesome flesh is forming. There are accordingly two eras in the life of the Christian. The one Paul describes as the time "when we were in the flesh"; the other is the true Anno Domini, the period of our life in Christ.

The significant fact of this new epoch in our history is the presence of Christ in the heart. Without this, man cannot be joined to God any more than steel can be welded without the flux of borax. "We cannot be loved of God apart from Christ, for the divine approval can go out only to that which is worthy. Neither can we be condemned if we are in Christ, for the divine disapprobation can fall only upon what is sinful, and he is without sin." * In prayer our acceptance is determined by the same nexus. If Christ's will covers, interpenetrates, and absorbs our will, there can be no conflict between our prayer and the sovereign wishes of God. "We can come with boldness as being in him 'that liveth and was dead,' and, being 'dead with him,' we shall be careful to bring that only required sacrifice of the Christian covenant, a crucified will." † Thus Christ prays through us.

Again, "since Christ and his attributes never part company, it is impossible to be made in him without being made into all that belongs to him." ‡ Here is the earnest of our sanctification. But "though this grace is conferred on each Christian as soon as he believes, it is nevertheless a gift held on deposit, 'hid with Christ in God,' to be drawn on through daily communion and gradual apprehension." §

Finally, the affinities thus created by union with Christ secure to his own the immortality which is his. "They that sleep in Jesus" have that in them which will respond to the resurrection summons as steel filings to the sweep of the mag-

---

* "In Christ," p. 119.   † Ibid., p. 142.
‡ Ibid., p. 168.   § Ibid., p. 170.

net above them.   Then the identity of life with Christ will have been attained through an identity of experience.

These first years in Boston were years of study and of spiritual exercise.   Private conferences were held semi-monthly in Gordon's house for the consideration of the deeper themes of scriptural teaching.   Associated with him in these studies were W. R. Nicholson, then rector of St. Paul's, and now bishop in the Reformed Episcopal Church, Mr. George C. Needham, Dr. H. M. Parsons, and others.   The reading upon which he fed included such books as Gurnall's "Christian Armor," Charnock's "Wisdom of our Fathers," and the body of Puritan divinity generally.   "It seems to me," he writes, "that the Puritan ministers held together both sides of the truth, and preserved their balance to a remarkable degree. They expounded most clearly the objective work of Christ, and they also unfolded his subjective work with a minuteness and a depth of insight quite beyond anything we witness in our day.   They wrote thus clearly because they had apprehended these things by a profound interior experience.   What tide-marks do the diaries and meditations which these good men left furnish of the heights to which the Spirit's floods rose in their souls!   We have a great lesson to learn of them concerning the culture of the inner life."

Among other books of which he was especially fond were Van Oosterzee's "Person and Work of the Redeemer," Vinet's "Outlines of Theology," Alford's works, the "Horæ Apocalypticæ" of Elliott, Edersheim's "Sketches of Jewish Life," the journals of Eugénie de Guérin, Uhlhorn's "Conflict of Christianity with Paganism"; the poems of Henry Vaughn, of Herbert, of Quarles, and of Donne; the works of Rothe, of R. Stier, of Birks, of Flavel, of Archer Butler, of Westcott, of Guinness, of Harnack; the lives of Joseph Alleine, of Robert Moffatt, of John Woolman, of Henry Martyn, and of David Brainerd.   The career of the last named exerted a powerful and lasting influence upon him. Years after, in describing a visit paid to Brainerd's grave, he writes:

"Does it savor of saint-worship or superstition to be thus exploring old graveyards, wading through snow-drifts, and deciphering ancient headstones on a cold day in midwinter? Perhaps so, on the face of it; but let us justify our conduct. What if the writer confesses that he has never received such spiritual impulse from any other human being as from him whose body has lain now for nearly a century and a half under that Northampton slab? For many years an old and worn volume of his life and journals has lain upon my study table, and no season has passed without a renewed pondering of its precious contents. 'If you would make men think well of you, make them think well of themselves,' is the maxim of Lord Chesterfield, which he regarded as embodying the highest worldly wisdom. On the contrary, the preacher and witness for Christ who makes us think meanly of ourselves is the one who does us most good, and ultimately wins our hearts. This is exactly the effect which the reading of Brainerd's memoirs has on one. Humiliation succeeds humiliation as we read on. 'How little have I prayed! how low has been my standard of consecration!' is the irresistible exclamation; and when we shut the book we are not praising Brainerd, but condemning ourselves, and resolving that, by the grace of God, we will follow Christ more closely in the future."

We should not, in summing up the influences which shaped Dr. Gordon's religious and theological opinions, omit those resulting from his contact with Brethrenism. In an interesting survey of the religious upheavals of the century, he describes the two movements, Tractarianism and Brethrenism, which, emanating from a common source, have affected so powerfully, yet so differently, the Christian life of England. After noting the important places which universities have occupied in religious movements generally, and after contrasting the opposite courses which Darby, in Dublin University, and Newman, in Oxford, took in their revolt against the current religious apathy in the Church of England, he calls attention to the insignificant contributions which the Tractarian reactionaries have made to biblical interpretation, as compared with the extraordinary productivity of Brethrenism. The Tractarian party left two works of exegesis—Pusey's " Daniel and the Minor Prophets " and Keble's " Metrical Version of the Psalms "—which barely pass the line of mediocrity. " But if we turn to the other party," he continues, " we see a movement almost ultra-biblical, and a body of men almost ultra-apostolical in their style and manner of life and service. It gathered to itself a strong body of scholars, mostly from the pulpits of the Church of England, who began to pour out biblical literature in floods—exposition and textual criticism, lexicons and dictionaries for aiding in the study of the Bible, synopses of Scripture, tract leaflets, etc. The Christian world has been fairly inundated with these issues, and it may be doubted if any body of Christians ever sent forth such a mass and such a variety of biblical literature in the same length of time.

" If we were to describe in a word the theological complexion of these writings, we should say that here we have high Calvinism, preaching free grace with a fullness and plainness never surpassed; practising believers' baptism, and writing treatises on its symbolism rarely equaled for deep spiritual insight; laying down a rule of life almost ascetic in its requirement of separation from the world and surrender of earthly possessions for Christ's sake; and holding with primitive apostolic fervor to the personal, literal, and ever-imminent coming of Christ as the hope of the church. It is our opinion that the best writings of this body have furnished the textbooks of modern evangelism, and largely determined its type of doctrine and preaching. Let us specify briefly.

"There is C. H. Mackintosh's 'Notes on Genesis,' 'Exo-dus,' etc., a work for which Mr. Spurgeon has expressed his high admiration, and which has had an immense circulation We know of hardly any modern treatise which is so full of the meat and marrow of the gospel as this, and which sets forth so clearly the fundamental doctrines of atonement and justifi-cation. There is 'The Blood of Jesus,' by William Reid—a small treatise, but one which has given to thousands of readers a new revelation of the simplicity of the gospel. There are the 'C. S. Tracts,' brief presentations of the gospel to the inquirer. They have been scattered far and wide, and have, in our opinion, never been surpassed as clear expositions of the way of life to the unconverted. Of less popular works, we might mention Darby's 'Synopsis of the Bible,' the expositions of Kelly, Newton, Tregelles, Soltau, Pridham, and Jukes. These books, especially those of the first three, have constituted the chief theological treasury of many of our evangelists. We can say for ourselves that, from the first time our eyes fell upon these treasures, we have nowhere else seen the gospel so luminously presented—the gospel of the grace of God, disencumbered of legalism and mysticism and tradition. Considered theologi-cally these are humble treatises. So was the 'Theologia Ger-manica,' out of which, through Luther, the German Refor-mation was born. So were the expositions of Peter Boehler, from which Wesley says he received his first true apprehension of saving faith. The springs of great reformations are often hidden and remote, but they rarely fail to be recognized in the end.

"Besides books, there were men. This little sect of which we are speaking has certainly shown us some apostolic char-acters. When George Müller set himself to live a life 'out and out for God,' and to prove in his own experience what can be accomplished by the single means of prayer and faith, many criticized, but few commended. When men like Darby

and Wigram forsook their aristocratic associations, and laid
down their great inherited wealth at the feet of Christ, going
forth in apostolic fashion, without scrip or purse, to preach
the gospel in every city, and in almost every European tongue,
none went before them to sound the trumpet of fame.   But
such examples are always and inevitably contagious ; and they
have doubtless affected the consecration of modern evangelism
quite as strongly as the books have influenced its doctrine.

" Such, we believe, after much thought and careful investigation and frequent conversations with those best qualified to
judge, is the real spring of the present evangelistic movement.
It demands a fearless candor to concede it, but we believe
that truth requires us to confess that we owe a great debt, both
in literature and in life, to the leaders of this ultra-Protestant
movement.   And we are glad to believe that the light which
it has thrown out by its immense biblical study and research
has been appropriated by many of the best preachers and
evangelists in our Protestant churches."

The summer of '76 Gordon spent with his wife in Europe.
Nothing especially noteworthy occurred in the three months'
visit.   The hoary churches and refectories of Oxford, the
gleaming peaks of the Jungfrau and of the Matterhorn, the
surf-like roar of London, the idyllic windings of the Rhine,
filled with interested pleasure the hearts of these, as of all
tourists.   In London he was specially drawn to the churches.
For the first and only time in his life after his ordination (with
the exception of a few Sundays of sickness and one solitary
Sabbath in New Hampton) he occupied a seat in the congregation.   The observations which he made from his new point
of view are acute and discriminating, and give us, naturally
enough, many intimations of the ideal and standard which he
had set for himself.

" ' The secret of power ' is much inquired after, and when
one demonstrates that he has real ability in preaching or in

teaching, there is forthwith great speculation as to how it was acquired. But it ought to be suggested at the outset that the secret of power is not some algebraic x—the unknown quantity in the problem of success, which can be figured out, and set by itself, and its exact value determined. Real power comes from an even proportion and nice adjustment of all the faculties of the man; and to imagine that there is some special secret which constitutes the philosopher's stone, that can transmute leaden failure into golden success, is to fall into a disastrous mistake. And so it has struck us again and again how utterly they come short who aim at power along some single line of culture or accomplishment.

" There were three preachers heard during a European journey who furnished a complete lesson on this point.

" There was, first, *the intellectual preacher.* He was such indeed; polished to the last degree, and dealing out real and carefully wrought thought. It was no ingenious serving up of scraps of borrowed opinion—no mere originality of literary pattern-working upon commonplace material. Here was a thinker, earnest, genuine, and thorough; and if one should want to hear such, we would commend him by all means to this divine. But though the congregation was exceptionally intelligent, it was evident that the number who could follow his discourse was very small. To them it was stimulating, no doubt. Yet how about the great numbers who could not follow it? Good food, and something for all, must be the rule in feeding the flock of God. But there, just in front of me, was a respectful, sedate hearer. He might have been a grocer or a butcher or a coal-dealer. At all events, his business was such as gave him little training or aptitude for the refinements of thought and the delicate shadings of style to which he was now listening. And so I set to watching his face. Determination to be faithful in attending to the services was written on every feature. He was holding the muscles of his face to their Sunday tension. I saw drowsiness and inattention pulling at them, but in vain. And when, under the loud and somewhat monotonous tones of the preacher, he half drowsed, he would start from the perilous edge of sleep, and open such a wakeful and applauding glance on the minister as fairly humbled me. For said I, 'What a pity that hungry souls should have to stretch their necks and strain their appetites to get their spiritual food, and that they should have to look such loyal amens at the preacher when really they do not understand what he is saying!' And so our good, patient, faithful hearer went out of church when the services were over. And if he had known the quotation, probably the truest confession he could have made would have been found in the lines of Tennyson's 'Northern Farmer, Old Style':

"'An' 'eerd 'un a-bummin' awaay loike a buzzard clock ower my 'ead,
   An' I never knawed whot a mean'd, but I thowt a 'ad summut to saay,
   An' I thowt a said whot a owt to 'a' said, an' I coom'd awaay.'

"Next we came upon *the unctuous preacher*. He made as much use of his heart and his handkerchief as the other did of his head and his learning. But who does not know how cheap the unction is that is merely poured upon the heart, and not pressed out of the heart by deep and genuine feeling? Ready-made emotion is not likely to fit a congregation very closely. If a preacher has no oil in his lamp, it matters little how profusely he pours oil on his head, or how lavishly it runs down his beard. In other words, fervor without light, feeling without truth, do not generally move one. When Robertson was discoursing on the love of God to sinners, and in the glow of his kindling thought a tear was seen to course down his cheek and fall upon his Bible, no wonder that they said that that was the most eloquent passage in his sermon.

There must be a certain amount of thought to give body to feeling; it is the beaten oil of the sanctuary which alone can feed true unction. Oil produced from the olive-press of Gethsemane—emotion born of true fellowship with the sufferings of Christ—this alone can beget genuine sympathy. But the preacher whom I am describing sought to work up feeling by pathetic exclamations and fond phrases, and the like. And so I was not surprised at the comment of a Norwegian musician, who chanced to be traveling in our company. In broken and entertaining English, he said, 'He did not seem to veel vat he says, and he did not says much.'

"The third preacher whom we heard impressed me neither by his remarkable culture nor by his remarkable pathos. He had enough of each, however; and the two elements were so evenly blended that neither was especially conspicuous. But he affected us very deeply. No admiration for the preacher's genius was awakened; no sense of his trying to make us weep was experienced. On the contrary, as he went on, we found ourselves thinking of our sins, and then adoring the Lamb of God who taketh away the sins of the world. In fact, we confess that we were disappointed. We went to hear a great preacher, and from beginning to end never thought of him as such, so much were we occupied with self, the great sinner.

"'Which now of these three?' The first made his sermon a work of art. That was evidently his business. To that end he was pressing on with all his might. 'And *by chance* there came down a certain priest that way.' To find a poor, wounded, half-dead sinner, and pour the oil of grace into his heart, was not what he was bent on. He was about other matters—attending to his *clerical* duties, minding his theology, etc.—and if he should discover a lost sinner in his way, it would be entirely by chance.

"The second preacher beamed unctuously upon his congregation, 'oozing all over with the fat affectionate smile,' and anon dissolving his smiles in a solution of tears.   But there was no grip of truth in all he said, no strong grappling with the conscience, no tears of penitence in the hearer's eyes reflecting tears of pity in the preacher's.   'And likewise a Levite came and looked' (with gold-bowed spectacles, no doubt, which had constantly to be wiped because of his emotion), 'and passed by on the other side.'

"The third preacher uttered a message which came straight home 'to men's business and bosoms.'   He was evidently bent on seeking out the sinner.   'This preaching finds me,' must have been the feeling of many a hearer.   'But a certain Samaritan, as he journeyed, *came where he was.*'   This is the preaching the world needs—not the discoursing in which the hearer gets glimpses, now and then, of the minister looking through the lattice of some flowery period, or emerging from some rhetorical circumlocution, only to disappear again into incomprehensibility.   The preaching which comes close to the heart, and finds it, and blesses it, is what is wanted."

On another Sunday Gordon had the interesting and novel experience of listening to his own words with the slight incidental modifications suitable to differing congregations.   Then indeed was a mirror set before his eyes.   For on going to a leading Presbyterian church he was surprised, when the text and headings were given out, to note how closely they followed a sermon scheme which he himself had used some months before in Boston.   As the sermon progressed from stage to stage, his own illustrations, his own metaphors, his very quotations, appeared as on an unfolding panorama.   The London minister had, Dr. Gordon afterward conjectured, read the sermon in a somewhat obscure American paper devoted to those prophetic exegeses with which he was closely in touch, and had reproduced it presumably by a process of unconscious cerebration.

For when Gordon shook hands with him, introducing himself at the meeting's end, he was invited without the least apparent constraint or embarrassment, which the common ownership of such a secret would naturally involve, to the minister's home, and spent the day with him in pleasant intercourse.

CHAPTER VII

THE TIDE TURNS

At work with Uncle John Vassar—The Moody meetings of '77—Incidents of the " inquiry room "—" A question of casuistry "—The redeemed men—Communion reform

AMONG all the influences which touched and vivified the early ministry at Clarendon Street, none was stronger than that of Uncle John Vassar, a devoted laborer for souls. " Far beyond any man whom I ever knew," wrote Gordon, " was it true of him that his citizenship was in heaven, and so filled was he with the glory and the power of the heavenly life that to many he seemed like a foreigner speaking an unknown tongue. I have never been so humbled and quickened by contact with any living man as with him. Hundreds of Christians, while sorrowing that they shall see his face no more for the present, will bless God as long as they live for the inspiration which they have received from his devoted life."

For five successive years, off and on, " Uncle John " labored with the Clarendon Street Church in his peculiar work of " spiritual census-taking," going through the streets of proud, cultivated, self-righteous Boston, ringing every door-bell, and confronting every household with the great question of the new birth. He was wont to describe himself as " only a shepherd-dog, ready to run after the lost sheep and bring them back to the Shepherd," and ever refused the honors and emoluments of the ministry. He would literally travail in prayer for the unconverted. "The nights which he spent at my home," writes Gordon, "were nights of prayer and pleading for my congregation and my ministry. Again and again would I hear him rising in the midnight hours to plead with God for the unsaved, till I had frequently to admonish him that he must not lose his sleep." And so he wrought and prayed and instructed the young minister, meekly teachable before such a master of spiritual things, in those hard-learned and rarely acquired secrets which open the way to the heart of hearts of sinful humanity.

The inspiration which this faithful man brought with him accrued principally to the pastor of Clarendon Street. The influence of Mr. Moody's meetings in 1877 affected both pastor and people. Indeed, this year was the turning-point, the climacteric which, after seven years of lethargic religious life, opened a new period of spiritual health. When the revival meetings were finished, Gordon realized that the crest of the hill had been passed, and that the crisis in the struggle for a spiritual as against a secular church was over.

These meetings, which were organized and carried on by Mr. Moody with all the executive ability and religious fervor for which he is distinguished, were held in a large Tabernacle —a great "tent," indeed, of brick and spruce timber, with nothing about it to attract but the gospel of Christ preached therein. This building stood within three hundred feet of the Clarendon Street Church, which was used from the beginning for overflow and "inquiry" meetings. The Tabernacle was thronged night after night by audiences of from five to seven thousand. People of all ranks and conditions attended. Excursion trains brought in thousands from all parts of New England. Seventy thousand families in Boston were personally visited. Great noon prayer-meetings were held daily in Tremont Temple by business men. Meetings were organized for young men, for boys, for women, for the intemperate—in short, for all classes in the community that were ready to help or be helped.

And at the center of all these operations stood the Clarendon Street Church, like a cemetery temporarily occupied by troops in battle. What a shattering and overturning of weather-stained, moss-grown traditions followed! What experiences of grace, what widening vistas of God's power, what instruction in personal religion, resulted from these six months of revival! A new window was built into the religious life of the church, letting in floods of light. The true purpose of a church's existence began to be emphasized. Drunkards and outcasts were daily reclaimed, and brought into fellowship. Christian evidences of the best sort, evidences which had to do with the present potency of a saving Christ, were multiplied to affluence, strengthening the faith of believers. The duty and opportunity of all in the work of the inquiry-room were asserted. A great education in methods of practical religious work resulted.

We get a glimpse of the character of this movement, as it proceeded month after month, in the following reminiscences from Dr. Gordon's own pen:

"In 1877, during Mr. Moody's meetings in Boston, there was an inquiry mee ing in our church. The house was full, and Mr. Moody sent me around to find workers to help. I came upon a woman with a baby. She was anxious to find Christ; for when I approached her and asked if she wanted to be saved, she said, 'That is what I came here for.'

"I stepped over to a gentleman on the front seat, a fine-looking man, and said, 'Are you a Christian?'

"'Yes, sir,' he answered.

"'I want you to go over there and talk to an inquirer.'

"'I never talked to an inquirer,' he replied.

"'But you are a Christian?'

"'Yes.'

" ' Here is a woman just ready to be led to Christ.'

" ' Excuse me. I should not know what to say to her.'

" Well, because I could not get him to go, I went over my-self and sat down beside the woman. But the baby was so restless that she could not give me her attention. The man kept watching us, and saw the situation. By and by he crept softly down and gave the baby some sweets, and took her in his arms and carried her to the other side of the church and held her for an hour, while I led the woman to Christ. He found that, if he could not lead a soul to Christ, he could hold the baby while some one else did. I think a special blessing rested upon that work; for not only was the mother saved, but that little girl came to Christ when she was twelve years old, and I haven't a more aggressive Christian in my church than that baby has grown to be."

" ' Did I tell a lie? '

" It was about as odd a question of casuistry as was ever propounded; and yet, as I thought of it afterward, it seemed to go about as deeply into the heart of redemption as any which could be asked.

" He was a real Irishman, whose brogue would identify him on the first interview. We have frequently noticed that when a genuine son of Erin becomes converted, and attempts to launch out into the language of Canaan, he provokes an irresistible smile on the faces of grave Christians. There is a certain quaintness of conception and expression which belongs peculiarly to the people of this race when dealing with re-ligious experience, of which we might give some very striking examples had we room. For this, however, we cannot now turn aside, but must come to our story.

" Patrick Daley was one of the first to profess conversion in connection with Mr. Moody's recent evangelistic services in Boston. He had been a stanch Roman Catholic by persuasion, but a desperate drunkard by practice.   With an over-powering desire to be saved from his evil habit, he so far broke through the prejudices of his religion as to go and listen to the great evangelist.   There he heard with astonishment and delight that the chief of sinners and the most hopeless of drunkards might find immediate forgiveness and deliverance through surrender to Jesus Christ.   He went into the inquiry-room, and trustingly accepted the Saviour, and entered into great peace and joy in believing.   With his conversion, he got rid not only of the heavy burden of his sin, but of the not less heavy burden of popish ceremonies and superstitions. All these he now counted loss for the excellency of the know-ledge of Christ Jesus the Lord, and descanted in no very temperate terms on the folly and abomination of the things in which he had formerly trusted.   Several weeks after his conversion, he approached me at the close of a meeting with his story and his question.

"'You see, your reverence, I know a good thing when I get it; and when I found salvation, I could not keep it to myself.   Peter Murphy lived in the upper story of the same tenement with me.   Murphy was a worse drunkard than I, if such a thing could be; and we had gone on many a spree together.   Well, when I got saved and washed clean in the blood of Christ, I was so happy I did not know what to do with myself.   So I went up to Murphy, and told him what I had got.

"'Poor Peter! he was just getting over a spree, and was pretty sick and sore, and just ready to do anything I told him.   So I got him to sign the pledge, and then told him that Jesus alone could help him keep it.   Then I got him on his knees, and made him pray and surrender to the Lord, as I had done.   You never see such a change in a man as there was in him for the next week.   I kept watch of him, and prayed for him, and helped him on the best I could, and, sure, he was a different man. Well, come Sunday morning, Joe Healey called round to pay his usual visit. This was the worst yet; for Healey used to come to see Murphy as regular as Sunday, always bringing a bottle of whisky with him, and these two would spree it all day, till they turned the whole house into a bedlam. Well, I saw Healey coming last Sunday morning, and I was afraid it would be all up with poor Murphy if he got with him. So when I went to the door to let him in, and he said, " Good-morning, Pat; is Murphy in? " I said, " *No; Murphy is out. He does not live here any longer;*" and in this way I sent Healey off, and saved Murphy from temptation.'

" Here was the burden of his question; for he continued:

" ' Did I tell a lie? What I meant was that the *old Murphy did not live there any more.* For you know Mr. Moody told us that when a man is converted he is a new creature; old things have passed away. And I believe that Murphy is a new creature, and that the old Murphy does not live any more in that attic. That is what I meant. Did I tell a lie?'

" Candid reader, what should I say? In the light of Paul's great saying, ' Nevertheless I live; *yet not I,* but Christ liveth in me,' can it be denied that Patrick Daley was right?

" It may be claimed that it is a dangerous kind of theological jugglery which we here encounter. ' What I hate, that I do,' says Paul. Alas! no one who knows the depths of an evil nature can deny that. ' If then I do that which I would not, I consent unto the law that it is good.' Yes; certainly that is true. ' Now then *it is no more I that do it,* but sin that dwelleth in me.' Ah! here is a conclusion which may well startle us. Can we prove an alibi at the judgment-seat? Can we swear the blame of our wrong-doing upon the inbred sin which dwelt within us, and expect to go scot-free ourselves? When the sheriff of the law comes knocking at our

door to arrest us and hale us away to prison, can we say,
' Old I doesn't live here any more ; the new man occupies the
house now '?

" It can hardly be denied that Paul's theology is very radical in just this direction. ' Unselfed and inchristed ' is the
phrase that has been employed to set forth the great transaction of spiritual renewal ; and observe how the apostle encourages us to serve a writ of ejection on the old tenant, our
evil self, and to bring in a new occupant of the premises :
' That ye put off concerning the former conversation the old
man, which is corrupt according to the deceitful lusts ; . . .
and that ye *put on* the new man, which after God is created in
righteousness and true holiness.' No betterment or reformation of the depraved tenant, who is always in hopeless ar-
rears with his landlord, but a peremptory order to move out!
Moreover, the Christian is considered to have done this very
thing—evicted his former self, and set its goods and chattels
out upon the sidewalk. ' Seeing that ye have put off the old
man with his deeds ; and have put on the new man, which is
renewed in knowledge after the image of Him that created
him.' So vividly and strongly did this conception take hold
of Martin Luther that he used to say, ' When any one comes
and knocks at the door of my heart and asks, " Who lives
here ? " I reply, " Martin Luther used to, but he has moved
out, and Jesus Christ now lives here." ' "

Before the meetings were ended nearly thirty reclaimed
drunkards had been received into the Clarendon Street Church.
The general opinion was that these men would not stand even
to the end of the year. Yet Gordon was able to say some
time after, in a Northfield address, " Of those who have continued their residence with us, all have remained steadfast,
as consistent, as devoted, and as useful members as we have,
a demonstration that God can instantly change a man from

the vilest and worst drunkard to one in the way to the highest saintship."

After his death a few pencilings were found among his papers describing the conversion of one of these men. He had started to write an eighth chapter for the fragment of spiritual autobiography which was issued posthumously under the title of "A Pastor's Dream." These few notes were found too late for publication. In the preceding chapters he had described the entrance of Christ into the church where he was preaching, and the effect which his presence had had on him. Continuing, he says:

"Why he visited our sanctuary on that Lord's day morning, and what gracious lessons he taught us concerning his power and his coming, we have learned in the previous chapters. But longing for yet greater blessings, we still press the question, 'But wherefore, O Master, camest thou in thither?' Was he searching, perchance, for a lost sheep? That were a sufficient reason, as he himself has taught us, why he should leave the ninety and nine which are safely sheltered, and go after the one which has strayed. Yes; but this would not seem to be the place to look for straying lambs. A beautiful Gothic church, richly carpeted and upholstered, and filled with a sober and respectable congregation, is not, as a rule, the resort of wretched outcasts. In the miserable slums, amid the reek and defilement of human sewage, we shall find such, and not in this elegant modern sanctuary. Thank God, however, there are exceptions to such a rule.

"No. 40 was the pew where, in vision, I saw the Master seated on that memorable Sunday morning. Directly behind, in the pew next to the door, is where, not in a dream, but in sad reality, I found the lost sheep. He had not strayed in by accident; he had been bleating about the fold for some hours with the vague hope of finding help; but Satan, with the premonition that he was about to be deprived of his prey, had made a last desperate effort to retain him.   Each saloon he had passed in his way to the church had smitten him with a fresh cup of alcoholic poison, till, sore broken in the place of dragons, and covered with the shadow of death, he had crept into this remote corner of the church and swooned away into a drunken sleep.   Humanly speaking it was only by the merest accident that I discovered him.   The congregation had dispersed after the evening service; the lights, excepting two or three near the door, had been turned off, when, passing down the aisle, I discovered what seemed to be a pile of filthy rags, beneath which, on examination, I found as wretched a specimen of ruined humanity as I ever set eyes on.   'Call a policeman.   Take him away to the lockup' would no doubt have . . ."

Here the pen dropped, never to be resumed.

The "wretched specimen of ruined humanity" became, through the miracle of conversion, a most extraordinary example of the transforming and sustaining power of God's Spirit.   For seventeen long years the man here referred to has, in the divine strength, been kept from falling.   The slave was freed; his family reunited in Christian fellowship.   No testimony has been more eloquent, because of its evident truth and because of its note of thankfulness, than this man's, so unfailingly given in the evening meetings of the church.   In season and out of season, at the shop and among the squalid wrecks at mission meetings, has he borne witness to God's presence.   And even on Boston Common, where Whitefield preached to the multitudes of an earlier generation with such power that tears might be seen on every cheek, the pitiable drunkard, now clean and whole and in his right mind, may be found on warm afternoons in the leafy months, setting forth the gospel of Christ to the motley crowds about him.

No one knows as well as Dr. Gordon's most intimate friends the complete and triumphant satisfaction which the conversion

of these ruined men gave him. No one else knows how
tender was the solicitude with which he watched their lives,
even as the Good Shepherd himself. The ninety and nine
just persons who need no repentance—who are busied with
literature, social life, and what not—doubtless felt how little
this man sympathized with their life, and how languid was his
interest in their enthusiasms. He was no social pet, no rev-
erend idol! His enthusiasm was for the poor, wretched,
submerged, helpless, and hopeless sinner. To such he gave
his heart and his time and his strength. The "redeemed
men" were to him the jewels of his church. In reclaimed
sinners he saw the flowering of the truth. They were as the
lotus growing out of the mud. We well remember his sigh of
relief on coming from the death-bed of one of these men at
the City Hospital. MacNamara was a miserable, drunken
beggar, with hardly three garments on him, when he first appeared at the pastor's home; but he was not beyond the reach
of Christ. Poor, weak man! though strong in the new
strength, falling, yet ever rising, and dying, finally, a triumphant death! "MacNamara is safe now," were the words on
Gordon's lips as he returned from the hospital that day. No
more anguish, no more heart-sorrow, for this child of his. He,
the under-shepherd, had passed him on to the great Shepherd
of the sheep, who carries the lambs in his bosom, and gently
leads them that are with young. *MacNamara is safe!*

The entrance of so many reformed men into the church
necessitated changes in the administration of the communion,
which have now become general. The cup of dragons could
not be offered to men whom it had tortured and poisoned.
Nor could it represent the perfect Sacrifice, the untainted
Passover. The first consideration was forced upon the church
by the presence of these members, newly emancipated from
the bondage of alcoholism. The second was the result of a
careful exegetical study, which led finally to the abandonment

of fermented elements altogether, and the substitution therefor of the pure juice of the grape and of unleavened Passover
bread. In justification of this supplanting of "that fallen
angel of creation, that right-hand minister of the evil one,"
an exhaustive study of the whole subject was published.
From this we can draw only a brief extract.

After commenting on the fact that the only two terms used
in Scripture in this connection are "the cup" and "the fruit of
the vine," and that the word "wine" is nowhere employed to
describe the symbolic blood; and after noting that the term
"fruit of the vine" could hardly signify fermented wine, since
the usages of the Jewish Passover, out of which the communion sprang, seem to forbid its employment by the rigid ex-
clusion of leaven; and after quoting statements of living
rabbis which interdict the use of wine in the Passover service
of to-day, he says:

"The use of fermented wine seems to mar the symbolism
of this divine ordinance. The crimson wine poured out
brings graphically before us Christ's blood which was shed for
the remission of sins; the drinking of the cup tells plainly of
our nourishment through the imparted life of Christ. But
there is another idea which should be suggested by this sacrament, the immaculateness of the Redeemer's blood.

"The Passover loaf was typical of Jesus Christ. It is important, therefore, that the symbols which point back to
Christ should be as significant as those which pointed forward
to him. The unleavened bread was rigidly insisted on as
the ceremonial prophecy of Christ; the unleavened bread was
used in instituting the memorial sacrament of Christ; and we
hold that the unleavened bread meets the typical requirements
and therefore should still be retained in the eucharist. We
apply the same principle to the cup. It is the symbol of 'the
precious blood of Christ, as of a lamb without blemish and
without spot.' Here is the one blood in which there is no

taint of hereditary sin, no trace of natural or acquired depravity. What can adequately symbolize the holy blood of him who, 'through the eternal Spirit, offered up himself *without spot* unto God?'

" Scripture declares that leaven signifies corruption; chemistry pronounces that fermentation is death. How then can this element typify Christ? Can corruption stand as the similitude of the Incorruptible One? Can death show forth him who is the Life? It may be fitting that those who are 'the degenerate plants of a strange vine'—the deniers of Christ's spotless humanity—should symbolize their faith by the cup in which the depravity of alcohol is working to produce all manner of concupiscence; but let the branches of the True Vine, who rejoice in the holiness of their Head, contend for the true fruit of the vine, and so keep the cup of the Lord innocent and undepraved till they drink it new in the kingdom of the Father."

CHAPTER VIII

REFORM FOR INDIVIDUAL AND STATE

The Boston Industrial Temporary Home—An answer to prayer—Wendell
Phillips and the drunkard—Crossett of North China—Advocacy of
prohibition—Coöperation with Joseph Cook in reform work—The
Prohibition party—Woman's cause

HOW to discriminate between the worthy and the unworthy
—between the man who is trying and the man who is lying
—is the eternal crux in the problem of charity. The Moody
meetings had brought to Dr. Gordon's attention, as never
before, the possibilities, the encouragements, and the dangers
inhering in work among drunkards. The futility of preaching to those whose stomachs are faint and empty became
speedily evident. The need, too, of a temporary refuge for
converted men, who without such a place would be likely to
drift back into old haunts, forced itself on him. The Industrial Temporary Home, an institution very like the Salvation
Army "shelters" of a later day, was started, therefore, for the
immediate relief of those out of work, and as a means of de-
termining the value and reality of professions made by men
of this class. The practical importance of the enterprise was
clear from the first. From the first, too, its peculiar difficulties were apparent. Embarrassing financial problems met the
committee in charge at every turn. The various superinten-
dents and matrons, who succeeded one another with ominous
rapidity, proved collectively incompetent. Trustees became
discouraged, resignation followed resignation, financial back-

ing was withdrawn; the craft was clearly water-logged and sinking.

Responsibility was shifted, finally, entirely upon Dr. Gordon's shoulders. For a term of years he carried almost alone the heavy weight of a work the only assured fruit of which was the annually recurring deficit. Burdened with this great care, he left the city one summer to take a brief vacation in the hill-country. A sense of deep disheartenment pressed heavily upon him. An undertaking promising, useful, necessary, was trembling on the edge of disruption. There was no human help in sight. He was driven, therefore, into the arms of God. Every morning during the whole summer he withdrew to a quiet place in the woods, a spot still, sun-dappled, and there laid before the Lord the discouragements and the needs of the work. Summer passed, and in early September he was back again in the city. Seated in his study a few days after his arrival, he was handed a note in unfamiliar writing, requesting an immediate interview. Replying to the summons and hunting up the address, he soon found himself in the chamber of an old man, in a quarter of the city long deserted by residents and given over now to the roar of traffic. The man was an entire stranger, a relic of a rapidly passing generation, inordinately fond of his properties, as was afterward learned. There he sat, dry, wizened, in skullcap, surrounded by a clutter of dust-covered documents and papers, a bottle of brandy at his left hand. His intentions were soon made known. He had learned during the summer of the Industrial Home, and had become convinced of the reasonableness and expediency of its method. He wished, therefore, to make provision for it in his will, and to get suggestions from Gordon looking toward the enlargement of the work and the placing of it upon a secure basis.

This day's interview was the first in a series of events which resulted in the complete solution of this problem of many weary years. The bequest when paid amounted to over twenty thousand dollars. A strong cabinet was formed for the more efficient care of the institution, composed of men able, generous, reliable—men who have stood by to the present day. As a result of further earnest prayer, a superintendent of exceptional ability and consecration, a converted horse-jockey, was brought unexpectedly to Dr. Gordon's notice, one who for many years has not only conducted the Home with superior executive skill, but has also helped to found homes of a like character in many of our Northern and Western cities. In a short time the institution was on a paying basis. At present nearly thirty-five thousand lodgings are provided annually, and about fifty thousand meals. Best of all, a successful rescue work is being carried on which has brought hundreds from the gutter into the church.

"It was the greatest lesson in faith I have ever had," said Gordon once, in recounting the experience. "From that day to this I have prayed with the greatest assurance of God's intervention in practical matters." From that day to his death, too, he labored for the Home, the last time that he was out before his final sickness being at its annual committee-meeting. His associates declared in resolutions after his death:

"He was, indeed, the central figure [in the work], being in a sense its founder, and always its devoted friend, giving to it unceasingly his time, his thought, his effort, and his prayers. . . . His devotion to the work of saving men was always prominent and supreme. In this respect we gladly concede that in service and sacrifice he has outstripped us all."

The following letter gives us an intimation of his constant interest in the Home:

"DEAR BROTHER ROBERTS: I have only now found time to reply to your letter. I appreciate more and more your work. It is *the* work for reaching men. I am sure there is no occasion for you to be disturbed in any way. So far as I can judge, it is going on well and satisfactorily. It requires much patience at your end of the line, and it requires much at this end to keep up with the door-bell, and to hear all the calls for help—a perfect stream this morning, giving us hardly a half-hour's rest. But we must all keep the two bears well fed and under constant control, namely, 'bear and forbear.' Both of these are liable to get out of their cages, and no-where is their good nature more taxed than at your Home and my home. May the God of peace keep our hearts and minds in perfect peace.

"Yours in Christ,
"A. J. GORDON."

In the early days of struggle and isolation, Gordon had been immensely encouraged by the sympathy which the first citizen of the commonwealth, Wendell Phillips, constantly showed to him in this undertaking. In some reminiscences of the great agitator, published shortly after his departure, he refers to this:

"In temperance work I saw more of Wendell Phillips's heart than anywhere else. He struck hard blows against the drink iniquity. But here he was not merely an iconoclast, bringing down his hammer upon license laws, which, next to fugitive-slave laws, he hated most intensely; he was a healer as well as a smiter. He used to come into the Home for re-forming inebriates, which we started at the time of the Moody and Sankey meetings, to inquire after the enterprise and give it his encouragement. He sometimes brought in poor, broken-down drunkards, to ask the help of our Christian workers on their behalf. His indignation against the rumseller, and the laws that sustained him, was matched only by his tender compassion toward the wretched victims of strong drink.

Once, with one of our Christian women, the question came
up as to the possibility of reclaiming the confirmed drunkard,
when she, with all the ardor of her conviction, declared that
there was certainly one way, viz., by the grace of God brought
to bear in a renewed heart. And I cannot describe the sympathetic tenderness with which he assented to the remark,
nor the spirit of humble self-distrust with which he alluded, in
a single sentence, to his own experience."

Others would occasionally stray into the Home besides
outcasts. Some ten years ago a minute was forwarded to the
State Department from the American consul in Shanghai,
describing the life of a Mr. Crossett, an independent missionary in China, who worked throughout the province of Shan-
tung, preaching, visiting prisons, nursing the sick, burying the
dead. He was much of an ascetic, living chiefly on rice,
millet, and water. The Chinese revered him, calling him the
Christian Buddha, and freely gave him food and lodging. A
little notice of him was published in the " Watchword " at the
time of his death:

" We were honored to know the man well. In the Industrial Home in Boston of which we are president—an institution to lodge and feed the homeless and stranger requiring
work, with the saw and ax as compensation—we first found
him. Being in the city as a stranger, he preferred to lodge
in this place, working for his board, to asking hospitality. An
educated man of keen, original mind, men called him very
eccentric. He was so since he made Christ his center, and
hence was thrown out of center with the customs and traditions of the world.

" Eccentricity is a relative term. The orthodoxy of one
age often becomes the heterodoxy of another. The faith of
primitive Christianity is at some points scouted as the fanaticism of latter-day Christianity. The first sign of alleged insanity which Mr. Crossett exhibited was in his laying hands

on the sick for their recovery. He learned it of his Chinese converts, they having learned it from the New Testament. He at first forbade them, but they challenged him by the Word of God whether they were not enjoined to do so. He had to concede it; then he practised it, and was set down as touched with insanity. . . . We had much sweet converse and prayer with him. May he rest in peace."

It is a rare thing indeed for one who has wrought any length of time among the poor, and for the rescue of drunkards, to fail to develop convictions upon the duty of the State in regard to the saloon. Monumental insane asylums, ever-widening potter's fields, and the vast, unending streams of miserable poverty—which, as investigators one and all, from Charles Booth to the humblest charity visitor, agree, flow from the doors of this institution as from a chief source—quicken indignation and stimulate belief in a "root-and-branch" policy. Gordon was no exception to this experience. "He was broad enough," wrote Dr. O. P. Gifford of him, "to look beyond the individual to the State. Some men make bricks; others make buildings. Some can never see beyond the unit; others can think of the sum. Dr. Gordon tried to help men who were in need, but he also strove for the health of the State. He was always ready to cast his vote and to raise his voice for prohibition. The Good Samaritan in the parable received commendation because he helped the man who had fallen among thieves. Dr. Gordon deserves greater commendation; for, while he ministered to the unfortunate through the Home, he hindered the robber through the State. He was not foolish enough to spend his money on bandages and oil, paying part of the bills, meanwhile, by licensing the brigands. He combined sympathy for the wronged with sense for the thief. The Pharisees might use the price of Christ to buy a potter's field; but Dr. Gordon had no patience with men who would sell humanity

and compromise with evil by taking money wherewith to buy
burying-grounds.   His great patience came nearest to exhaustion when he saw politicians putting the State in pawn
for license fees, and professing Christians casting votes to
strengthen the politicians, and sharing the spoils. . . . In
pulpit and platform he never flinched in his advocacy of total
abstinence for the individual and prohibition for the State.
Like the pillar of Israel's wanderings, he was light for those
who sought liberty, but lightning for the Egyptians who followed to enslave."

No consideration of expediency ever affected him. The
opportunism of the so-called high-license system he opposed
on grounds of conscience with utmost vigor.   " ' The moral
law,' " he used to say, quoting Vinet, " ' is an arithmetic in
which there are only even numbers, no fractions.   In other
words, there are no half-duties in God's requirements.' If
we cannot enforce our view we can at least witness against
any other which compromises with this disreputable iniquity.
There is a power in steady, year-after-year protest which will
make itself felt in the long run."

One can hardly deny now that his moral intuitions have
been, in the light of the continuous and complete failure of
half-measures, entirely justified.   The saloon, with its Gar-
gantua appetite, goes on swallowing everything we prize—
virtue, honor, wealth, integrity, political purity, the sanctities
of the home.   "The new barbarism," as they fitly call it in
France, yearly extends its sway.   Only one policy has in any
degree driven it back—the policy of prohibitive extinction.

Every one familiar with the life of Boston knows how difficult it is for moral reform to get a foothold on its congealed
and slippery respectability.   The traditions of reform are up-
held by ostracized men.   Phillips in the last generation and
Joseph Cook in our day have been social pariahs for the
truth's sake, cast out in the one case by the Cotton Whigs,

and in the other by a dull, rich, respectable bourgeoisie. "This Joseph," remarked Gordon once, referring to Mr. Cook, "like that other Joseph, whose branches ran over the wall, has been sorely shot at by the archers. But we rejoice that, like that same Joseph, his bow to-day abides in strength." Side by side, the two wrought, supporting not what was politic, but what was right. It is interesting to think of the old veteran of antislavery giving them his blessing as he himself left the stage.

"There is a grand movement in the way of temperance on foot," said Gordon one day, in a little speech at the Monday lectureship, "led by what Wendell Phillips used to call 'the Beacon Street reformers.' He sat yonder one morning, almost the last time I ever saw him, and after he heard what was said here, remarked to me as he went out, 'Well, I might as well retire; the temperance cause is in good hands; I think we can safely leave it there.' . . . A certain class of reformers have a theory that the way to destroy low dives is by high license. These men say, 'Why cannot we unite, bring together all the temperance forces—the license men and the Prohibitionists, the high-license men and the low-license men? Why cannot we all unite, and present a solid front?' Why not? Because two men cannot pull in the same direction when one has his face toward the north and the other has his face toward the south. There is just the difference between license and prohibition. They pull in opposite directions, and there is no use to try to compromise or bridge over the difficulty. I remember that Frances Power Cobbe tells us that she heard two Irishmen talking in London, and that one of them said to a stranger, 'Can you tell me how far it is to Hampstead Heath?' 'Ten miles,' was the reply. He turned to his friend and said, 'That makes it five miles apiece; we can easily do that.' How far is it to the abolition of the liquor traffic? The whole length of prohibition. We must go the whole distance, every one of us. It is no use to divide it up between high license and low license. We have got to go the whole way."

At every opportunity he bore testimony against the unrighteous traffic. "There is no matter nearer my heart," he wrote to a Kansas judge whom he was urging to take charge of certain resolutions on the subject at the annual denominational gathering, "than the prohibition of the liquor traffic. If you will come to Chicago and take the stroke-oar, I will pull behind you to the best of my ability." And at another meeting of the same character in Boston, when a humble brother with a sound conscience introduced out of due course a resolution protesting against the exportation of Medford rum to West Africa and was duly suppressed by the scrupulous parliamentarian in the chair, Gordon started to his feet with the exclamation, "Order or no order, we cannot as Christians afford to table that resolution!" The protest was carried with a cheer.

His political connections during the last decade of his life were determined by his convictions on this point. With Arnold, he had "an intense abhorrence of all party ties save that one tie which binds a man to the party of Christ against wickedness." Moral issues with him transcended all others. The defeat or victory of either of the dominant "realm-ruining parties" was, he felt, a matter of comparative unimportance. When the Prohibition party, therefore, was organized in 1884, he joined himself to it, assisted in the establishment of its organ, the New York "Voice," contributed to its campaign funds, and spoke repeatedly at its public meetings. It was a period of heated controversy. The defection of a large contingent of voters from the Republican party resulted in its defeat for the first time in a quarter-century. Much petty persecution of Prohibitionists followed. Ministers who had not been cajoled by the "catnip-tea resolutions" of the politicians were crowded out of their churches. The leaders in the secession were hung or burned in effigy. Warmth of opinion was engendered between friends who disagreed. We get a suggestion of this in the following letter:

" I was sorry after you left that I had my discussion on the issues of the day. It is a time of deep agitation, and there are great issues at stake. It will not be always easy to keep cordial feelings between friends who differ. I sympathize with your tender regard for the old party. As long as I read only the Boston ' Journal ' I felt very much the same. But I have been reading widely since I came home and examining carefully, and I have perfect rest and, peace in the position which I have taken. I believe that in the providence of God the time has come for the readjustment of parties. That readjustment may come through the setting aside of some things that are dear to us, but I pray God it may come.

" I have not the slightest desire to change you, for I know you are as set as I am in what you believe. But I want you to read all sides, that you may see your pastor is not utterly unreasonable and erratic. So will you kindly read some things which I may send you from time to time? You will find them interesting.

" To-day is the anniversary of our marriage. Wendell Phillips told me that had it not been for his wife, he might not have been an antislavery man. I think my wife's clear, strong convictions, coupled with her self-denying work for the wretched victims of drink, have done not a little to confirm my convictions.

" Yours cordially,
" A. J. GORDON."

Gordon's opinions on questions of moral and social reform always rang true like a bell without flaw, on whatever side they were struck. The extinction of the saloon, the relief of the unemployed, unrestrained freedom of speech, the emancipation of women, the protection of Chinese immigrants, the defense of the secular, State-controlled schools against ultramontanism—for all these things he spoke as only a man of positive religious convictions can. He was, as he said of another, a citizen "with iron in his blood and blood in his cheek, who could strike vigorously for the right and blush visibly for the wrong." * Scores of times did he confront legislative committees in the green room of the State capitol or in the chambers of the city council to plead for some just law or to protest against some iniquitous measure. His championship of woman's cause was constant and chivalric. Those who speak of

> " Women sobbing out of sight
> Because men make the laws,"

run the risk, perhaps, of seeming strained in their opinions and even fanatical to people with quiet homes and a protected family life. It is the experiences in bare garrets, the pastoral contacts with unobserved though none the less sadly existent suffering among women, which teach wisdom on this point. That women, therefore, might have opportunity not merely to correct the laws which men make, but to pass others which they have not made and seem not to care to make—laws for the protection of girlhood, for the relief of women wage-earners, for the defense of woman's kingdom, the home, against our licensed Kurds, the saloon-keepers—he advocated their complete enfranchisement and their entrance into every political and social privilege enjoyed by man.

* Memorial address, Hon. Richard Fletcher, Supreme Court of Massachusetts.

CHAPTER IX

ON THE HIGHWAYS

Arrested for preaching on Boston Common—The New England Evangelization Society—How to reach the unchurched—Address at Plymouth,
"Forefathers' Day"

IN the June of 1885 an incident occurred which illustrates
how willingly this most unobtrusive and modest of men
stood when necessary, even at the expense of much personal
humiliation, for the common rights of American citizenship.
"For the simplest, devoutest, and most peaceful preaching of
the word of the Son of man" on Boston Common Dr. Gordon was summoned to court and fined by the same city
government which, as if to emphasize the deep gulf fixed between the instincts and purposes of the Irish Catholic and
American Protestant elements in the community, was honoring almost at the same time a vulgar and brutal pugilist with
a public meeting in Music Hall and with a public presentation by the mayor * of a diamond-studded belt. It is interesting to note further, as suggestive of the amiable tendencies of
Romanism and as disclosing the real hand back of the puppets
of the city council, that five years after this, when for the first
time the Irish canaille controlled the entire city government
of Boston, a Romanist † who had been made chief of police
in Calcutta signalized his régime by forbidding open-air
preaching in that city and by arresting the venerable Caius
McDonald for a violation of the ordinance. *Semper et ubique!*

* Hon. Hugh O'Brien. † Sir Henry L. Harrison.

Gordon's arrest was only one in a series.   Mr. H. L. Hastings had been put in jail for reading on Flagstaff Hill without note or comment passages from three chapters of the Bible.   Rev. W. L. Davis, for similar breaches of the public peace, was imprisoned for more than a year in close confinement in Murderers' Row, Charlestown Prison, allowed no exercise, insulted by turnkeys, and given insufficient food until scurvy set in.   Tract-distribution was stopped by the police. A worthy and devout lady was arrested and taken to a police station merely because she had sung a portion of a hymn to a poor unfortunate on the street.   Petty persecutions of others engaged in outdoor religious work followed.   The legal justification for these outrages was deduced from an ordinance passed during the Civil War forbidding meetings on public grounds unless permission had been previously granted. From 1862 to 1882 such permits were easily procured.   In 1882 the Y. M. C. A., which for fifteen years had conducted open-air services, applied for them as usual.   They were refused.   In 1883 they applied again and were refused.   In 1884 their application to the chairman of the Common Council was not even answered.   The following year they organized a meeting on the Common to test the action of the municipal authorities.   It was for addressing this meeting that Dr. Gordon was arrested and fined.   In court Judge Adams declared that the by-law precluded objectionable persons alone from speaking, and that any responsible people could obtain permits.   This decision made it clear that the committee on the Common had administered the statute in question arbitrarily.   Appeal was immediately made for permission to use the Common during the remainder of the season.   This was denied until legal measures were taken to obtain it.

That such scandalous crimes against free speech should be committed, of all places, on Boston Common, where one hundred and forty-five years before Whitefield had addressed thirty thousand people in the open air and where every foot of ground was consecrated to freedom by the memories of the Revolution, was sufficiently humiliating. That they should be perpetrated upon men whose traditions of personal liberty ran back to the folkmotes of the German forests, traditions enunciated once for all and in classic form by John Milton and Jeremy Taylor two hundred years before, was a further aggravation. But that the perpetrators should be irredeemable aliens, whose fathers were savage kerns in the peat-bogs long after Naseby and Lexington, was perhaps the most odious feature in the whole proceeding. Public indignation was aroused. Professor Austin Phelps wrote: " Freedom of speech is too sacred a right to be subjected to the petty tyrannies of the O's and Mac's so significantly numerous in the nomenclature of our city government. Restriction of free speech on Boston Common is as much out of place there as a whipping-post." Dr. Brooks and Dr. A. P. Peabody wrote in a similar vein. Petitions for the repeal of the ordinance, numerously signed by representative men, were sent in. The city government, under the pressure, granted four evenings for hearings on the subject of street-preaching. These meetings, which packed City Hall to the roof, were a memorable protest against an obnoxious municipal regulation. Speeches in behalf of repeal were made by Dr. A. H. Plumb, Dr. Brooke Herford, Joseph Cook, and A. J. Gordon. The gag-law was not rescinded, however, and still stands a menace to liberty of speech. But thanks to this vigorous agitation against it, it has practically fallen into disuse.

Open-air preaching was not, then, to be suppressed by an Hibernicized city government. The New England Evangelistic Association, founded within eighteen months, made it an especial feature of its work. Dr. Gordon frequently spoke under its auspices, now in Roxbury from the tail of a cart, now by the arching surf at Crescent Beach, now on the Com-

mon itself. For many years he served as chairman of the
examining committee, taking great interest in the selection
and guidance of young men and women in these outdoor
and house-to-house enterprises. He always cherished a deep
interest in efforts to reach the unevangelized, and lamented
the drift of churches, so general in American cities, from
needy into prosperous localities. Writing of the situation in
Boston, he said:

". . . The usage has been for the churches to retreat before the incoming tide of poverty and illiteracy as it has
swept over the older part of the city, and to cover their retreat
by throwing out a picket-line of mission stations. Only two
original churches remain on the ground first occupied by the
gospel in Boston. The sepulchers of Increase and Cotton
Mather are with us to this day; they sleep hard by the scene
of their useful labors. But the churches to which they ministered have moved on with all their neighbors, except old
Christ Church and the later Baptist Bethel. Nothing so
tends to disaffect the common people with the gospel as to
move the church away from them, on the ground that it
must follow wealth and fashion. I cannot tell how many
non-church-goers I have met whose sore spot I have found,
by probing, to be just this: 'The church left me, and so I left
the church; they cared nothing for me, and I care nothing
for them.' It is a natural retaliation for the violation of that
divine law, 'The rich and poor meet together: the Lord is the
maker of them all.' Dr. Chalmers used to say, 'A house-
going minister makes a church-going people.' Of course.
Let the people see that the church cares enough for them to
follow them into their homes with its ministry of help and
blessing, and to stay by those homes for their spiritual protection, and they will not desert it. The law is just as inevitable that a house-leaving church will make a church-leav-
ing people. Most of the churches that were born at the north

end of the city are now huddled together at the south end and on the Back Bay—the newest portions of the town—so close that they can almost catch each other's eavesdroppings. Some of them ought to have moved; but some ought to have remained, or at least to have left their sanctuaries with a sufficient body to maintain worship. Now we are planting missions among this large unchurched population. But the original hold can never be recovered in this way. Move out your palace-cars from the assembled passengers, and then back in a cheaper train with a more economical service, and you need not be surprised to hear them say, 'No, thank you, we do not ride second-class.' So we do not doubt that a considerable number among the honest and decent middle class have been estranged from the sanctuary by this careless habit of church-moving, the tabernacle following those whom it most needs instead of staying with those who most need it."

After describing some from his church who preach out of doors, he goes on to say: "These have led the way which I verily believe the ministry ought to follow. I have watched them going upon the Common, where thousands gather on a summer day, or upon the circus ground, thronged with an expectant crowd waiting for a show; and as they have lifted up their voices hundreds have gathered about and listened with utmost attention to their words. Here is a lesson. These people could not be drawn to church, but they listen when the church is brought to them; and when the crowd disperses there is generally left a residuum of those who would like to hear further, and who, upon conversation, promise to meet the speaker at the church next Sabbath morning. What now if the great body of ordained preachers would go out each Sunday afternoon upon the commons and squares and public gardens and parks and tell the simple story of the gospel? I know of no solution of the problem, How shall our churches reach the masses? at once so simple

and so practicable as this.   And I would have each minister
go as the pastor of his church.   Let the people know that
the church cares enough for them to send its ministers after
them.

". . . We talk about the dangerous classes.   The danger
lies in the separation of the classes—those who are the salt of
the earth keeping by themselves instead of coming into contact with that which tends to corruption.   If the great mass
of Christians would come into heart-to-heart relation with the
so-called dangerous class much might be done to change its
character.   But here is where we fail.   We have too many
family churches and too few missionary churches.   Custom is
inexorable in its demands, and it is exceedingly difficult for
us to admit the propriety or utility of side-tracks running off
from the main lines of our ministry to reach the unprivileged.
We praise God indeed that our Redeemer is one who can
have compassion on the ignorant and on them that are out
of the way ; but how far we should go out of the way is quite
another question.   The regular thoroughfare can command
unlimited capital for its extension, and no matter how costly
the rolling-stock of quartet choirs, Gothic arches, memorial
windows, and all that, the funds can generally be raised for
it.   But for an unsurveyed and unchartered extension into the
highways and hedges it is always very difficult to get stock-
holders.   The reason is that we shrink from the unusual and
the extraordinary.   Fashion controls our religion very much
as it controls the cut of our garments.   The most grotesque
styles are worn upon our backs if custom so order, and the
most absurd contrivances of medieval art are sanctioned in
our churches if they are laid down on the fashion-plate of
ecclesiastical architecture.   Custom is a pope whose bulls few
have the courage to resist."

On the 19th of December of this year Dr. Gordon spoke
at the annual Forefathers' celebration in old Plymouth.   The

speakers were drawn from various professions and from all denominations, James Russell Lowell being the most distinguished. There was there, as usual, a large contingent of the liberal stripe—as unconscious apparently of any incongruity in their celebration of the heroic faith of Puritanism as Romans of the Lower Empire might have been in honoring the fathers of the Twelve Tables. For the dry gravelly bed may indeed continue to believe itself the stream long after the cooling waters have sought other channels. To such Gordon's address seems largely directed:

"I count myself highly honored in being called to participate in the festivities of this occasion. For though I cannot trace my lineage, natural or ecclesiastical, to Plymouth Rock, in common with all New Englanders, I cherish a profound interest in its history and principles. You remember that in speaking of the rock which Moses smote in the wilderness to give water to the Israelites the Scriptures call it 'that spiritual rock which followed them.' Plymouth Rock does not remain in Plymouth alone; it has followed the sons of the Pilgrims in all their migrations, its grain and grit wrought into their constitution, and rendering them the most stalwart race that has yet appeared on this continent. And without desiring that this noble rock should grow less, I do wish that a strong solution, a powerful tincture of it might be prepared and administered far and wide to those politicians without principle, to those civilians without conscience, and to those clergymen without creed, in which this generation so abounds. Then, perchance, observers like Ralph Waldo Emerson might not have to lament the 'dapper liberalities,' as he names them, which have rendered our generation so 'frivolous and ungirt as compared with the former and Puritan age.'

"Mr. President, it was my fortune to be hatched ecclesiastically on Roger Williams's rock, situated in Narragansett Bay. I would not say to the sons of the Puritans, 'Our rock

is not as your rock.' It *is* as your rock, the same geological
and theological formation. And while the adherents of the
' standing order' are complaining that Plymouth Rock is dis-
integrating and crumbling in the atmosphere of modern doubt
and liberal thought, I am glad to say that our rock is as firm
and compact as ever, so that we could undertake to furnish
underpinning for any number of new churches and new States,
provided the demand is for ' a church without a bishop and a
state without a king.' And this suggests a theory of ecclesiastical evolution which I have formulated, but have never
before ventured to make public. The followers of Roger
Williams, after two hundred and fifty years, have grown to
two millions, and the principles of Roger Williams—soul-
liberty and religious toleration—have been gradually appropriated by all churches and governments till they have become almost universally accepted. This is certainly a remarkable triumph. How shall we account for it? Well, you
remember that quaint old Thomas Fuller explains figuratively
the wide-spread diffusion of the doctrines of Wickliffe, and
that Wordsworth puts the same into verse, telling us how the
reformer's body was dug up and burned by his enemies, and
how, his ashes being cast into the little brook, it bore them

> " ' Into the Avon; Avon to the tide
> Of Severn; Severn to the narrow seas;
> Into main ocean they. . . .
> Thus the bold teacher's doctrine, sanctified
> By truth, shall spread throughout the world dispersed.'

" It was even so with Roger Williams. He was buried on
one of the slopes of Providence Hill. An apple-tree grew
above his grave, spreading its branches widely and striking its
roots deeply, and bearing year by year a heavy burden of
fruit. How widely that fruit was scattered and eaten, how its
seeds were diffused and reproduced here and there, I need

not conjecture. Suffice it to say that while a college student in that goodly city I saw the bones of Roger Williams disinterred, and, strange to relate, it was discovered that the taproot of that apple-tree had struck down and followed the whole length of the stubborn Baptist's spinal column, appropriating and absorbing its substance till not a vestige of the vertebræ remained. And thus that invincible backbone of Roger Williams, whom a critical Massachusetts statesman stigmatized as 'contentiously conscientious,' was 'spread throughout the world dispersed,' and reproduced in generations of· his adherents. Blessed are they who are so fortunate as to have their theology enriched by such strong phosphites.

"But, Mr. President, I must not obtrude family issues into this most catholic celebration. More can truthfully be said to the praise of the worthies whose names we honor to-day than any of us shall have time to express. In the first place, of whom could it ever more truly be said that 'they builded better than they knew'? Who supposes they ever dreamed of the noble republic whose germ and principles they bore in the hold of the 'Mayflower'? They were simply dutiful servants of the Most High, not architects of their own fortunes; and, like Abraham, they obeyed the voice of God and went out, not knowing whither they went, that they might inherit a land which he should afterward give them. Had they been mindful of that country whence they came out they might have had opportunity to return, but now they sought a better country, and God gave them one which far surpassed their thoughts. I remember to have read that, years after its completion, General Jackson's campaign at New Orleans was sharply criticized in Congress, and Judge Douglass, in a masterly speech, vindicated it. Afterward meeting the judge, the general cordially thanked him, and said, 'I always knew that I was right in what I did at New Orleans, but I never knew why I was right until I read your speech.' The remark may awaken a smile, but there is something deeply philosophical in it. The thinker must come after the actor to interpret his conduct for him. As the great master takes up some rude melody of the troubadour and sets it to music, so thinkers have to set to logic the deeds of the world's great actors. Instinct is greater than reason, because it reads the mind of God, yet knows it not. It was a divine instinct which guided the helm of the 'Mayflower,' and it was a divine instinct which guided the footsteps of the Pilgrims to this spot; and it is for us to-day to exult in the clear reasonableness of what they did.

"In another sense, these forefathers were great thinkers, for they thought God's thoughts after him, careless of the contradiction which those thoughts might bring to our human logic. This was their intellectual heroism, that they believed God though they thereby made every man a liar. It is the fashion nowadays to admire the Puritan and decry Puritanism. But it was the doctrine that made the man, and not the man the doctrine. Iron in the thinker's brain is just as needful, if he is to grasp and master the dark problems of the universe, as iron in the blacksmith's blood is needful if he is to weld and mould the iron bar which he holds in his hand. And our Puritan fathers had the iron from the hills of eternal truth so wrought into their blood that they have sent down a current of stalwart convictions which a score of generations have not outgrown. May this be the lesson which we gain from our visit to this New England shrine to-day—that fidelity to God is the surest way of fidelity to man. The truest humanity is that which is born of the truest divinity. And therefore, if we would realize the prayer of George Fox, the Quaker—of being 'baptized into a sense of all conditions'—let us know that we must be baptized into God's truth as well as into God's love. This, then, shall be my closing sentiment: as the

Pilgrim fathers are marching on year by year in the culture and wealth and greatness which their sons have wrought out after them, may the Pilgrim sons fall back year by year upon the piety and virtue and conscience which their fathers wrought out before them."

CHAPTER X

The establishment of the " Watchword "—Its aim, scope, and history

FEW question the degeneracy of the American daily newspaper and the degrading influence which it exerts in our
social system. It has become a hoarse-throated tale-monger,
its output being not much better than an endlessly issued
chronique scandal use. This for the news column. The editorial page also exhibits the most unworthy traits. The
proverbial timidity of capital finds here its complete expression. The daily paper would never for truth's sake offend
the smallest fraction of its paying constituency. It is as cal-
culating as those state-churchmen who, as Marx says, would
give up the entire Thirty-nine Articles rather than one thirty-
ninth of their income. It is ever heard "bawling forth judgments unashamèd all day long," and these judgments are
shaped notoriously by the counting-room. The result, of
course, is the extreme of unreliability and a proneness to
darken the counsel of the "leader" by words without conviction.

This decadence of the secular press has been a standing invitation to religious weeklies to assume a leadership and to
acquire a confidence which the daily paper has long since
forfeited. They have the more naturally taken upon themselves this leadership inasmuch as the receding emphasis laid
on denominational distinctions has, in some degree, atrophied

a former function and given them scope for the new work. But this important and valuable service has deflected attention from a still more necessary and too easily neglected line of teaching. We find very little stimulus to the culture of the inner life in the average religious weekly. It is occupied with exterior church life, with missions, education, the affairs of the denomination, and, in an increasing ratio, with the news of the whole swinging globe.

This semi-secularization of the religious press and the clear need of some publication entirely given up to the things of the closet led Gordon to issue, in the fall of 1878, an unobtrusive little monthly devoted wholly to the spiritual life. The name adopted was the "Watchword," and the motto at the head of the first page read: "Watch ye: stand fast in the faith. Let all things be done with charity."

The first number began with a commentary upon these words, into which was woven a statement of the purpose of the undertaking. After remarking upon the apparent hardihood involved in the launching of another religious paper, he says:

" *The primitive faith* is proclaimed by a great multitude both of preachers and of papers, but as there can never be too many engaged in setting forth the doctrines of grace, we may be welcomed in undertaking the same work with methods somewhat different from those in general use. We propose to make use of Bible readings and brief Scripture expositions and narrations of personal experiences of the work of grace, thus presenting the doctrines of grace biblically rather than theologically, experimentally rather than controversially.

" *The primitive hope* we believe to be sadly obscured and neglected by the great mass of Christians in our day. That hope in the apostolic age was the personal reappearing of the Lord from heaven—'looking for that blessed hope, and the glorious appearing of the great God and our Saviour Jesus Christ.' To the first disciples this event was imminent and inspiring, and constituted the most powerful motive to activity and consecration.   But so dark is the eclipse into which this hope has been thrown that its avowal is almost certain, nowadays, to bring down upon one the charge of fanaticism. Braving that charge and rejoicing profoundly in the wonderful awakening to this truth which the last twenty-five years have witnessed, we shall have much to say upon it and upon closely related topics.

"*The primitive charity* we may in slight measure illustrate and magnify if in the discussion of these and kindred themes we shall exhibit that forbearance toward those who differ from us which we conceive to be according to the spirit of Christ. Here is a field, certainly, which offers magnificent possibilities. There is a commendable zeal for soundness in the faith among many of our religious journals.   But in the sharp contention for the faith once delivered to the saints many think they hear too often the clash of carnal weapons.   Soundness in the faith by all means, but let us not forget the injunction of the apostle that we should 'be sound in faith, *in charity*, in patience.'   'The heart is the best theologian,' it has been said; and also, we may add, the worst heretic when it defends the truth in uncharity and bitterness."

The temper of the new publication was deeply Christian and pietistic.   How well the editor succeeded in giving practical expression to the last article of the above program is well known by all who ever read the paper.   There was, however, no loud profession of undenominational charity.   The stereotyped formulas of comprehension were altogether wanting here.   The spirit of fellowship with all Christians was too deep and its current too calmly powerful to indulge in frothy and declamatory phrases.

In fact, the line of cleavage followed quite other than denominational lines.   It was transverse, grouping associates and contributors from all churches, whose main bond of fellowship seemed to be the love of the Lord's appearing. W. S. Rainsford, Professor Duffield of Princeton, S. H. Tyng, Jr., George C. Needham, and W. L. Mackay of Hull, England, were among the contributors—a pledge of able and catholic management. Its clientèle was extensive among that diaspora of patient and loving souls who, in distant hamlet and in crowded city, walk through life with the upward gaze, cherishing "the hope." To them it was a silent, freshening influence, like the hidden springs and veins of water which percolate from the mount of vision. It was in its editorial writing edifying, full of sober, lucid reflection, providing that soul-nourishment, that bread which the world knows not of. It was full of meaty expositions of Scripture, quaint, yet not fantastic, bearing always the mark of deep insight and singularly luminous in expression. Short sketches of the lives of saints, of missionaries, and of martyrs served as encouragement to those whose lives seemed hopelessly environed with commonplace. There were frequent quotations, too, from those wonderfully quaint and unfailingly apposite unfolders of the Word, the Puritan divines of the Commonwealth. He must have been a careless reader indeed who has not seen, at one time or another, the faces of Marshall and of Brook, of Gurnall, of John Owen, of Thomas Manton, of Joseph Alleine, peering through the print of these columns.

There was, in the earlier years, a special column for ministers, replete with mingled admonition and encouragement. It was here that Dr. Gordon sought to deepen the sense of responsibility and to lay bare the secrets of power, to stimulate hunger for souls and to inculcate interest in the whole world in those who were being narrowed by the centripetal tendency of parochial duties.

The undertaking was not begun without misgiving on the part of friends and family. To the bantering remark that every little minister sought, as his ultimate ambition, to have an "organ," he would reply that he felt as clearly called to this work as to the ministry. It is difficult to express what it cost in every direction. It was conducted in quiet defiance of mercantile principles. He spoke of much of the writing which appears in religious weeklies, flanked by columns of questionable advertising, as giving the impression of an invalid limping between crutches. Advertisement, as diverting attention from the purely devotional tone of the paper, and as suggestive of money-making, was therefore discarded. For many years the enterprise was conducted at a financial loss. The expense in labor, care, and personal attention was incomputable, but very real and very great. The experience of hymn-book making had left Gordon with a peculiar nervous weakness which made the preparation of copy almost the severest work in which he could engage. The Monday mornings devoted to this work were the most painfully laborious days in the year. "Our aim," he remarks, "is to do our utmost in opening the Word of God and leading our readers into evangelical truth. So far the effort has not, of course, paid financially, but, what is far better, it has cost. Time, pains, money, and labor have been freely given. With the multitude of religious sheets which go forth every week, it will still be a question with many whether ours is called for. Each reader must now decide that question for himself." And then he adds characteristically, "We do not propose, as the manner of some is, to print the letters of commendation which we have received. That would seem to us like egotism. We do not believe that there is any 'editorial we' large enough to hide a man's shame when he gets behind it to praise himself, or to read in solemn falsetto the compliments which others have passed upon him. The injunction, 'Let another praise thee, and not thine own lips,' is certainly violated when we repeat another's praises in an assumed tone or in a changed voice."

CHAPTER XI

TRUTH AND COUNTERFEIT

Christian Science — Its genesis and doctrine — Dr. Gordon's indictment of it — Healing by faith — Remarkable answers to prayer in Dr. Gordon's experience

THE early eighties saw the rise and development of a new delusion in that city which has proved, spite of its claim to the highest culture, so prolific in such growths. "Christian Science" is the misnomer by which it goes. Its Christianity has in it more of parody than of actuality. Of science, in the accepted sense of the word, there is not even what the chemists call a trace. This is clear from a cursory reading of its text-book, "Science and Health," a work nebulous to the point of mystification, badly written, and bearing in its own body its self-evidencing refutation. The spring of this superstition is, we are inclined to believe, in "transcendentalism." We recognize the old Emersonian "pass" of the hand, the worn trick of subjectivism, in the declaration, for example, that "decaying flower, withering grass, blighted and gnarled oak, ferocious beasts, sicknesses of all sorts and all qualities, are but the falsities of matter, the changing images of mortal mind; not in reality substance, but only belief in it." The elusive opinions of the Concord philosophy running underground here come to the surface again, muddy, defiled, yet recognizable. For Gnosticism runs through the same cycle in Boston as in Alexandria. Thaumaturgy ends in theurgy, Iamblichus succeeds Plotinus, Mrs. Eddy follows Emerson and Alcott.

These delusions have their rise and fall like the trajectory
of an arrow, reaching the heights of popular interest only to
drop finally into obscurity and neglect.   It was so with spirit-
ism, whose great, gloomy fane still towers on a prominent
Boston thoroughfare, though the influence of its uncanny
creed is now a thing of the past.   It must be so shortly with
this new wonder-working system.   For, as if its own claims
to be an inspired commentary on Jesus' words—a new revelation again "opened to humanity after a long night of materialism (i.e., nineteen centuries) through the spiritual understanding," a new apocalypse as pretentious as that of Sweden-
borg or of the Utah Saints—were not enough to confute and
destroy it, it has, in later years, developed a curious special
cultus of which the author of "Science and Health" seems
to be the subject.   Her words are given equal authority with
those of Jesus himself, if one may judge by the impartiality
with which quotations from her book alternate with those
from the New Testament on the walls of the "First Church
of Christ, Scientist."   As priestess of the new dispensation,
and as revealer of the arcana, she is reverenced with almost
Delphic honors.   The black haircloth rocking-chair in which
her book was written is an object of veneration by the sect.
The very plumbing of her boudoir has been gold-plated, while
her apartments have been decorated by her followers with an
elegance worthy of Schoenbrunn or Balmoral, and comically
suggestive of Hood's lines:

> " Only propose to blow a bubble,
>   And Lord! what thousands will subscribe for soap!"

Surely the next phase of the movement must be dissolution.
There can be nothing beyond!

In the April "Congregationalist" of 1885 appeared a long
article by Gordon, which, circulated later by the thousand
in pamphlet form, proved an effective antitoxin for the cure

of this wide-spread malady. The clogged, heavy, illogical style, weighted with a pseudo-philosophical phraseology, is cut through and through by this keen little pamphlet, clear and clean as a rapier, till nothing remains of the system but waving, torn shreds. Its subjective and unwarrantable quotations of Scripture are exposed. This in itself was no hard task, however, for the unreality and falsity of this new mongrel idealism lies bare and naked upon every page of its text-book.

The pamphlet is entitled " Christian Science tested by Scripture." From it we make these excerpts:

"Whatever results this system may effect in healing the body, it has given grounds for the suspicion that, as affecting the heart, it is a system of spiritual malpractice and is leading its subjects away from the simple faith of the gospel into a vague and transcendental misbelief. It is indeed an insidious delusion. Its large use of the Bible, its strenuous demand for holiness and self-abnegation in its disciples, the results apparently effected in its ministry to the sick—these are powerful considerations for attracting converts by giving them the impression that they are getting some finer quality of Christianity. Its philosophy, briefly stated, is this: Evil is not; sin, sickness, and death are unreal; 'matter and the mortal body are nothing but a belief and illusion;' 'there is neither a personal Deity, a personal devil, nor a personal man.' Let us test these propositions by Scripture.

Christian Science	*Holy Scripture*
Jesus never ransomed man by paying the debt that sin incurs; whosoever sins must suffer.—II., 189.	In whom we have redemption through his blood, even the forgiveness of sins.—Col. i. 14.
Sin is not forgiven; we cannot escape its penalty.—II., 165.	If we confess our sins, he is faithful and just to forgive us our sins, and to cleanse us from all unrighteousness.—1 John i. 9.

Christian Science	*Holy Scripture*
Petitioning a personal Deity is a misapprehension of the source and means of all good and blessedness; therefore it cannot be beneficial.—II., 170.	In everything by prayer and supplication with thanksgiving let your requests be made known unto God.—Phil. iv. 6.
Asking God to pardon sin is a vain repetition such as the heathen use. Habitual goodness is praying without ceasing.—II., 173.	For thy name's sake pardon mine iniquity.—David, Ps. xxv. 11. And forgive us our sins.—Luke xi. 4.
The belief that man has a separate life or soul from God is the error that Jesus came to destroy.—II., 90.	From everlasting to everlasting thou art God.—Ps. xc. 2. The soul that sinneth, it shall die.—Ezek. xviii. 20.
Science decides matter or the mortal body to be nothing but a belief and an illusion.—II., 193.	Let not sin therefore reign in your mortal body.—Rom. vi. 12. He shall also quicken your mortal bodies by his Spirit that dwelleth in you.—Rom. viii. 11.
Man is coeternal and coexistent with God, and they are inseparable in divine science.—I., 173.	So God created man in his own image, in the image of God created he him.—Gen. i. 27.

"Beyond these palpable contradictions of the Word of God, we must confess also the shock which it gives to hear Jesus constantly spoken of as a metaphysician and demonstrator of Christian Science—'the most scientific man that ever trod the globe;' to be told that the cause of his agony in the garden was that he was touched with 'the utter error of a belief of life in matter'; that on the cross he was giving the world 'an example and proof of divine science'; that his Christianity 'destroyed sin, sickness, and death because it was metaphysics, and denied personal sense, bore the cross, and reached the right hand of a perfect principle.' . . .

"Every text-book which we have examined on the subject brings this art of healing into acknowledged connection with pantheistic and Buddhistic principles. The mind which acts on mind is irreverently confounded with the eternal Mind. For example, in 'The Primitive Mind Cure,' by W. F. Evans, the author, after quoting one who declares that an *idea* directed upon the seat of a supposed ailment causes a stream of nervous energy to flow toward the secreting organ, says: 'This nervous energy I prefer to call the universal, divine life-principle in nature, the *akasa* of the Hindu metaphysics, an all-pervading, omnipresent, vivific principle of life and motion, identical in its higher aspects with the Holy Spirit of the gospels.' This we call pantheism of the most revolting type, a confounding of the third person of the blessed Trinity with a secretion of the nerves. In this book, too, is evolutionism of a very profane sort. 'As the cabala expresses it, the mineral becomes a plant, the plant an animal, the animal a man, and man becomes divine. This is the divine Man, the Christ of Paul, at the same time a divine personage and a universal, humanized principle of life and light.' After telling us that the Christ is the 'universal spirit,' the 'all-pervading, divine presence,' it is declared that, 'owing to the unexampled spiritual evolution of the man Jesus, his individual life became merged and blended into unity with the Only-Begotten of the Father, the universal Christ.' All this and much more of the same quality there is, which we would not quote except to warn Christians who are swallowing without suspicion this book and others of the same family. It is a sort of witches' caldron, in which every conceivable heathen and Christian heresy is found seething and simmering to produce the subtle essence called 'mental medicine.'

"Now, reading in a work lies like this, and seeing on almost every page its connection with theosophy, esoteric Buddhism, cabalism, and pantheism, the roots of these doctrines all the while being so artlessly entwined with apparently devout and reverent exposition of Scripture as to deceive the very elect; and then turning to the metaphysical healers who are going to their patients, some of them, at least, filled with the evil philosophy of this manual, and winning such reputed success as to have caused a rare stir in our country, what shall we say?

"We say two things, viz., that there may be some psychic force here, mind-contagion or what not, which experts can show to account for the whole matter; or there may be something deeper. For us, we have the strongest conviction of the existence of a personal devil, not omnipotent, but endowed with an infernal ingenuity. It has been his steady policy either to parody Christianity by inventing spurious imitations, or to adulterate it with such heathen mixtures as to 'turn the truth of God into a lie.' The literature of Christian Science presents clearly enough such a pagan adulteration of the religion of Christ; and we greatly fear that 'the prince of the power of the air' may be appropriating and reinforcing whatever occult principle of healing there may be in this system, and using it to accredit his own gospel.

"It will be hardly necessary, after what has been said, to distinguish 'Christian Science' from the 'prayer of faith,' which is said in Scripture to 'save the sick.' No one who believes this promise or makes use of it has ever, so far as we know, considered that its fulfilment depends on the action of mind upon mind. All who credit 'faith-cures,' as they are sometimes called, hold that they are the result of God's direct and supernatural action upon the body of the sufferer. 'Christian Science' pointedly denies the efficacy of prayer for the recovery of the sick. It says: 'Asking God to heal the sick has no effect to gain the ear of love, beyond its ever presence. The only beneficial effect it has is mind acting on the body through a stronger faith to heal it; but this is one belief casting out another—a belief in a personal God casting out a belief in sickness, and not giving the understanding of the principle that heals.' ('Science and Health,' ii., 171.)

Here the antagonism between two things that differ is so marked that we only need to call attention to it.

"All this we have written from no love of controversy and from no personal ill will toward those whom we criticize, but for the warning of Christians, lest they be beguiled away from the simplicity that is in Christ. Let such as would abide in the truth give heed to the clear denials of Scripture indicated in the quotations above; and then remember the warnings of St. Paul to avoid the '*oppositions of science falsely so called: which some professing have erred concerning the faith.*' And when this science talks about Jesus Christ's '*supposed life in matter*,' let them remember that some in the days of St. John spoke precisely thus—'Gnostics' or 'scientists' they were called —and that of them the gentle apostle is supposed to have written when he said, 'For many deceivers are entered into the world, *who confess not that Jesus Christ is come in the flesh.* This is a deceiver and an antichrist.' And finally, remembering the saying of Calvin, which accords with Scripture and the universal testimony of the early church, that 'Satan perverts the things which otherwise are truly works of God, and misemploys miracles to obscure the glory of God,' let us, with sober watchfulness, pray daily as our Lord has taught us (R. V.), 'Lead us not into temptation, but deliver us from the Evil One.'"

"Bar-Jesus the sorcerer forever dogs the steps of Christ Jesus the healer as he walks through the sick-wards of the world," wrote Gordon later, "and whoever encounters his satanic miracles should infer that the Lord is not far off performing gracious works through the prayers and faith of his servants." The charlatanry of spiritualism and Christian Science, as well as Romish appeals to bones and vestments and shrines, was, he believed, the devil's travesty upon a vital truth. That these wrought cures he did not deny, for "*all power*" * is

* "Whose coming is . . . with all power and signs and lying wonders" (2 Thess. ii. 9).

ascribed to the adversary. The impulse, however, of which these cures were an expression he believed to be from below, its purpose being the exaltation of evil systems to the discredit of God's supernatural workings. " God never puts a man upon the stage that Satan does not immediately bring forward an ape."*   " Yet let us not abandon our wheat-field," Gordon would say, " because the devil has sown tares. The fact that he sows tares is his testimony to the genuineness of the wheat."

" The Ministry of Healing," published somewhat before this time, discusses the subject at length from his point of view. Miracles occurred in apostolic times. They occurred subsequently, according to patristic testimony. With the periodical renaissance of vigorous religious life in such movements as Pietism, Methodism, etc., have come almost invariably the same manifestations of God's willingness to heal. The tree of life, whose leaves are for the healing of the nations, bears its fruit every month. " The test is, 'if thou believest,' not if thou wast born in Palestine and within the limits of the first Christian century."   In the early church healing by faith as enjoined by James seems to have been a sacrament pointing forward to the restitution and renewal of mankind, as baptism symbolized the resurrection, and as the communion pointed to the coming of Christ. " But while the prayer of faith which saves us is the simplest exercise of the heart, the prayer of faith which saves the sick is the most exacting."   This being so, the practice fell largely into disuse, the only suggestion of it which survives in formal ecclesiastical life being extreme unction, " wherein an ordinance for life is perverted into an ordinance for death."

He was inclined to believe further that Jesus endured vicariously our sicknesses † as well as our sins, and also that " the restoration of the sick in Christ's ministry was an enacted

---

* Godet.   † Matt. viii. 17.

prediction of the final redemption of the body, a pulse-beat from the heart of him who is the resurrection and the life, giving a slight foretaste of our full recovery at his appearing and kingdom." Of this he felt the striking words in Hebrews to be premonitory where Christians are spoken of as those who have tasted the good Word of God and the powers of the age to come. "The age to come," said he, "is the resurrection age, the time of the redemption of the body. We know the powers of that age not simply by prediction and promise, but by experience. Every miracle is a foretaste thereof, a sign of its universal healing and restitution. The driftwood and floating vegetation which met the eye of Columbus as he was keeping lookout upon his ship assured him of his proximity to the new world which he was seeking. His study of geography had convinced him of the existence of that world. But now he tasted its powers; he saw and handled its actual first-fruits. So it is with us voyagers to the world to come, the millennial age, and time of the restitution of all things. As those who have known and credited our Lord's miracles while on earth, or have experienced the wonders of recovery which he has wrought as he still stretches out his hand to heal, we have tasted the powers of the coming age."

"Miracles of healing" he characterized, therefore, as "manifestations of nature's perfect health, lucid intervals granted to our deranged and suffering humanity; not catastrophes, but exhibitions of that divine order which shall be brought in when redemption is completed" in the resurrection. That those who spiritualize into thin air the New Testament teaching of the resurrection of the body should deride the possibility of bodily healing by faith in Christ was not surprising to him. The denial of the greater includes the denial of the less. He was wont to remark on the grim irony of the fact that in the history of the church, when the departure of the spirit at death began to be confused with the return of Christ with resurrection powers, we should then first find miracles of healing alleged by contact with the bones of dead saints and martyrs instead of miracles of healing through the prayer of faith offered to the living Christ. The current sentimental estimate which makes of death not " the last enemy," but a good angel, a messenger of release, finds its counterpart in the opinion which describes death's adjutant, sickness, as a servant of the Most High. To an article which contended that the miracles of cure recorded in the New Testament were for those on a lower plane, and that others, like Paul, of finer organization can have a fuller spiritual life in bodily weakness than in good health, he replied:

"We appeal to experience, and ask whether our readers have found it easier to maintain communion with God when they have been prostrated with illness and racked with pain than when they have been in buoyant health. We have found just the opposite to be true—that sickness and debility are a great drawback to devotion. We appeal to Scripture again, and ask whether, because Paul's thorn in the flesh was over-ruled to his spiritual chastening, he did not nevertheless speak the truth when he called it a messenger of Satan. An old writer says, ' The Lord often sharpens his saints on the devil's grindstone.' This we admit most fully; but we do not there-fore advise that that grindstone be set up as a part of the furniture of the Lord's house. We question not that out-breaking sin is often overruled for the final salvation of the offender, as in the case of one who declared in a public ad-dress that had he never been a drunkard he probably should never have become a Christian. His statement can be readily credited; yet we would not recommend drunkenness as a pre-paratory dispensation to grace, for sin is of the devil. In a word, we must distinguish between what our Lord overrules and what he ordains. If in his vast mercy he thwarts the Evil One, making sin and sickness work to our good, we must not therefore sanctify these things into an ordinance, lest we make Christ the minister of sin."

Curiously enough, while prayer for the sick is almost the commonest form of petition among Christians, a belief in the efficacy of such prayer and in the direct answer to the call for healing is freely scouted as fanaticism. "Therefore we need," said Gordon, "less praying for the sick rather than more; only the less should be real and deep and intelligent and believing." The divine help is not to be invoked lightly or as a substitute for God's natural provision in medicine and hygiene. Nor is it a grace for those without depth of spiritual life or for those with whom exercise in prayer is not habitual and prevailing. Yet if the superior faith of prophets and apostles is brought forward to discourage this practice it should still be remembered that to the injunction in James to "pray one for another, that ye may be healed," is added a significant note on the powerfully effective prayers of Elias, "*a man subject to like passions as we are.*"

To the objection that prayers for the sick are often, apparently, unanswered, he replied with a disarming *tu quoque*. "Holding such views as we Christians do," he would say, "in regard to the efficacy of prayer for the conversion of souls, and resting on the plain declaration of God our Saviour that he will have all men saved, how can we explain the fact that the mass of men go down to death unreconciled to God? We must remember both Melita and Miletum. In one place Paul healed the father of Publius by his prayers; in the other he left Trophimus sick."

He realized, nevertheless, the great perplexities in the whole matter. "I have little to say in regard to the principles of divine healing," he says in a letter, "but am looking constantly for light. It is a subject full of difficulties, and I shrink more and more from undertaking any philosophy of it. I do my best with every case which comes before me."

When the sick sought him out he prayed with them in quietness and reserve.   Many remarkable answers were vouchsafed.   The statements of some of the healed are subjoined:

Rev. Joseph C. Young, Boston, Mass.:

" In 1887 there appeared a growth on my lip.   When first noticed it was very small, but gradually increased until it seriously interfered with my preaching.   A physician of good standing, after two examinations, told me that it was cancer and that I had better put my house in order, as he believed I had only a short time to live.   Though believing in healing by faith, I had no appropriating faith to claim the promise *for myself*, yet I constantly sought divine guidance.   For a week I had no light. At the end of this time the promise in James v.14 came into my mind like a new revelation.   I had read and quoted it to others hundreds of times, but now it came direct to me with an indescribable force.   I believed it immediately.   Then came a perplexity—who were the elders of the church?   Who could offer the prayer of faith for me?   I knew many in Brooklyn, my home, and in New York, who professed faith in this promise, but I had no inclination to call them.   I made the matter a subject of special prayer for some days, and the name of Dr. Gordon, with whom I was only slightly acquainted, was so vividly thrust into my mind that I accepted it as an answer to my prayer.   The appointment was made to meet him in Boston with Mr. McElwain and Dr. Peck.   I told them why I had come, and asked if they could take the promise in James and pray in faith for my healing.   They replied that they could, and Dr. Gordon prayed, anointing me according to the instructions.   I was in the study only a short time, and went away almost immediately after the prayer.   I had no more pain or trouble from the cancer, and within a few weeks all signs of it had disappeared.   It has never returned.   The promise was believed, the prayer was offered, I was healed. . . . I give this testimony with some reluctance. It is not a subject to be too much advertised. The Spirit heals according to the will of God, not according to our will. There has been too much fleshly formulating of theories on this as on all other teachings of the Bible, and for that reason less of the power of God manifested."

Mr. Mial Davis, a lumber-merchant of Fitchburg, Mass., writes:

" Next to my conversion, the divine healing in the study of dear Dr. Gordon was the most remarkable experience of my life. In 1889 I was prostrated. The right thigh seemed to lose its vitality to such a degree that it seemed for a time impossible to bring life back to it. Some of my friends wished to remove me to the Massachusetts General Hospital to see if amputation could not save me. I said no; I was ready to die. Years of prostration followed. At intervals I could go about with crutch or cane; at other times I was confined to my bed. I could do little or nothing at my business. My mind finally turned to the study of healing by faith. After correspondence I forced myself, in great weakness, on crutches to Dr. Gordon's study. He laid his hand upon my heart and, oh, what a prayer for my recovery, what pleading with God! Brother McElwain's prayer followed, then my own poor prayer. Oh, what a miniature transfiguration of Jesus was there! The very place was holy ground. That was the day of days to me. You probably know how I went ' walking and leaping, praising God.' I rose from my knees after all of us had prayed, went out on the sidewalk to go to the depot. I felt that new life had come to my knee and limb from thigh to foot. I walked up and down the cars while on my way home, praising God and giving him the glory. I had worn rubber bands round my knee, leg, and ankle, but the next morning I did not put them on and never have worn them since. My crutches and cane were laid aside.

I have been able to do far more church work and business than ever I expected to do. . . ."

Miss Emma Davis, Southboro, Mass., writes:

" I suffered for years from seasons of utter prostration and acute suffering, with insomnia frequent and prolonged. My left side was a little, weak, shrunken thing, and my spine was badly curved, the right side being much too large and bowed. A few years since, when my attention was called to the Lord's healing, I was about as full of unbelief and prejudice as one could be. But prejudice began to melt away under the light of the Word, and I began to believe that possibly I might be helped. I consecrated myself to God as never before, dear friends prayed earnestly in my behalf, and, as fully as I knew how, I placed my case in the hands of the great Physician. For a while I was better. Then new ills came upon me until it seemed at times as though my very reason would leave me. . . . About this time I was most definitely led to write to Dr. Gordon. An interview followed. He seemed fearful lest I should fix my faith on the human agency instead of on the divine. He said most emphatically, ' I have no power.' ' But,' replied I, ' you have faith in the One who has.' He smiled, and asked some very searching questions as to my faith to receive, as to consecration, and the use of God-given health.

" He appointed a day when he would with others pray with me for my healing. When I came to his study I was suffering intensely. With others he prayed for me, placing his hands on my head. I felt no change. Reaching home, I was soon prostrated with the old misery, suffering terribly night and day for nearly two weeks, but over and over again came to me the words, ' Fear not, only believe;' and there was a deep stillness and peace in my soul, beyond anything I had ever experienced. The trial of faith was fiery, but I knew deliverance was near. One morning about the middle of April I woke without a pain in my body, and, as I then expressed it, 'they are all carried away into the wilderness.' With a new song in my heart, even praises to God, and with faithful promises, I rose up to serve anywhere the Lord might indicate. It is now almost four years, and I have had no return of my old pains or sickness. The change in my deformity is most marked. All the pads and artificial means of relief are dispensed with. . . . Until my healing I was always over-tired, and the more tired the more pain and insomnia. Now no matter how much I exert myself I wake fresh and rested in the mornings. . . . Can any one explain away this sudden lifting of nearly thirty years' misery?"

Mrs. Gertrude Floyd Cole (deceased),—statement of husband:

"She was a fragile girl from her youth up, a few days at school being sufficient to exhaust her for weeks. Yet she was ever a person of great piety and of a pronounced spiritual life. Coming to Boston, she found work as a sewing-woman. The confinement brought on consumption of the most malignant type, accompanied by severe hemorrhages. The physician pronounced her case hopeless. Dr. Gordon, on one of his visits, the last preceding his departure to the country, conversed with the dying girl. He asked her if she could rely on the Lord Jesus Christ to raise her up, human aid having done all in its power. She said that she could, and that henceforth she surrendered herself to Christ. He prayed the prayer of faith as recorded in James, and left her in God's hands. She abandoned medicine, but sank beyond all indications of life, and was pronounced to have passed away. She did indeed pass into the world of eternal life, and heard that which cannot be recorded other than that she was told that her life-work was not yet complete. While the attendants were making ready for her burial, she showed signs of returning life. From that hour her hemorrhages ceased and a warm and grateful healing sensation permeated her lungs, and she was raised to health. Dr. Gordon, on returning from the country in the fall, met her on the street and did not know her, so perfectly had she recovered. This was his first intimation of her healing. She lived many years, married, engaged in Christian work, and died finally, though not of consumption."

CHAPTER XII

AMONG STUDENTS

The Princeton College meetings—Difficulties met and overcome—Contact
with President McCosh—Work at other colleges

IN the opening weeks of 1884 a door to new opportunities
and new activities was opened.   Dr. James McCosh, the
venerable president of Princeton College, had heard of Dr.
Gordon through his Northfield labors and wrote urging him
to come to Princeton, there to undertake special religious
work among the students.   The field was new and untried,
and of especial difficulty and delicacy withal.   Few will
question the natural tendency to levity which prevails in a
student community.   Youth, freedom from home restraints,
the contagion of diverse acquaintance, and the ignorance of
those severe and disillusioning experiences of maturer years
combine to make a product almost inaccessible to sober and
religious influences.   There were, furthermore, exceptional
circumstances which, all unknown to the visitor, worked
greatly to his prejudice and disadvantage.   Take the train to
Manhattan Field, New York, any day when the bill-boards
announce some special intercollegiate fête.   Listen to the
hoarse cheering, rising like the surf of the Atlantic.   Watch
the waving colors, the excited thousands, the gladiatorial
struggle over a pigskin foot-ball.   It is on such occasions, if
ever, that college students occupy a large place in the public
eye.   How irritated they would be if kept home and packed

off *en masse* to college chapel! Yet this was very much the case with the discontented, angry youths who, by some recent and perverse enactment, found themselves gathered to hear an unknown preacher from Boston at the very hour upon which they had pitched for some gala festival of athleticism. That the preacher enjoyed the service quite as little as the boys themselves is seen from the following letter:

" PRINCETON, N. J., February 4, 1884.

"MY DEAR WIFE: I will give you a little account of the work, thanking God for what he has graciously given. The first day was the toughest experience I have ever had. The students have been free, hitherto, to come to the prayer-day services or not—they have largely chosen not to come—till this year their attendance was made compulsory. My first address was to this compelled crowd, many of them disgusted that their holiday had been turned into a holy day. They sat before me facing at all angles, ogling and squirming and showing pla nly enough that they did not propose to be solemnized. I was never so taken off my pins in my life. I sweat and floundered about and made an utter fizzle. All the grave and dignified faculty sat ranged on either side. I came home and dried my clothes and went back to the evening service with fear and trembling. That was not compulsory, and I got on much better. Still, I was so discouraged that I determined to start for home on Friday morning. But I feel that the Lord overruled my rash purpose. A large delegation of students, who appreciated exactly the trial under which I had labored, came to see me, and insisted that I should stay. I consented, and began to visit the young men at their rooms. Sunday morning I preached again before students and faculty. There was a great change; no compulsion, but all were out and very attentive. In the afternoon again deeply solemn meeting. The good old president arose and made a most solemn appeal, saying, 'Young men, you have heard the gospel to-day so plainly declared that you are without excuse if you do not accept Christ.'

" In the evening the students who were Christians planned for meetings in their rooms, inviting those in their respective halls to come in. I started at seven o'clock to visit these meetings. I found them all crowded. In the first one I struck, ten rose at my invitation to indicate their purpose to follow Christ. I went from building to building among the meetings, finding in almost every one those who were ready to stand up. I visited six of these, and I judge there must have been twenty who confessed Christ in different rooms. My reception among the students was most cordial and affectionate. I think the Lord has given me their hearts, and my first discouragement has been turned into great joy. I have addressed the theological students and have met many of them in private for prayer and conference. A good work has certainly begun. I shall stay to-day at least to see it furthered. It has been a peculiar and valuable experience.

" Much love to you and to all. The Lord bless you. Pray, all of you, that I may not labor in vain or run in vain.

" Yours affectionately,

" GORDON."

The effect which his personality and his earnest words had upon the students may be gathered from the following admirable notes written by one who was at the time in the senior class at Princeton and who took a deep interest in the whole movement :

" In November, 1883, the Interseminary Missionary Alliance met at Hartford. It was composed of delegates from theological institutions, but a large contingent from Princeton College went up and were permitted to enjoy the feast of good things, without participating in the discussions.

Dr. Gordon was one of the chief speakers, and gave at an evening session a powerful address on the enduement of the Holy Spirit for service. He held a consecration meeting at the close of the session at which nearly all the young men remained, even till nearly the midnight hour. It was a remarkably tender and spiritual service. He spoke very modestly and reverently of his own experience in receiving this enduement of the Spirit some years before. The Princeton students, like all the rest, were greatly drawn to Dr. Gordon. When the ' Day of Prayer for Colleges ' drew near, the latter part of January, those of us who had heard him at Hartford were a unit in desiring him to preach on that day, and through our efforts he was invited and came. Recitations were suspended for the day, and the students were required to attend service at eleven o'clock. The beautiful Marquand Chapel was filled with students, professors, people from the town, and students from the theological seminary. The sermon was excellent and made a fine impression, but the preacher was far from being himself.

" I remember very distinctly, in talking with him several years later regarding that service, he said it was one of the most trying experiences of his life. Everything around him was new, and everybody was strange; he was right in the heart of the conservatism of the great Presbyterian Church, and all about him were seated its ablest representatives. He was requested to remain over Sunday, which he did, and in the meantime conducted services as he had opportunity. But before he had concluded the meetings of Sunday he had recovered himself and had won all hearts. In spite of the earnest request that he stay and continue the good work which had sprung up among the students during his brief visit, he felt obliged to return to his own charge. For the next week or two we carried on special religious services with some degree of success; but finally it was decided that we must have Dr. Gordon return. At our earnest solicitation, indorsed by Dr. McCosh, he came back and was with us for perhaps ten days. He preached each evening in Murray Hall, and from nine till eleven o'clock went from dormitory to dormitory to conduct prayer and inquiry meetings. All the students that could be induced to attend were summoned from the section of the hall in which the meeting was held — a dozen, twenty, or more. A great many in those meetings made a profession of faith in Christ. They were gatherings never to be forgotten. One memorable feature was his teaching inquirers to pray. All bowed the head, and then Dr. Gordon would offer up a simple, earnest prayer of self-surrender and consecration to God, followed, sentence by sentence, by a chorus of half a dozen voices. Many of the rougher fellows of the college were deeply moved in these meetings, to which they came when they would not attend a public meeting.

"The students throughout the college were delighted with Dr. Gordon. Those who are familiar with such matters know how hard it is to suit an audience of undergraduates. I am sure there was less of criticism passed upon him than upon any other man who came before the students while I was in the institution. The professors as well as the students were pleased. Professor Raymond, of the chair of oratory, said the quality of Dr. Gordon's voice was unsurpassed; indeed, he had heard but one speaker who equaled him in this respect. He thought if his natural gift were cultivated, he would have marvelous power as a speaker.

"Dr. McCosh was in most hearty sympathy with the work. He was present at very many of the public meetings, and always urged their importance upon the students. Those who ever met Dr. McCosh will readily understand that he had absolutely no gift as an evangelist. He was wholly lacking in that tact, grace, and delicacy which one must possess who would conduct a successful inquiry meeting, among students especially. Frequently at the close of the meeting, as a matter of courtesy, the preacher would ask if the president had anything to say. He always had something to say by way of commendation of the work and of him who conducted it. Indeed, he seemed unable to find words to express his appreciation of the preacher. With his broad Scotch accent, which was well-nigh unintelligible to those not familiar with his speech, he would invariably inform us that ' Dr. Gourdon is the looveliest mon I iver had in me house. And if I iver h'ard the gospel preached in me life, it has been from the lips of Dr. Gourdon.' This sentiment was expressed with much feeling, evidently to the embarrassment of the preacher, and a good deal to the amusement of the students.

"It is doubtful if Dr. Gordon ever had a greater triumph, so to speak, than he had at Princeton. He showed himself to be by nature a prince among men, and by grace a man of God indeed. During that religious awakening, which continued a number of weeks, we had the assistance of some of the most noted preachers we could command, such as Drs. John Hall and Charles Cuthbert Hall, of New York, Drs. Pierson and Mutchmore, of Philadelphia, besides Professors Hodge, Patton, and Paxton, of the seminary. But none of these, and not even Mr. Moody, who had been at the college some years before, was received as was our own great leader. It was remarked by those who had been connected with the college a long time that not within their recollection had any one met with Dr. Gordon's reception. This chapter in his life will always stand as a significant indication of his influence among men, and especially among young men in college, than whom a more critical class cannot be found. Most truthfully may it be said of Dr. Gordon, 'As a prince he had power with God and with men, and prevailed.'"

During the daytime—which, as he said, "passes not a little

slowly, as I can do nothing among the students until the evening, my work beginning at 7 P.M., and continuing until eleven "—he stayed at the Nassau House, "in order to give the students a better opportunity to come and see me, though I have two or three cordial invitations to professors' homes." After the evening services were over he went usually to Dr. McCosh's house and there spent the night. We get a glimpse of the delightful intercourse which he had in these late hours with the veteran president in certain charming reminiscences which he wrote out just after Dr. McCosh's death and within three months of his own departure. He says:

"Some ten years ago, when invited by the students of Princeton to address them on the 'Day of Prayer for Colleges,' the president wrote confirming the invitation, and adding, 'Of course you will live with me while in Princeton.' I cannot say that I was entirely at ease in his dignified presence the first hour after entering his house, or that he was entirely free in his confidence toward a stranger till he should know who and what manner of man he might be. But, being invited to remain over Sunday, and the ice having been broken in the evening of that day, so that more than a score of young men came forward as inquirers, the good man at once laid aside all reserve, and from that hour put his whole heart into the work, attending every public meeting, and urging on the students at every session of college prayers the importance of giving attention to their spiritual welfare. The services continued for two weeks, very soon taking this turn in order to reach the students: preaching in the chapel at five daily, and then night meetings in the various halls, beginning at 9 P.M. and continuing till 12 P.M. It was in these gatherings that the personal work was done.

"When I returned to the president's house at the close of these midnight meetings Dr. McCosh would invariably be found waiting, with a warm fire on the hearthstone and a table spread with refreshments, always eager to hear what new names had been added to the list of inquirers. There could hardly have been greater joy in heaven over repenting sinners than there was in his heart as the names were read to him from my note-book night after night; and then he would talk them over and lift them up before the Lord, that he would by his Spirit make thorough work in their hearts and keep them from falling back.

"And now, the day's work being over for president and preacher, the former was ready to talk, to tell you about the men and the experiences associated with his early life, to be drawn out on points of doctrine and controversy, to answer all the questions you might propound, no matter if you should continue till two or three in the morning. He would never g've the slightest intimation that he desired to retire."

The talk ran largely on religious movements in Scotland. Many and interesting were the stories which were told of the heroic days of the Disruption. Irving, McCheyne, Chalmers, Duff, were all there in the dim twilight of the blazing fire's penumbra. They laughed heartily, too, over the mishaps which had befallen Matthew Arnold in his then recent visit to the college. For he had mailed his acceptance of an invitation to lecture there to Dr. Churchill, of Andover, sending instead a hearty expression of thanks for Dr. Churchill's hospitality to Dr. McCosh. And then, to cap all, he had missed the Princeton station and was obliged to walk eleven miles, coming finally into the little college town, spattered with mud, sitting on the high seat of a butcher-cart.

At last, when the fire had burned to the last ash, the long night sessions would break up.

"Thank God," says Gordon in closing his reminiscences, "for a great scholar who was able to yoke up the deepest philosophy with the simplest faith; who, with all his learning, kept the heart of a child toward the Saviour. How much he

owed for the purity of his faith and the simplicity of his piety
and the stalwartness of his convictions to these friends of his
early days whom he so loved and revered—Chalmers and
McCheyne and the Bonars! Almost as remarkably as Dr.
Wayland, in Brown, did President McCosh combine the intellectual and the evangelistic spirit. Pointing to a chair
standing before the open fire in one of those midnight talks,
he said, ' He came back some years after his graduation and
knelt with me by that chair and confessed Christ. I believed
he would do so, for I never forgot him nor ceased to pray for
him after he left college.' He had been speaking of a very
able but skeptical man with whom he had ' dealt much,' to use
his own phrase, during his student days. Such college presidents are to be sought for and prayed for in these days. May
God multiply their number."

Gordon's work among college students did not end here.
At the Northfield college conferences his influence upon
young men was always marked. To mention one case only,
Mr. Robert P. Wilder, the original and most prominent leader
in the Student Volunteer Movement, since grown to such
proportions, has declared in a recent letter that to A. J. Gordon and to J. Hudson Taylor he owes more for the development of his spiritual life than to any others, living or dead.
Others have made like statements. In later years, in addition
to the addresses given at these college conferences, he spoke
at various times at Yale, Amherst, Rutgers, Mount Holyoke,
Williams, at Princeton again, and at Brown, always with
great acceptance, and in several of the colleges named conducted series of religious meetings with the attendant personal
work described above.

CHAPTER XIII

MISSIONS OR MAMMON?

The Congo Mission bequeathed to the A. B. M. U.—Dr. Gordon's fight against its abandonment—"The cooking-stove apostasy"—Address at Evangelical Alliance, "The Responsibility Growing out of our Perils and Opportunities"

IN the fall of '84 the Livingstone Inland Mission, founded by Mr. and Mrs. Grattan Guinness of London, was handed over to the American Baptist Missionary Union. This mission was organized immediately after Stanley emerged from the gloom of interior Africa in '77. By this time its stations were planted all up and down the Lower Congo. Twenty-five men and women were in the field, acclimatized and instructed in the vernacular. Translations of a large part of the Scriptures had been made into many Congoese dialects. Schools were in running operation. A steamer for itinerating purposes plied from station to station. All the preliminary expenses, all the discouragements of frequent sicknesses and early deaths, which accompany missionary pioneering, had been borne by the founders. The mission with all its equipment was bequeathed without conditions to the American Baptists, who had been contemplating opening work in Africa, as to "those who believe in maintaining every word and ordinance of God."

The gift was accepted at the Detroit meeting of the denomination in '84. A reaction of timid conservatism, however, followed soon after. The value of the gift did not seem to be fully appreciated. The difficulties ahead loomed large against the black sky of boundless African heathenism. A cry for "concentration of interests" went abroad, and pressure was brought to bear from many quarters looking to the return of the missionaries and the abandonment of the field.

It was at this juncture that Dr. Gordon set himself to stem the tide. Earnestly did he appeal to his own church and to local conferences to resist the retrenchment. With his pen he addressed the denomination at large. A pointed tract, "The Ship Jesus," emphasizing the American debt to Africa, was written, and became widely influential. Finally he took the field with Dr. Sims, who had worked many years in this mission, and went from city to city over all the country east of the Mississippi, pleading for the evangelization of the Congo Valley. With statesman-like prevision he showed the strategic opportunities of the mission. With burning words he denounced the proposed desertion of those who were holding the outposts. He aptly recalled the history of the great and flourishing Telugu Mission and the demands for its abandonment which had been made in its days of weakness. He denied the "lack of interest" which many were urging as a reason for withdrawal. "When the doctor would feel the pulse of a patient," said he, "he lays his finger on the wrist, where the walls of flesh are the thinnest. Who will say that we may not detect the missionary pulse and learn something of the moving of the Spirit by noting the expressions of Christ's poor saints who have sent up their little gifts—in some instances the widow's all—because the burden for Africa is on their hearts? I have rarely read anything more touching than some letters of this sort which have been received; and there have been hundreds of these small donations. How can the Union, having opened its treasury and invited contributions to the Congo Mission, and in response having received gifts from hundreds of donors, many of them, as I know, the fruit of the most conscientious self-sacrifice, fail now to fulfil the trust which the acceptance of such gifts involves?

"No! let us, pastors and editors, laymen and workmen for Christ, shut our ears to this talk about 'giving up,' and raise the cry, 'Give.' Let us emphasize the cry by entering upon a course of self-denial which we have not known before, in economizing in our living and cutting off our luxuries, that we may have more to give. The American Baptists need the Congo almost as much as the Congo needs them. They need the tremendous appeal of its misery, its darkness, and its ruin to rouse them to their old-time heroism and self-denial. Ethiopia is at last stretching out her hands to God; she is also stretching out her hands to us. How can we answer at the bar of God if, with all our yet unused resources, we turn away from the call, and withdraw our hands from Ethiopia?"

The response to these appeals was such as to place the Congo Mission beyond even the suggestion of abandonment. Gordon was able to write from Asbury Park, where the question came up for final settlement at the annual meetings of the denomination, the following triumphant words:

"Praise the Lord! The Congo Mission has gone up with a shout—gone up, that is to say, with the strong and unanimous voice of all the people to possess the land. I wish you could have seen and heard the enthusiasm of the meeting yesterday. The Lord hath done great things for us, whereof we are glad."

"Dr. Gordon's best monument," wrote after his death one who knows more of this crisis than any other, "is the Congo Mission. He saved it!"

The increasing tendency in Protestant churches to adopt unworthy methods for raising money, and the growth of church amusements and "vestry junketings" to the detriment of the spiritual life, was severely rebuked in an address which

Dr. Gordon delivered about this time. " Machinery," he said, "is taking the place of life in our churches. If money is needed for carrying on the Lord's work, the first resort is not to fasting and prayer, but to festivals and fairs. Now eating strawberries and cream in the interest of foreign missions stands in immeasurable contrast with foregoing butter and sugar, as the poor Salvationist does, in order to save thereby to help the gospel." He aptly characterized the series of noisome enterprises for filching dollars from unwilling pockets —the rainbow teas, the chocolate drills, the operettas, the bazaars, the clam-bakes, the minstrel shows, the broom drills, the kermesses, the oyster suppers, and so on to the end of the whole wretched category—as a new heresy, a heresy of conduct, "the cooking-stove apostasy." The new methods of "compelling them to come in" were branded as a compulsion of the senses rather than of the heart. The extravagant billboards, advertising church services in the language of the opera-bouffe poster, he felt to be a dishonor and a reproach to the Lord Christ. Of the "entertainments" which they hawked, he said in his last message to the church:

" Certain insects conceal their presence by assuming the color of the tree or leaf on which they prey. Church amusements are simply parasites hiding under a religious exterior, while they eat out the life of Christianity."

His opposition to these things dated back to the earliest years of his ministry. His own church, never much tainted with the canker, had silently and gradually, with the development of a new and higher religious consciousness, cast aside all such devices.

This address awakened, together with a wide favorable response, much adverse criticism, as is always the case when extensive and popular abuses are attacked. In reply to these criticisms a counter-reply, printed in part below, was sent forth:

"To invent a new phrase may give one renown, but it may be as perilous as to invent a new explosive unless one is prepared to be blown up by his own compound. They were thrown off in the heat of fervid utterance—this expression, 'the cooking-stove apostasy,' and that other, 'the amusement heresy'—and now they are coming back without having cooled at all in the course of their travels. One suggests that the author must have relapsed into incorrigible Puritanism, and wonders if he has never heard of the love-feast of the early church, in which a simple meal was sanctified to the salutary use of Christians, and made a means of nourishing their social joys. To which we reply that we have so heard, and that we remember how quickly this feast degenerated, and brought in such abuses that it called out the stern rebuke of the apostle, 'What! have ye not houses to eat and to drink in? or despise ye the church of God?' Thus it is that innocent things are so easily spoiled by our misuse unless we are very watchful. This is exactly our point. Another critic brings the accusation of pessimism. As though that were more dangerous than the shallow optimism which glides over the surfaces of things and complacently refuses to believe that there may be perilous depths below! We desire to be neither an optimist nor a pessimist, but a truthist; and such we humbly believe we are, in giving the note of warning suggested by these phrases. . . .

"An excellent and sober Christian of fifty years' standing in one of our churches meets us and says, 'You are right, brother, in your note of warning. I am done with church sociables. I have never objected to such gatherings accompanied by a simple meal, nor do I now object. But when I found at the beginning of the year that our church had engaged a colored man to furnish the supper; and when I saw him there, with his white vest and white gloves and professional cookery, I said, "No more of this."' By which he meant to say, we judge, that there may be danger of getting a ministry of three orders in our churches—pastor, deacons, and caterer, the last in white vestments manipulating the ritual of pies and cakes. And we think his alarm is well grounded. Usage sanctifies the most incredible innovations in the course of time. It is far easier to start a thing than to stop it, and we commend the wisdom of this man who stepped out when the caterer stepped in, saying, 'We have no such custom, neither the churches of God.' . . .

"To denounce theater-going from that pulpit in which the theater has actually been set up is, we take it, a very ineffective proceeding. There is no question in our mind as to which is the more objectionable for Christians, to go to the playhouse, or to bring the playhouse into the church. . . .

"To one who asks why the *work* of Christian women in preparing delicacies to be sold at a church festival, or in making goods at a church fair, is not just as acceptable to the Lord as money, especially when they have not the latter to give, we reply, the work *is* acceptable; but the principle of raising money in this way for the cause of Christ is what we object to. To get an equivalent in food or goods for the money put into the Lord's treasury robs the offering of its richest element—that of sacrifice. The very savor and sweetness of a gift in the sight of God are contained in this, as abundant Scriptures show. In God's reckoning the value of an offering depends as much on what it costs the giver as on what it nets the receiver. Therefore the treasury of the Lord is vastly more enriched by the widow's mite than by the widow's muffins. . . .

"'But what can poor churches in the country do, where money is scarce?' asks another. Let them do a little in the right way, rather than much in the wrong way. 'For the honor of Christ I pray that the heathen may never learn how the American Christians raise money for missions,' writes a

returned missionary in a recent article.   And what advantage
financially would it be for them to learn?   The Bassein Baptist
Christians out of their poverty give more per head for missions
than the Baptist Christians of Massachusetts with all their
wealth ; that is, they give more without these modern methods
than we do with them.   As for attracting people to the sanctuary, which is the principal aim of church suppers and entertainments, what is gained in that direction compared with the
immense spiritual loss incurred?   In a certain body of Christians in New England one hundred and fifty-one churches report not a single accession by conversion during the last year.
We know something of the ecclesiastical machinery by which
these churches are carried on, and how almost universally the
devices which we are considering enter into their established
order.   Is not the record sad enough, and does it not seem
to call out the pathetic question of the Lord, 'Wherefore do
ye spend money for that which is not bread? and your labor
for that which satisfieth not?'   And by way of contrast,
my poor brother, a pastor from Russia, is sitting by me while
I write.   He never heard of a church entertainment or church
supper till he came to this country, and has not a single
wheel of our church machinery in his system.   Constantly
persecuted, seven times imprisoned, once sent into exile, and
with no place to gather his flock except his own private
house, yet without any of our modern appliances, he has baptized in the region about his home four hundred converts during the last two years.   Does not this suggest how much
more the Lord can do without our modern improvements
than with them? . . .

" On the whole, it may be a question whether we have not
laid undue stress of late on the mere question of drawing the
masses.   Christianity has repulsions as well as attractions, and
these two are so perfectly adjusted as to hold off those who
care only for the loaves and fishes, while drawing in such as

are ordained to eternal life. The same voice which says, 'Come unto me, all ye that labor and are heavy-laden,' also says, 'If any man will come after me, let him deny himself, and take up his cross, and follow me.' The operation of this twofold constraint of tenderness and severity is very strikingly told in two sentences from the Acts of the Apostles: 'And believers were the more added to the Lord;' 'And of the rest durst no man join himself to them.' To enervate our own spiritual life in our effort to draw the masses will be a very great price to pay for our success, if we gain it. Satan takes all ways to destroy the church. Heaven help us if, having resisted the encroachments of Arianism, we should now be seduced by this folly of vegetarianism. To deny the cross in our creed is a fearful thing; to deny it in life may be even worse. 'For many walk, of whom I have told you often, and now tell you even weeping, that they are *the enemies of the cross of Christ:* whose end is destruction, whose God is their belly, and whose glory is in their shame, who mind earthly things.'"

In December, 1887, Dr. Gordon addressed the meeting of the Evangelical Alliance in Washington on "The Responsibility Growing out of our Perils and Opportunities." He spoke in part as follows:

"We are accustomed to say that responsibility is measured by opportunity. That is certainly one of its measures. But there are two factors necessary to constitute an opportunity—the ability and the occasion. There may be the ability without the occasion, or there may be the occasion without the ability. In either case we have but half an opportunity, and this cannot evoke any very great responsibility. But where both are present in large degree—ability and occasion—the upper and nether millstones of accountability have come together, and woe be to the Christian who gets between them. For if new corn is not ground into bread for a suffering world,

the owner of the corn will be ground.   If he does not give
his substance he will be in danger of losing his soul.   It is
estimated that eight billions of dollars are to-day treasured
up in the hands of Protestant Christians in the United States
—a sum so great that it staggers our arithmetic to compute
it.   That is one element of our ability.   Into our doors the
untaught and unregenerate populations of the Old World are
pouring by the hundreds of thousands every year, while
through our doors we can look out upon every nation of the
globe as a field ripe for missionary harvest.   Here is our occasion.   It is enough to startle one into alarm to think of the
stupendous obligation created by the conjunction of these
two elements. . . .

"If we look at the great laboring-class we hear from
some of its representatives the impatient murmurings of communism.   I know of no answer to such at once so subduing
and so potent as the divine communism which is presented in
the New Testament.   I open the first chapter of the church's
history and read this remarkable statement concerning the
primitive Christians: 'And all that believed were together,
and had all things common; and sold their possessions and
goods, and parted them to all men, as every man had need. . . .
Neither said any of them that aught of the things which he
possessed was his own.'   At once I hear the current comment on this text that it represents only a provisional and
temporary condition of things, and was not intended for a
permanent model.   Yes, that is the way we are apt to look
upon ideals which are too high for our faith or too hard for
our selfishness.   It is the exegesis of covetousness and self-
interest that has largely fixed this interpretation upon the text.
As a matter of fact there is not the slightest intimation anywhere that this feature of the primitive church was intended
to be transitory.   I for one am profoundly grateful for this
lofty and divinely appointed example of Christian commu-

nism. Of course in translating this example into practical experience we must take into account all the modifying texts: 'If any will not work, neither shall he eat,' which excommunicates from our community all the shiftless and idle; and 'If any provide not for his own, and specially for those of his own house, he hath denied the faith, and is worse than an infidel,' which enjoins upon us the duty of making decent provision for the family. What we find as a resultant is this: that the church, according to its primitive ideal, is the one institution in which every man's wealth is under mortgage to every man's want, every man's success to every man's service. No laborer in any part of the field should lack the means for prosecuting his work so long as any fellow-disciple elsewhere has ability to supply his lack. This, I believe, was the divine communism on which the church was founded, and by which it was intended to be perpetuated. And if we could present to the discontented working-classes to-day this fresh, unsullied ideal in active operation it would be the most powerful answer possible to their bitter complaint of the selfishness and unsympathy of men. . . .

"Two centuries ago quaint Thomas Fuller said, 'If any suppose that society can be peaceful while one half is prospered and the other half pinched, let him try whether he can laugh with one side of his face while he weeps with the other.' We are not concerned, however, with those outside the church, but those within. As surely as darkness follows sunset will the alienation of the masses follow sanctimonious selfishness in the church. . . . The church millionaire stands at exact antipodes to the church millennial, and in proportion as the former flourishes the latter will be hopelessly deferred. It is not an orthodox creed that repels the masses, but an orthodox greed. Let a Christian in any community stand forth conspicuously as honest as the law of Moses, yet building up an immense fortune by grinding the faces of the poor, compelling them all the while to turn the grindstone, and he will wean a whole generation from the gospel. . . . We have no power to prevent men of the world from heaping up colossal fortunes. But our gospel plainly forbids Christians to do it. 'Lay not up for yourselves treasures upon earth,' said Jesus to his disciples for all time. It requires no very skilful exegesis to explain the text; but it would require a very ingenious exegesis to explain it away.

"Dr. McGlynn told the exact truth when he recently declared the corruption of the church traceable to two things—Roman gold and Roman purple. As fast as the church became a coffer for hoarding coveted wealth she became a coffin for enshrining a dead Christianity. And to-day the scandal of Christendom is exhibited to our gaze in a pope claiming to be the true and only Vicar of Christ, living in a palace with six hundred attendants, and enjoying a personal income of a million and a half dollars annually. Oh, if, according to the dream of devout Catholics of the middle ages, some *papa angelicus* were to arise, an angel-pope who would fling out this vast and prodigal church wealth among his penniless subjects, while he himself once more took up the primitive commission and went forth without purse or scrip, what an 'anti-poverty' argument would that be for men and angels to witness! I say all this not to cast gratuitous contempt on Rome, but to bring a solemn warning to America. That eight billions of hoarded money constitutes a tremendous danger. I cannot see how the church can keep hold of it and be able at the same time to take hold of the million hands of poverty and illiteracy and spiritual destitution which are stretched out for help. . . .

"In this world, as well as in the world to come, there is an impassable gulf between Dives and Lazarus. If the church deliberately chooses the company of Dives, putting on purple and fine linen and faring sumptuously every day, she cannot keep with Lazarus. The attempt may be made to effect conciliation by tossing biscuits across the gulf. But this will not do. It is not money that is wanted, to bring the disaffected masses into sympathy with the church, so much as fellowship. The word *koinonia*, 'community,' or 'having in common,' is a great characteristic word of the New Testament. The church is a heavenly commonwealth, in which there is a community of life with the Head and a community of goods with the members and a community of sympathy with the world. If only the church could once more stand forth transfigured in its primitive ideal, it would be certain to repeat its primitive conquests. Let the ministers of our great metropolitan churches who enjoy munificent salaries begin the reform by becoming like the chief apostle—poor, that they may make many rich; and let the millionaire pewholders follow their lead by parting their goods to such as have need. Then see if the growing spirit of communism will not be speedily arrested, not by the counter-irritant of ridicule, but by the emollient of Christ-like example. . . .

"If we look to the upper and best-educated classes of society we are confronted with a wide-spread and growing agnosticism. And what is agnosticism? It is culture ending in ignorance, as the highest mountain-peaks are lost in clouds. I would not deride or pour contempt on this tendency lest I be guilty of what an old writer has called 'beating a cripple over the head with his own crutches.' A loud-mouthed and boastful infidelity may awaken our contempt, but a lame faith, stretching out its hands toward the great mysteries of life and eternity, deserves to be pitied rather than pelted. And so I have delighted to quote to men of this school the words of Scripture concerning our great High Priest, 'who can have compassion on the ignorant [the *agnoöusin*, the agnostics], and on them that are out of the way.'

"But how shall the church meet this growing sentiment

outside the church? I may surprise you when I answer, With a humble Christian agnosticism.

" Christianity is not a system of philosophy, but a revelation to faith. The attempt to survey and map out its doctrines according to our logic charts has always proved injurious. If theologians insist upon being wise above what is written, neologians, by a natural reaction, will be ignorant below what is written. I am a most decided believer in a positive gospel, and concerning everything that has been revealed I think we may be just as sure as concerning the conclusions of mathematics. But not everything which we desire to know has been revealed. The gospel exhibits a divine reserve as well as a divine revelation, and the same voice of the great Teacher which declares concerning one realm of truth, ' To you it is given to know,' declares concerning another realm, ' It is not for you to know.'

" Now while upon such questions as, for example, the resurrection of the body at Christ's second coming there is a flood of light from Scripture, upon the state and employments of the soul between death and resurrection hardly a ray of light has been thrown. And while the most positive information has been vouchsafed as to what God will do for the heathen who hear and believe the gospel, he has nowhere informed us exactly what will be the ground and method of his dealings with those heathen who have never heard it. Yet such minute surveys of the *terra incognita* of the intermediate state have been attempted, and such learned conclusions concerning this mystery of the heathen's accountability have been put forth, that great religious bodies have been set in battle array, and vast missionary interests have been imperiled. If the most learned man in the whole fraternity of theologians had long ago faced these questions with a positive and dogmatic ' I don't know,' he would have been worthy to be counted ' a prophet, and more than a prophet.'

"It has been the misfortune of Christian philosophers from the beginning that they have made theology 'dark with excess of light.' The heresies which have afflicted the church have, almost without exception, been invented by learned scholars; and the speculations which have blighted the faith of believers have generally been hatched and brooded in the theological schools. The great mass of plain and practical Christians have, as a rule, kept the faith in its purity; for they have been content to believe more than they know, and to accept more than they can understand. Reason and faith are like the two compartments of an hour-glass: when one is full the other is empty. Those who have determined to know all things, revealed and unrevealed, have often thereby reduced their faith to the minimum, and so doing have contracted the very faculty by which we are to apprehend God.

"Now what I am urging is this, that as sumptuous wealth in the hands of the church has always proved a curse, so a sumptuous learning in the schools of theology has proved too frequently a blight upon the faith and piety of Christians. Agnosticism is the spiritual pauperism which stands over against the theological and philosophical wealth with which men attempt to endow the gospel. Paul declares that in giving the gospel God 'destroyed the wisdom of the wise.' If this wisdom of the wise gets installed in our theological chairs and presides there, it will in turn destroy the gospel. It is written that 'when the world by wisdom knew not God, it pleased God by the foolishness of preaching to save them that believe.' If the wisdom of this world attempts to reverse this order, and to please men by the learnedness of preaching, it will darken and bewilder those that would believe.

"Here, I solemnly conceive, is one of the most serious perils to which our Protestant ministry is exposed to-day, viz., that it shall be impoverished by excess of learning, that it shall attach the first importance to German learning and to

Greek philosophy, instead of going forth with the humble
equipment of the Word of God.   I am perpetually chagrined
to see how much better many of the unschooled lay preachers
of our time can handle the Scriptures than many clergymen
who have passed through the theological curriculum.   I do
not undervalue the seminary in saying this, but beg that we
should consider the point at which it is most conspicuously
failing.   I wish, for one, that no more chairs might be endowed in our theological institutions for teaching the relations
of Christianity to science; that those courses in polemics,
which stuff men's heads full of the history of all the heresies
which have afflicted the church from the beginning, might be
shortened more and more, and that the time thus saved might
be given to studying the Bible and practising with the 'sword
of the Spirit.'

"Magnificent and far surpassing all that has gone before
is the electr c light; but the shadow which it casts is the dark-
est and den est that ever yet fell upon earth.   And I believe
that in New England, where the light of philosophic Christianity has been the most brilliant and the intellectual lenses
and reflectors for its diffusion the most clear and polished,
the shadows of agnosticism and atheism fall most darkly.

"Would that our teachers of theology were content to know
less that they might know more, that they were less endued
with the spirit of modern thought and more deeply baptized
by that Spirit that has been sent to us 'that we might know
the things that are freely given to us of God.'"

CHAPTER XIV

"SEASONABLY OUT OF SEASON"

Northfield and its conferences — Dr. Gordon's spiritual experiences —
Work at Seabright — Summer ministries in New Hampshire and on
the Atlantic

THERE are few lovelier spots than Northfield. The
broad Connecticut flowing with many a sweeping bend
between green hills and rich intervales, the "sweet aisles of
the wilderness" stretching beyond the town, and the long
street lined with elms, which, like the clustered pillars of a
church, meet overhead in green vaulting with a fan-tracery of
foliage, unite to give to it a peculiar attractiveness. The conferences here, which have come to fill so important a place in
the current life of American Christianity, were first organized
by Mr. Moody in 1882. The old camp-meeting of the stormy
and emotional type was a thing of the past; the system of
summer schools, so widely developed nowadays, was as yet
in its infancy. Into the Northfield plan both ideas enter.
The demonstrative zeal of the earlier institution is tempered
and corrected by sober Scripture study, while to the quiet,
meditative, scholastic tone of a summer school of theology an
element of enthusiasm and of practicality is added by the
presence of evangelists, missionaries, and working pastors.
Here gather summer after summer the evangelists Whittle,
Needham, Munhall, Mills, Chapman, and the rest who go
from town to town and from city to city, preaching, as
did the Franciscans of old, to men of all sorts and condi-

tions.   Able, faithful, self-denying workers in city slums are here too, and of those from heathen fields not a few: Hudson Taylor, the organizer and forger of that great instrument for the evangelization of China, the Inland Mission; Bishop Thoburn, the statesman missionary, who has wrought in India a work second only to that of Duff and of Martyn; Ashmore, with his unshaken faith in China as a great figure in the enlarged Christendom to be; Chamberlain of the Arcot Mission, Post of Syria, and scores of others.   For speakers and teachers the great globe itself is ransacked, the best men in the world-church being brought into service.   Hither have come the courtly, piquant Drummond from Edinburgh, Pierson, mighty in the Scriptures, Andrew Murray, the saintly mystic of South Africa, Andrew Bonar, John McNeill, F. B. Meyer, Webb-Peploe, and more of equal note.   Their message is intensified and multiplied in that they preach to the preachers and lead the leaders of the people.   Yet hundreds of laymen as well gather about them, the most devout and earnest in the churches.   These are brought into relation with missionaries and Christian workers.   A medium of contact is thus established fruitful in its influence.   Finally, the wholesome interdenominationalism of the place establishes the best bonds of Christian unity.

Dr. Gordon's connection with these conferences runs back almost to the beginning.   Summer after summer he resigned his much-needed rest that he might give to eager hearers his view of the truth.   To Mr. Moody he was as a right hand. Often did the great evangelist dwell upon his readiness to do any service, to take any place, to stand in any gap.   "I cannot thank you enough," he wrote one summer, when his absence had thrown the whole charge of the conference upon Dr. Gordon, "for your great help at Northfield.   All the letters I have got from there speak in the highest terms of your generalship.   I know of no one who could have taken your place. *It will now answer the question what is going to become of the work when I am gone.* May the Lord reward you a thousandfold."

Of the addresses which he delivered here one writes:*

"His preaching was as far as possible from any mere oratorical performance. He had the graces of the finished speaker, but they were all invested with the higher grace of God's ambassador. He taught with authority, but it was with a derived and deputed authority. Among all the renowned speakers át the Northfield Conference, he was *facile princeps;* and the address he gave there last summer on the Holy Spirit has been pronounced by competent judges the most complete ever given, even from that platform of great teachers. There was this supreme charm in his utterances, that, while those who are less taught of the Spirit seek to defend the inspiration and inerrancy of the Word of God, he so exhibited its wonders, so led the way into its mysteries, so unfolded its hidden riches, and showed such articulated and organic unity in all its parts and members, that doubt was disarmed, and scholarly 'criticism' hesitated to use the scientific scalpel upon a body of truth instinct with the living Spirit of God!"

The Student Volunteer Movement, which, wonderful as it is, bids fair to be but the spray of the incoming tide of missionary activity, dates back to the conference of '86. The gathering of representatives from the colleges of the nation— a constituency of more than two hundred and fifty thousand young men and women—is an important feature of Northfield summers. The healthy, sunbrowned, muscular Christianity of the afternoon athletic fields, and the missionary enthusiasm of the conference hours, delighted Dr. Gordon's heart. For the amusing competition in national bombast 'twixt English and American at the Fourth of July fête, with

* Dr. Arthur T. Pierson.

all the contending and ridiculous claims to national precedence, he had a keen relish.   But his chief gratification, of
course, was that of the teacher with apt and willing pupils.
Upon these perfervid and eager hearts his influence was great
and beneficent.

"I was announced this afternoon," he writes, "with quite
a flourish of trumpets, but fear, from my excessive weariness,
that I responded but with a jews'-harp. . . . I would not
have missed the summer school.   It is an event great in results.   The missionary enthusiasm has been a feature which
has astonished us all.   It came to be the ruling idea when I
left, and over sixty names were down as pledged to that work.
Almost the entire delegation from Princeton was included.   I
could but rejoice at the demonstration given that the children
of godly and self-denying parents do follow in the way of the
fathers and mothers; for there were nearly ten missionary
sons there, all of them on fire with missionary zeal; and all
but one, who is a confirmed invalid, are bent on returning to
the foreign field.   Indeed, this one says that it is his greatest
regret that he is deprived of this privilege.   And so I have
given him a long talk to-day on divine healing.   I hope he
may yet lay hold of this."

And at another time he writes to his wife:

"It is really so that a great opportunity has been open before me.   Doctrines which are so obvious and plain to me
seem so strange to many to whom I minister.   I think we
planted seeds on Mount Hermon which, by the grace of God,
will yield a good harvest.   The day I came away they were
to have a consecration meeting.   Mr. Moody said, 'All who
want such a meeting, and are ready to yield themselves
wholly to God, come.'   I expected a remarkable time.   The
questions which they asked about the work of the Holy Spirit
are the hardest I have to answer.   Questions of experience
are so much more difficult than questions of doctrine.   For

while 'the testimony of the Lord is sure," the testimony of
consciousness is very variable, like the impression on the sea
beach, which the next wave may change. So after Mr.
Moody had given his experience of the baptism of the Spirit
because the students called for it, I confessed to much shrinking and reluctance when they made the same demand of me.
The boys would have all that could be known both of doctrine
and experience. A hungrier crowd one rarely finds; may the
Lord give us more and more to tell. . . . Mr. Moody inquired tenderly for you. He seems set on seeing you at
Northfield this year. So have the axles of baby's chariot
greased, and have the canopy swung for the journey. That
princely carriage, with its sweet-faced occupant, often comes
before me in my waking visions, and or ever I am aware my
soul makes me like the chariots of Ammi-nadib, and I am
impatient to go near and join myself to that chariot. Love
to all, and blessings on the little one especially."

And again, after describing the Northfield convocation of
'85 as a great meeting of men of many tongues and of diverse
denominational connections, he says, " Notwithstanding this
variety of denominational standing, there was absolute harmony in doctrinal deliverances. We doubt if a convention
made up of any one of the above-named bodies could be held
fourteen days and preserve such entire unanimity of sentiment. Indeed, we are persuaded that those who have mastered
and who correctly maintain the three A's of Christianity —the
Atonement, the Advocacy, and the Advent—will find themselves in close accord on all other points. One entire day was
given to the doctrine of the Lord's second coming. All the
speakers held strongly to the premillennial advent, and found in
it the key-note which brought their whole system into accord."

One of the interesting features of Gordon's later ministry
at Northfield was the evening baptism in the lake which has,
since his death, been called after his name. These services

were of great solemnity. The assembled people, the soft
singing in the eventide air, the majestic baptismal formula,
" Know ye not that so many of us as were baptized into Jesus
Christ were baptized into his death? " the face as it had been
the face of an angel, the broken waters, and the resurrection
chant at the end—these things can never be forgotten by
those who stood by the water's edge.

The letters which follow touch closely upon Northfield, and
illustrate from Dr. Gordon's personal experience the doctrine
of " enduement for service," which he preached with so much
power at the conferences.

" Dr. Gordon," writes Mr. George C. Needham, " unlike
some Christians, believed there was something always beyond.
This he ever sought to attain.   Fifteen years ago, during the
first Northfield convention, he was desirous to secure what he
yet needed as a saint and servant of Christ.   Toward the
close of those memorable ten days, spent more in prayer than
in preaching, my beloved friend joined me in a midnight hour
of great heart-searching and infilling of the Spirit.   He read
with peculiar tenderness our Lord's intercessory prayer of
John xvii.   The union of the believer with Christ and the
Father, as taught by our Lord in that chapter, called out fervent exclamations, while with deep pathos he continued reading.   During united prayer which followed the holy man
poured out his soul with a freedom and unction indescribable.
I never heard him boast of any spiritual attainment reached
during that midnight hour.   Soul experiences were to him
very sacred, and not to be rehearsed on every ordinary occasion.   But I have no doubt that he received then a divine
touch which further ennobled his personal life and made his
ministry of ever-increasing spirituality and of ever-widening
breadth of sympathy."

The work at Northfield finished, he had hurried down to
the New Jersey coast to preach on Sunday at Seabright.

" It's a great way," he writes, "people have of coming to the beach, living in wooden cottages of three or four little rooms—the sand knee-deep, no cooling shade, but 'sacred high, eternal noon,' and the glare of the sun intensifying the noonday. Moody cannot endure the sea-shore. His green fields and ever-shadowing hills and deep-rolling Connecticut are his paradise. So my native hills and quiet shades at New Hampton are to me. I long to be back thereto. . . . Mrs. A—— has instituted beach meetings for the fishermen and sea-side rabble, and not only they came out yesterday, but a great company of the gay and fashionable. It was a fine sight, but not an easy service to manage, since the breakers are very noisy, and the sound of many waters is a very unequal rival when brought into competition with my voice. However, I think I made them hear. May the Lord bless the Word."

Of the humble, self-denying work of the afternoon previous —a ministry which we believe should be connected with the midnight hour at Northfield—he does not speak. It came out after his death in the following note:

" I want to add my name to the long list of those to whom dear Dr. Gordon brought almost the greatest spiritual blessing that I ever had. No one knew how much he was to me; he never knew. At Seabright, years ago, he kindly, and without our having any especial claim upon him, came to us to preach in the chapel and the little reading-room where the fishermen met. Many a time have I seen him on his knees beside those common, rough men, praying and leading them into the kingdom of God. I remember how new to me his way was of leading sinners to Christ. I learned a little about it from him. I remember his once coming from Northfield after the August conference. He seemed filled with the Spirit; he could not talk commonplaces. He said he had had a great blessing. He went to his room, and came out shortly after and said he was going down to the fisher village, and asked

the way. He did not come back until we were at dinner—
that hot afternoon. He had visited the beer and liquor saloons
and prayed with the men there, and had been among the
shanties. I know more than one family saved that day. His
dear kind sympathy and instruction and his family prayers—
oh, how much they were in our home! His book, 'The Twofold Life,' is one of the few religious books I keep on my
table and near my heart. He gave it me on my birthday
some years ago. Whenever he came to New York he made
us a real pastoral visit."

His ministry in his native town was continuous through all
the summers of his life. As regularly as the day of rest settled
down on the quiet hills, could he be seen, with Bible under
his arm, walking the long, maple-shaded village street to the
little white meeting-house with its importunately resonant bell.
In later years it was his special joy to preach in the afternoons
also, in a church building dismantled and long disused. Situated near the line of an adjacent township, the "Dana Meeting-house" was central to several communities, and on occasion could draw on a widely scattered constituency of back
farms as well. On many occasions Dr. Gordon held here
all-day services, preaching twice or thrice, and conducting inquiry meetings. What a delight these informal gatherings
were to him! How he would revel in illustration drawn
from the every-day life of the farm! The oxen bearing the
yoke, the sheep straying on the mountain-side, the seed thrown
into the fresh furrow—how admirably were the parables of
the gospels translated into the homely correspondences of New
England country life! His great gifts of illustration and of
story-telling were used with charming appositeness and simplicity. And very eagerly did the matter-of-fact people drink
in these practical and pictorial expositions of the words of
Christ. We shall never forget those still August afternoons,
the long grass waving lazily in the occasional breezes, the

THE DANA MEETING-HOUSE.

woolly masses of clouds heaped on the steel-blue sky-fields, the motley teams tied to the dilapidated fences and to the low branches of trees, and that mellifluous voice sending its full diapason out of the open windows and doors. Inside, the people sat in old-fashioned box pews, facing in all directions, and in the high pulpit—so high that his head could not have been much more than two feet from the ceiling—stood the preacher. On the shelf-like desk lay the familiar worn Greek Testament, open to some chapter in Colossians or Luke which was to serve as the subject-matter of the discourse. Scripture was compared with Scripture, words were traced from gospel to epistle, and from epistle back to prophecy, and then placed in such collocation as to bring out in full force the profound verities. How our hearts burned within us as we sat in those quaint boxes and listened anew to the recital of the blessed truths and hopes! Here were no metaphysics to confound and weary untaught souls, no prideful rhetoric, no worldly display of learning, but rather "simple Christ to simple men" —just such homely teaching as Latimer employed in the villages of sixteenth-century England, and as Whitefield used hard by the coal-pits of Lancashire.

Nor was the summer work in New Hampshire confined to his own town. He was for some years a sort of bishop— without the lawn and title of ecclesiasticism—to the dismantled churches of the abandoned farms. What more characteristic of the real, the primitive bishop than this work of strengthening and stablishing the perishing churches of a half-deserted country? How characteristic, too, of Gordon's humility of spirit! Why should he, with his great, prosperous city church, care to trouble himself with these poor, decadent, cross-roads meeting-houses, with their bare handful of unspiritual, unlettered folk! Surely no man needed more the "total rest" of his few weeks. To none would the summer days have passed more delightfully with the last volume of history or of current theological discussion; but his meat and drink was to do the will of Him that sent him. His labor and his recreation, his toilsome life and his brief vacations, had but one aim and interest. The extension of God's kingdom in New Hampshire was to him as important as its advancement in the crowded cities of India and China, or along the watercourses of central Africa. And so "out of season" he preached and worked, as well as in those months which are assigned for the formal duties of the pulpit.

The extent of this rural work is surprising when we recall it in detail. He bore many little constituencies on his heart and mind. Now he would arrange for furnishing this country church with hymn-books, now for the systematic visitation of some neglected region, now for the supply of some unoccupied pulpit by the students of his training-school. Several years since he aided in the reorganization of a church in the little town of Salisbury, Webster's birthplace, and had the great joy of placing over it one of the stanch "redeemed men" of Clarendon Street—one who had been saved from the horrible pit and the miry clay of drunkenness. The summer before his death he went up to Jefferson, in the far north of the State, after a laborious week's convention in Maine, and with the usual ten days of Northfield before him. The church there, after having been closed many years, had been resuscitated by the labor of one of his students—a woman. At her earnest solicitation, foregoing his own wish to join his family, and at the expense of all the vexations which insufficient and untimely railroad connections imply, he spent a Sunday there, preaching, baptizing, administering the communion, and exhorting the infant church to unity, godliness, and patient labor.

It was his often expressed belief that "the deadness and dearth everywhere here" could be arrested only by the preaching of common men who knew the Scriptures and eschewed philosophizing. He longed for a renaissance of the class of "farmer preachers" with which his boyhood had been familiar. "Three of the four churches which stood in the town where I am staying this summer," he once said in a Northfield address, "were manned by farmers. When higher education came they felt themselves crowded out, and the class is lost to us. I believe in the farmer preachers. They knew the Bible from cover to cover. I wish we had that class in the country to-day to preach to the people, and I hope God will send down a vision of his Spirit that will inspire these men to go forward and preach just as they used to. When the fashion came on of being educated, they made the mistake of trying to appear as the educated, and began to read their sermons. With these men we could renew the religious life of New England."

Nor was this summer ministry suspended even in mid-ocean. In crossing the Atlantic, Gordon invariably sought out the un-privileged and taught them. He describes in a letter written in '88 the meetings which he held one Sunday in the crowded, fetid steerage of a Cunarder:

"Sunday afternoon we got permission to hold service among the steerage passengers. They were of all nationalities and all creeds, and were not ready at once to gather for a religious and Protestant service. So I went down into the hold, and preached to the men and women in their bunks, or as they sat lounging and smoking on the floor. Though dis-inclined at first to hear, they soon became attentive, and lis-tened with deep interest as I preached to them of the Good Shepherd going after the lost sheep. Meanwhile Mrs. Gordon had started singing on the deck among the same class, and, with the help of a few Christian friends, had held their atten-tion till I came up and preached to them also. This service was quietly listened to, though with some interruptions. When I announced to the people that 'there is none other name under

heaven given among men, whereby we must be saved,' a
Catholic Irishman, with just enough of his national beverage
aboard to make him mellow and religious, stepped out and
crossed himself very devoutly, exclaiming, ' That's so, your
riverance! Jesus Christ is the Saviour, and St. Peter is head
of the church—St. Peter whom he commanded to walk on
the water.   Think of that, my friends '—pointing out over the
waves—' think of St. Peter walking on the sea.'   And so he
went on in a very noisy but friendly way to vindicate the
primacy of St. Peter, the head of the apostolate, till the crowd
insisted that he be quiet that the preacher might finish his
sermon.   Then I proceeded, urging the people that they were
sinners in need of pardon, till a socialist, sitting on the bulk-
head with his pipe in his mouth, cried out, ' Preach to Jay
Gould.   He is the sinner that needs praying for.'   And so he
gave us something of a talk on the tyranny of capital and the
oppression of labor.   Thus we closed, but not without finding
warm-hearted Christians, Swede and Scotch especially, and a
Welsh Methodist, who led the singing and became thereafter
my faithful helper and co-laborer among his shipmates.   A
good opportunity is afforded on shipboard for giving the
gospel if we are mindful of the Lord's words, ' As ye go,
preach.'   This public introduction has given us some opportunities for personal talks on board, which we trust may not
be without fruit."

CHAPTER XV

A CHARACTER SKETCH

Personal appearance — Traits and characteristics — Work among poor — Home life

WHAT we are about to say of Dr. Gordon's personal character may seem to those unacquainted with him suggestive of that method of chronicling men's lives which consists in suppressing or ignoring faults and in unduly magnifying virtues; but to those who ever shared his companionship it will seem an inadequate estimate of a personality superlative in its sweetness and saintliness. We cannot desist from applying to him what he once wrote of John Woolman, to whose " Journal " he so frequently acknowledged his indebtedness:

" We dare not indorse the verdict of one who has called him ' the man who, in all the centuries since the advent of Christ, lived nearest to the divine pattern.' It is impossible to give such solitary preëminence to any disciple of Christ. We have called him, above all whom we have known, a disciple of the Holy Ghost and the most worthy exemplar of ' the love of the Spirit.' " Qualities which we look upon in ourselves as attainments we think of here as natural and inevitable traits of one who wore so manifestly the white rose of a pure life.

In personal appearance he was of massive form and well proportioned. His hair had turned early from chestnut to silver. He seemed never to have had any long period of middle life. The transition from spring to fall, from youthfulness to the grayness and gravity of age, was direct. In meditation his face appeared to some a little severe; in relaxation none could be more gracious and genial. In his last years the light of heaven played about his features. This radiancy, which was but the symbol of the life within, was startling at times. On one occasion an Irish servant-girl opened the door for him at a house where he was calling, and on announcing him said that she had forgotten his name, but that he certainly had the face of an angel. This strange spiritual light was neither the silver shimmer of the hair nor the deep benignity of the far-shining pupil, nor the calm of the features. It seemed to be all these suffused with something else too subtle for description, something ethereal, rare, beatific.

In his daily walk he was beyond criticism. "He and his sermons are one," they were wont to say of John Tauler. It could be repeated here. "If Dr. Gordon should sin," said a Boston minister, "I should lose my faith in God." What others commit of the Scriptures to memory he committed to practice. "We now know what 'the life hid with Christ' is," said his people of him. "It has been visibly exemplified before us."

Neither could sins of omission be well charged upon one whose whole life was spent in a round of ceaseless and self-denying effort for others. "The man whose hands are full," he would say, "is generally found to be the one most efficient in the service of Christ. The strings of the viol must be taut in order that they may be fitted to make music. So our energies must be keyed to a pitch of activity to make us efficient Christians." His diligence was extraordinary.*

---

* His letters indicate this throughout. In the first of the three following extracts he refers to his labors on Monday, usually thought to be the minister's rest-day after the strain of the Sabbath:

" I have just returned from my fifth service to-day. Ten o'clock at the

Seven days each week were as full as continuous demands on his time could make them. He never refused to speak at a meeting or to act on a committee where it was possible for him to do so without conflict with other engagements. His door-bell, which he called "almost the greatest trial of my life," rang from morning till night, announcing applicants for advice or sympathy or pecuniary help. We get a suggestion of its diligent jingling in the following note, which describes his return from a summer vacation and the swarm of callers who waylaid him on his first appearance:

"We reached Boston safely and speedily, and were home at 2 P.M. A royal welcome awaited us—all my clients and dependents having scented my coming from afar. Dr. A——— was at the house awaiting me to consult about the interests of China, and that great empire with a third of the human race was considered and its vast interests disposed of in twenty minutes. Then D——— came in to grapple with the affairs of the training-school and its more than a dozen applicants waiting to be attended to. While I was in consultation with him a young Scotchman came for help and counsel. Having spent his 'little all' in search for employment, and being now penniless, he had heard of me, and had been anxiously looking for my arrival as the one ray of light in his dark prospect.

Congregational ministers' meeting, address on the Sunday question; 3 P.M., Executive Committee meeting at Tremont Temple; 4 P.M., Bethel Board; 7:30, Standing Committee meeting at the church; 8:30, Sunday-school Union meeting at the church. Ought not one to get tired out and talked out? But I came home full of joy. Four came before us for baptism—and such conversions as I have rarely seen."

"I am wanted at two places this evening, both important, for 'no license' and for 'church extension.' Am on the fence as to which to choose."

" . . . Oh that I were three and could make for myself three tabernacles of usefulness—one for Boston, one for Raleigh, and one for the Missionary Union urging me to go to Pittsburg next week!"

While talking with him another edged his way into the parlor wearing that peculiar look of sanctimonious sheepishness which I can never certainly interpret whether the bearer waits to profess religion or to get married. In this case it was the latter, and the transaction awaits completion. It was nearly dark before I got through with these, and I had sat down for a hurried meditation on my Sunday's sermon when the bell rang, and I found a man panting for breath on the front steps, so exhausted that he could not get his wind sufficiently to articulate for some minutes. I recognized him as an old offender of twelve years' standing, but I did not on that account shut up my bowels of compassion against him. A tall, lank, long-haired man with a bundle of documents under his arm was the next. He wanted me to assist in calling a great meeting to expose the iniquities of Freemasonry, and made my blood curdle by reciting the formula of initiation used in this order. Well, you see I had a royal greeting home."

His patience was, from a psychological point of view, marvelous. Such constant intrusions, such various and frequent interruptions, such unremitting labor, such continuous expenditure of vitality, would have kept most men in a chronic condition of nervous irritability. Yet no one ever reported a single outbreak of petulance, a single expression of impatience, in his whole career. His heart kept a "high, calm, spheric frame," undisturbed by the exasperating incidents which beset every one who has to deal largely with the helpless, the broken, and the weak. For it could be said of him, as Erasmus said of Sir Thomas More, that he was "patron-general to all poor devils." "Let scientific charity look after the worthy poor," he used often to say; "my mission is to the unworthy." And it must be said, in justice to him, that he had a fairly representative and numerous constituency of this class. He would laughingly speak of the two tramps, whom he overheard one evening when walking along a neighboring street, one of whom sententiously remarked, "It's wan eighty-two" (the number of Dr. Gordon's house); and again of a half-intoxicated wastrel who inquired of him while passing "where the institooshun on Brookline Street" was, referring also to his home. Yet these personifications of poverty and sin who came to his lower porch for charity were treated with an unfailing courtesy and tenderness. "'Remember them that are in bonds, as bound with them,'" he was wont to say. "If you are temperate and prosperous and fortunate, you are called upon to share the sorrows of the drunkard's wife and the trial of the widow's poverty and the pain of the sick man's couch. *As bound with them!* 'I don't sign my name to any man's bond,' says a shrewd business man. In business that may be a right principle, but in religion we are called on to be bondsmen for any poor, suffering brother who asks it of us. If sickness has put a mortgage on his body, or poverty has fixed an attachment on his goods, the Bible tells us we must consent to be bound with him."

That he lived up to this high standard the day of his funeral attested. He doubtless knew many a face in the throng of poor that passed his coffin that morning, though they were strangers to all others. "Dr. Gordon's study," writes a well-known pastor,* "was in the back of the church, in the second story, directly over the rear entrance. Wishing to see him one day, I shook and rattled the door. The window of the study slowly opened, his face appeared, and when I told him what I wanted, he took his key from his pocket and tossed it down with the words, 'Come up.' He lived above the rest of us, but was always ready to share the heights with any who wished, and tossed the key to his secrets to any who sought them. He always worked with door open for all who cared enough for him and his to seek, knock, and climb. A thousand might pass the silent study on the noisy street and give

* Rev. O. P. Gifford, D.D.

no thought to him, but whenever a man wanted what he had, the want was met as soon as help was sought. No book in his library was too good to be loaned, no experience too deep to be shared, no hour too busy to be yielded to the life in need. With the upward look and the upper room he partook with the apostles of the baptism of the Spirit, and sought to make practical application of the truth to life."

His unwearied patience in committees, where contending opinions pulled and tugged like the four horses in Plato's fable, was often remarked. The most outrageous filibustering never ruffled his pellucid temper. The same evenness and control were conspicuous in his letters. Nothing could be more vexing than the assurance with which problems in eschatology, so easy to propound, so impossible to solve, were put before him by unknown correspondents in Iowa or in Texas, as if he were a new oracle holding in his breast the secrets of the age to come. These he would answer as best he could in his slow, cramped, peculiar handwriting. Sometimes, of course, such answers were necessarily concise. At one time he wrote a mere outline of his view, and added, in closing, his regrets that he had then no time to amplify. He received a reply some months later in which the writer remarked, " It is certainly fortunate for me that your time was so limited. I have already spent nine weeks in attempting to decipher the handwriting of your note, and am not nearly done yet!" His correspondence was extensive, and, like Molinos, he directed by this means the spiritual life of a widely distributed circle of Christians.

The same trait of patient considerateness was prominent in his estimate of others, especially of those with whom he disagreed. "We believe we ought to contend earnestly for the faith once delivered to the saints," he once said, "but in doing this *we should seek to be like the saints once delivered to the faith.*" He always aimed to keep experimental religion to the front and the conflicting theories of belief in the back-ground. "Theology begets strife; salvation genders unity. The saints fight over doctrine; they weep together over sin-ners." In his utterances no man was ever more circumspect. His tongue was as completely subject to his will as ever Hebrew slave to Egyptian taskmaster. Exaggerations, harsh comments, misinterpretations, caricatures, distortions, rash or thoughtless statements, never fell from his lips. He never had, therefore, to retreat from the positions which his words had chosen and fortified.

Criticism and opposition he endured without recrimination. "A Christian," he says, "should be a patient, undaunted, undiscouraged torch-bearer for Christ. If a storm of abuse should chance to break upon him, he is to stand in statue-like indifference to it all, holding forth the Word of life. If blasts of ridicule dash him in the face, he is to take it as silently and as imperturbably as the bronze figure takes the tempest. It is the man who stands that moves the world." And again, "The opprobrium of truth identifies us with Christ in the tenderest and closest sense. It was not, surely, greediness for contempt which led Paul to glory in the cross of our Lord Jesus Christ. By it, he tells us, he was crucified unto the world, and the world unto him. That which cut him off from men joined him the more closely to the Lord; that which oppressed him from the human side liberated him to-ward the divine." Yet this meekness was "never to the abatement of firmness in maintaining principle. His upright-ness was inflexible, and when need arose intrepid. The hand that could carry the grapes of Eshcol with a touch so delicate as not to disturb their bloom could, when occasion demanded, seize the sword of the Lord and hew Agag to pieces before him." * The unpopularity of a doctrine had nothing to do with his adhesion thereto. For him there was but one test—

* Dr. Arthur T. Pierson, article in " Missionary Review," April, 1895.

the will of Jesus Christ.   His obedience to God was as unquestioning as that of the legionaries to Cæsar.   Much as he disliked controversy, the imminent probability of trouble never tempted him to curtail or conceal the least essential of his convictions.   " Better the church militant battling for the truth than the church complaisant surrendering the truth for the sake of peace.   The Prince of Peace is a man of war. Let us be less afraid of contention for the truth than of communion with error."

In nothing, indeed, was he greater than in that rare grace, humility.   "The way to see the divine light," says an old proverb, " is to put out thine own candle."   Simeon Stylites was not more sensible of his unworthiness.   Unlike him, however, Gordon never, by dwelling on his unworthiness, betrayed a consciousness of this humility.   He quietly implied it by giving to others the precedence at all times.   " Who of us is, after all, worthy, Mr. Roberts? " he once said to the superintendent of the Industrial Home, when interceding for some vagabond who had forfeited all claims on charity by his ingratitude and dishonesty.   And at another time he writes:

"As to the absence of my kindred from church—well, I am sorry.   How easy it is to backslide!   I feel this myself, and wonder what I should be without the stimulus of helpful circumstances."

And again, writing from Northfield to his wife:

" How wonderful it all is that I, so little time ago washing wool and tending the cards in the place where you are, should be here in this mount of privilege, with such honor put upon me as teacher and co-laborer with the greatest and best!   To God be all the glory.   How little could I have foreseen all this!   How little could I have brought it about!"

In a letter written to a friend in London soon after his return in '88, we find this striking sentence, " Redemption from beginning to end is a problem in loss and gain, in which—

strange paradox!—the magnitude of our gain is determined by the multitude of our losses. The highest bidder for the crown of glory is the lowliest bearer of the cross of self-denial." These maxims were adopted as a working program for his daily life. Self-renunciation became to him the primary law of conduct. In the larger and more noteworthy sacrifices of life this rule is often not so exacting as might at first appear. Signing checks for good causes, registering one's name in subscription lists, discommoding one's self for good friends—there are in all these hidden but recognizable compensations which return to us like those indemnifying benefits which politicians claim to find in indirect taxes. It is a joy to be the "servant of the servants of God." There is a perceptibly suffusing pleasure even in stripping off one's coat and handing it to the beggar, as St. Martin did, provided the act is noted by observing eyes. But the real, the crucial test comes in the little crucifixions, the unnoticed and apparently insignificant self-denials. It is hard to be the servant of the ungrateful and the unworthy. It is hard to pay the direct, the summary assessments on one's convenience and leisure. To ride late in dreary cars that some little county conference may have the inspiration of your thought and the impulse of your words; to intervene in behalf of unpopular causes when, if your friends are not scandalized, they are at least silent; to resign the brief moment of rest at the fireside, putting on coat and hat and going out into the cold, that some man may have his bed or some woman her groceries—in short, to stand ready to be spent to the last fragment of personal comfort, to empty one's pockets of all the small change of unoccupied time, this indeed is the trial of one's unselfishness. It was in these ungrudging services that the rarer and more superlative excellences of Dr. Gordon's character were most conspicuous. Bonhomie and kind-heartedness he had in no limited measure; but far beyond this was the high genius for self-abnegation.

As with Luther, love of music was one of his most striking characteristics. Though without a musician's training, he edited with peculiar discrimination two hymn-books, and wrote admirable and much-used tunes for fifteen or more hymns.

Hymnology was, indeed, his only diversion, a spring of refreshment and a means of relaxation after tension, as fiction is to most men. Matching in spare moments old hymns to new tunes, writing either hymns or tunes as the case required, humming into being new melodies as he went to sleep, singing the old ones with his family till all throats were hoarse and all lungs weary save his own—here was his unfailing resource. And so responsive was he to music that a few chords would often suffice to bring him downstairs to the side of the piano, as if an invisible, yet no less potent, spell were working.

His setting of the well-known words, "My Jesus, I Love Thee," is familiar wherever hymns are sung by men and women of the English tongue. It was sung by thousands in jerseys and bonnets on that sad day when the mother of the Salvation Army was laid away to rest. Many have been the interesting incidents connected with it. On one occasion in New York, after some great meeting, he was met by a handsome and stately young woman who had been a singer of distinction in opera. Disillusioned of a career of excitement, sick at heart of the pride of life, filled with yearning for she hardly knew what, she had sat down at the piano in the reception-room of the hotel where she was staying, and opening haphazard a hymnal which lay on the rack, had played the first number she turned to. It was "My Jesus, I Love Thee." She sang verse after verse. Before she had finished she had gone through the whole experience—tears, repentance, forgiveness, peace! For more than a year, now, she had given herself to humble mission work in the metropolis.

At another time, after he had spoken at a large meeting in a Canadian city, at which the provost of the town presided, this hymn was given out. It was sung with great power and fervor by the congregation. Happening to look at the chairman, he was surprised to see him giving way to emotions of uncontrollable grief. After the services were over he went with him to his home. In the quiet of his library he told Gordon how his only son had passed away some weeks before in his arms singing the same blessed hymn.

Like Luther, too, he was, above all, fond of children. None knew better than his own with what tenderness he could share their sorrows, with what almost vicarious willingness he hurried to take upon himself their difficulties and their trials. A note to a little five-year-old nephew, printed in roman letters and capitally illustrated, which lies before us is worthy to be placed alongside the great Reformer's singularly beautiful letter to his boy Hans. No one ever had a surer entrance into children's hearts. No one ever better knew what to say to them on all occasions. His addresses to the children of the church—so simple, so transparent, so charming—were the wonder of all. But those who knew him in his home relations understood the secret of their charm. It sprang from an acquaintance with child character which results only from long companionship and sympathy.

As a teller of marvelous tales he had few equals. What multiplex incident! What extraordinary involutions! What unexpected dénouements! His art was that of the magician who draws yard upon yard of ribbon from his mouth. For these stories were nigh endless, and ran night after night, like the plays in Chinese theaters. That of " Guggles "—the name is sufficiently suggestive of its droll character—was perhaps his masterpiece. His elaborate improvisations on themes drawn from Grimm ran a close second. Never was he happier than in the nursery with a lapful of babies hypnotized by his thrilling incidents and vivid descriptions. " Tell Theodora how constantly I think of her, and that I am getting some five-story stories to tell her at bedtime when I get home," he writes from Canada in the midst of an arduous missionary campaign.

His drawings, too, were always in great requisition. With that irresistible power of enchantment which seemed to dwell in the stub of his pencil he summoned them forth from the paper—rows of sleepy listeners in church, files of bald-pated deacons, groups of fantastic faces suggestive, in their physiognomic eccentricities, of the innumerable oddities who turned up weekly at his home with bizarre theories and quaint explanations of prophecy. I have since thought, in calling to mind these sketches, that while he sat patiently drawing for a group of interested heads about him, he was all the time enjoying a mild revenge in these caricatures, and that inwardly there was much quiet satisfaction over the distorted noses and undisciplined hair.

One of his specialties in the pictorial line had to do with the escapades and activities of a little brownie folk made of straight lines and minute capital circles. The battles of these linear people, their winter sports and summer rambles, their household mishaps, their ludicrous employments, constituted a perpetual vaudeville of nonsense for children and grandchildren.

Furthermore, he possessed—oh, rare delight of youngsters! —an almost Helvetic skill in wood-carving. To recount the various amusing and play-provoking things which his deft fingers whittled out would be to give an inventory of the contents of a well-stocked toy-shop. Miniature farming tools, houses, barns, churches, animals, were released one by one from the enveloping thraldom of a pine block by his emancipating penknife, as Ariel was released from the riven oak. Besides this, he would make watering-carts out of tomato cans mounted on wheels, transparencies for campaign purposes out of old soap-boxes, and "keroogians," an invention of his own—

bits of glass of various lengths strung on strings, and arranged in the order of the notes of the scale—on which he would play long "kinder symphonies," to the infinite amusement of little folks.

This ingenuity was apparent even in the discipline of children. Who ever used his gift of imagination more cleverly in the unwelcome task of getting an appetiteless three-year-old to eat? This is how he managed. Froebel himself could not have done better:

"Theodora is well and happy. She does not eat any better than ever, but Elsie and I manage that. To-day the milk-cup was a steam fire-engine and her mouth the tenement where the conflagration was raging. I rang the table-bell violently, and as the engine rushed down the street she allowed the fire to be put out to the extent of a cupful of milk poured in."

A letter or two will illustrate these traits. In the first the Congo Mission and his last baby occupy him alternately. In the last his children in New Hampton are sent some timely advice.

"My constant thought has been of you, mother and child, Iadora * and Theodora. Everybody I met, whether from the far West or frozen North, congratulated me and inquired for you both. I have really hardly waked up to the event that has taken place in our home as viewed by the great public, and wonder now that I have been so reserved and so self-contained. I knew, or thought I knew, that we had a well-spring of joy in our house, but how far the streams thereof had flowed to make glad the great Baptist constituency, I had not taken in till, by the warm grasp of the hand from scores at every station crowding round to do us honor, I was made fully aware of it. All seemed to have known it whom I met on the train—that is, that another olive plant had sprouted about my table—and even the hackmen, as I stepped out from the cars at various points along the line, nudged and

* " I adore her," of course.

winked at each other, whispering I know not what except, 'That is the proud parson.' . . .

"Theodora still continues to be the brightest star in the Milky Way. Give the little dairymaid my best wishes for success in her earliest occupation. . . . Mr. H——'s son came in for a little time in the evening, and sat, with cigar in hand, and sometimes in mouth, talking of the virtues of his dead father and of his prospective departure for the beach to spend the summer. And I thought of that good father's profound interest in the Congo Mission, and wondered why he did not leave his fortune to that work instead of endowing one solitary son to smoke and saunter at summer resorts. I hope our children may be endued, but not endowed, especially Theodora now pasturing in the land of milk and honey. May she get strength and sustenance therefrom to bless the world. I believe your own temperate living and temperance lecturing will bear rich fruit in children and children's children. May it prove so especially with Theodora. May she be a living stone polished after the similitude of a palace. On the cars the prospects of the Congo Mission were much talked of by all whom I met. Generally the voice was favorable and the sentiments strong. I am in for it, and am bound to organize a new society to carry it on unless justice is done it. With myself for president, and you for collector, and Arthur and Helen for home and foreign secretaries, we could do it. Haley, Ernest, Elsie, and Theodora will of course be on the executive committee. The last, I am sure, under the tuition of her present appetite, would be ready to vote for large supplies. I sincerely trust that the little maiden may be delivered from colic, and that the winds in her little cave of Æolus may be laid and kept at rest. I speak, of course, paregorically. Now may the God of peace be with you all, protecting, keeping, guarding you. May he cause all grace to abound in you always."

"DEAR CHILDREN: How I envy you the joy of being together in that lovely retreat. Now I send you my list of cautions and instructions. They are as follows:

"1. Give ample time for prayers each morning. Examinations are over, and there need be no hurrying off now. Sing a hymn and take turns in leading.

"2. Do not rush too rapidly into farm work, but begin very slowly till you get inured to it, and look out for sunstroke.

"3. Have a good solid three hours of reading aloud.

"4. Don't run any risk in going into the river. Go together if at all, and watch over each other.

"5. Look out for the horse. Ἴδε τὸν ἵππον. Go slow with him till you find out his temper.

"Pray for us that the Word of the Lord may abound through us."

It was in his boyhood home that the geniality of his disposition came out most clearly. Relieved for a few weeks from the innumerable cares of pastoral life in the city, his spirits took on fresh sparkle and animation in the quiet and tender air of the New Hampshire country. With what enthusiasm did he enter into the simple rustic joys! What delight did he take in rambling over the rough pastures with his children for blueberries, in organizing excursions to far-away hilltops and to distant lakes, in riding homeward at dusk singing the evening hymns of Lyte and Keble, while the glow was still living in the west and the whippoorwills were beginning their chant in the hollows! In later life these intervals of rest and recreation steadily narrowed as the calls for service became more frequent and more urgent. Summer conventions broke into small fragments the short furloughs, while an enormous correspondence, the ceaseless rolls of printers' proof, and the continuous intrusion of the outer world gave to what was left the uneasy hurried character of a half-holiday. Yet, brief as they were, these days were the regenerating tonic which, in anticipation, in retrospect, and in immediate enjoyment, strengthened him to accomplish the tasks of thirty years.

" The happiest and most exalted moments I have ever known in this life," he writes, " are those when I stand on some high outlook of my New Hampshire home, and gaze off upon the blue hills in the distance, and see those hills rising range upon range, as though they were the very portals of Beulah land. There is something indescribable in these mountain-top experiences, and they never fail to lift me out of myself and bring me nearer to God. I shall see the King in his beauty, and the land of far distances. . . . I have just revisited many scenes of my early walks in this so familiar place. I remember a tree where I used to go as a boy to pray. Only the stump of it remains; but I could call it to witness, while kneeling there, that God had done exceeding abundantly above all that I thought or asked. What a change! Who could have dreamed it!"

In New Hampton the abstracted look disappeared, the tense determination of spirit relaxed. The mental pictures clustering about him here so different from those of the city life as almost to suggest a double personality. One remembers him reading, with rich intonation, " High Tide on the Coast of Lincolnshire " to his sick child, while the butterflies came in the windows and the leaves rippled in the breeze; or standing, watch in hand, in the perspective of the long bridge over the Pemigewasset, timing his little sons as they raced to the other side after their evening's bath in the river. In later years we see him climbing a hill path, a St. Christopher of the mountainside, with his eldest grandson astride his shoulders and grasping that transfigured forehead; or, again, driving a rackful of city children to the village, complacently silent amid the clatter of tongues and the shrill singing of gospel hymns.

The coming of these children to New Hampton was during

many years a feature of his vacations. He was not content to enjoy in selfish meditation, far from the sorrow and poverty behind him, the sweet influences of the summer hills, the quiet companionship of nature. There were white faces and puny frames which needed the regenerating touch of mountain air. There were tired mothers to whom a change of surroundings and work would mean a renewed lease of life. How could he leave such in the straitened warrens of the city while he himself was drinking in the air of enlarged landscapes and of distant vistas? So for a dozen years or more he had with him, in an unoccupied farm-house not far from his own home, from fifteen to twenty-five poor children. And as to expense? Well, this was how it was met. From his own purse he contributed much; friends in the home church helped further; but for their immediate support vegetables, supplies, and cooked food were sent in by farmers from the neighboring districts in response to the requests which he always made from the pulpit of the village church. "I have ministered unto you in spiritual things," he would say; "minister ye to the temporal necessities of these little ones." And so even the vacations were unreservedly given over to good works. The local church received a vitalizing impulse on Sundays from one deep taught in the Word and ever ready to communicate, and the impulse realized itself practically in a tender and helpful charity. What a delight these children were to him! What a fatherly interest he took in them all! On one occasion, when a little girl was sent up unexpectedly, and no place could be found for her to sleep, he went to work with hammer and saw and scantling and built a bed for her, hardly finishing it before night arrived. The last summer of his life was unusually successful in this direction. In a letter to his wife he writes:

"To-day there was a lawn picnic for the children on the farm. Many of the townspeople turned out, and the children appeared beautifully. The kindness of the people has been superabundant; more than could be eaten has been supplied. I thanked them publicly. The Dana Meeting-house people feel defrauded that they have had so little hand in the business. I promised them a chance next year."

And again:

" I felt this afternoon that a sight of the joy of the children on the farm, as they ran to meet me, was more than a compensation for all the trouble they have made you and the rest. It is an unspeakable treat to them, and they are already mourning the shortness of the time remaining for their stay. They are going down this evening to sing to blind Uncle Isaac. They execute ' I have a song I love to sing ' with real power."

The tenderness which exhibited itself in his relations to children extended even to the weakest animals. All things both great and small shared his kindness. Many a manumitted mouse has doubtless wondered at the good fortune which befell him on being caught in the trap of which a large man with silver hair and a kind face was the owner; for it invariably meant freedom. In an affluent home on Commonwealth Avenue there lives even now a well-fed cat bearing the name " Adoniram," who perhaps recalls that wild snowy night when a hospitable door was unaccountably opened for him by the same man with the same kind face. And to one friend at least a verse in an early chapter of Matthew recurred as he saw the same man hunting, with a palpitating, unfeathered sparrow in his closed palm, for the nest of horsehair whence the birdling had dropped.

CHAPTER XVI

INTERMEZZO

Dr. Gordon's humor—Negroid and other stories—Quaint experiences—
Pastoral incidents

AS has been intimated, Dr. Gordon had a fund of humor
which was inexhaustible—humor of a clean, quaint,
pointed, genial type with never a suggestion of malice or un-
friendliness. He was a great maker of puns. This might
have been suspected by an acute attendant on his preaching.
He never, indeed, indulged in anything approaching levity
in the pulpit. But the striking antitheses and clever allitera-
tions which rose and jumped, now and then, like trout in a
pool, disclosed what he was likely to be at his dinner-table.
This vein of humor often bubbled out in happy characterizations or in bright repartee. A petition for the removal of a
noble and useful man from a post of great responsibility was
once shown him. Glancing at the list of Adullamites who
had signed it he said wittily, " They are of three classes, I see :
figureheads, soreheads, deadheads." At another time, when at
Northfield in charge of the conference, a telegram was received
from Mr. Moody saying that he could not be present, but that
he had three helpers, Meyer, Pierson, and Pentecost, who would
take his place, and adding an encouraging Scripture reference.
Gordon retorted immediately with a counter-reference (1 Cor.
xvi. 17) : " I am glad of the coming of Stephanas and Fortu-
natus and Achaicus : for that which was lacking on your part
they have supplied."

Those who find any incompatibility between humor and sanctity forget, doubtless, that the same Maker who brought into being the archangels created as well the bill of the toucan and the bray of the ass. Humor is—we say it reverently—a divine attribute.

Dr. Gordon's table talk was brimming with this quality. Discussions over the deep things of Scripture or the vexed problems of missionary polity were frequently followed by the free play of anecdote and a restrained raillery. If there happened to be an equally skilful *raconteur* present, stories flew back and forth as balls on a tennis-court. Then indeed did iron sharpen iron. A story was never told merely for the sake of telling, but always in response to some other or in illustration of the point under discussion. Quaint pastoral experiences, comic coincidences, laughable adventures, would come out one by one as the conversation enticed them. There was a long cyclus of negroid stories which had to do with the "colored" mission of his church, and another series pertaining to the children of Erin, with whom his pastoral and philanthropic work brought him occasionally in touch. The emergence of these stories was always preceded by a premonitory suffusion over his face of quiet fun, as of the light which glimmers before the dawn.

It was his often expressed intention to write out a brief volume of the amusing experiences which lightened his long pastorate; but for this *entr'acte* undertaking he never to the last found time. Most of the anecdotes which so amused his friends have vanished with him. Yet a few have been collected by diligent effort, and are reproduced in the following pages, that those unacquainted with his family life may get a new insight into his character.

The first of these we are able to give in his own words. It was written out at the time when he was calling attention to the excesses in church amusements. The old deacon whose story he tells was a leading member of the Ebenezer Baptist Church.   His opinions on theological currents and counter-currents were given in all confidence to the friendly pastor, and were marked by a shrewdness on which the latter often commented.   Surprised, no doubt, would he be if he were to know how wide has been the circulation of his astute and pithy Africanisms.   On one occasion they were rehearsed before a group of Edinburgh professors, to the amusement of all, especially of Dr. Calderwood, the eminent writer on ethics, who carefully preserved them in his note-book.   Our carpet-beating Epictetus is, however, to this day unaware of his fame.

One epigram always pleased Dr. Gordon.   "The black deacon of our mission church," he wrote, "gave us a very significant answer not long since.   He was complaining of his Ethiopian pastor that he did not expound the Word. When we expressed surprise and remarked that we had supposed he did, he replied, 'He can take the Bible apart as good as any man I ever seed, but he can't put it together again.'   This in learned phraseology would mean that he excelled in destructive criticism, but not in constructive."

I

"'I kicks ag'in' it, sah!'

"Such was the vehement exclamation of Brother Moses, as I met him one day in front of an aristocratic mansion where he was busily at work dusting carpets, trimming the lawn, etc.

"But before I rehearse his sidewalk discourse I must tell my reader something about this ebony sage, whom I have known now for more than twenty-five years.   Like the singer in the Canticles, he is 'black, but comely.'   Not that he has any natural beauty to attract one, but when he becomes animated upon spiritual themes the listener forgets his dark

visage and thick features, and the ' beauty of the Lord' seems
to shine out in his face.

"My first acquaintance with Moses began thus:

"Soon after the close of the war, when a considerable influx
of freedmen toward the North had set in, a Unitarian neighbor
said to me one day, 'I wish you would call in and see my
colored man, who has recently come to me from the South.
I assure you he is a character. He seems to take a great
interest in the welfare of my soul, and, as he is of your persuasion, I would like you to make his acquaintance. By all
means get him to tell you of his "experience."'

"I called one morning, according to request, and found
Moses busy in the stable polishing the harnesses and beguiling
his labors with the weird strains of an old plantation melody.

"After a pleasant introduction and some interchange of
Christian fellowship, I said:

"' Brother Moses, I wish you would tell me your Christian
experience if you can spare time for it.'

"' I allers has time enough for dat, sah,' he replied, ' and
allers shall till I puts off dis clay tabernacle, and den I'll hab
all eternity to tell it in.' And then a shine came into his
dusky visage more brilliant than that which he was imparting
to his master's leather.

"' It was on de sixth day ob October, 1853,' he continued,
' at three o'clock in de mornin', in massa's corn-field in ole
Virginny, dat de Lord spoke peace to my soul. You see, I
had been a-mournin' for weeks, yet all de while more or less
confidential in myself, and settin' store by de heaps ob good
works and prayers and repentin's I'd done. But at last dese
deceitful refuges began to gib way, and de foundations ob de
great deep broke up in my soul, and for three days and nights
I could neither eat nor drink nor sleep, a-mournin' and a-wail-
in' for my sins. At last, nigh sunrise in de third day, out in
de corn-field, I sez, "Lord, you must save dis despairin'

sinner or he'll die. I know I'se wicked and vile and rebellious,
but den you'se all-merciful and forgivin'. Dat's your reputation, Lord, and I begs you for de sake of your great name to
show mercy and not judgment." And so I cried and pleaded
dere on de ground. Den de Lord 'peared to me in de visions
ob de mornin' and reached out his hand to me; but he didn't
reach it out to me flatways as though he had any bread ob
life to gib to my hungry soul. Time hadn't come yet for
dat. But he reached out his hand edgeways toward me;
and if dat hand had been a sharp two-edged sword it couldn't
cut me open quicker'n it did; separatin' de j'ints and de mar-
rer, and layin' bare de corruption ob my heart. I never
dreamed what a heap ob blackness dere was in dat heart till
dat mornin'. But just den I heerd a mighty noise, which
made me tremble from head to foot, and I sez, "Lord,
what's dat rumblin'?" And he sez, "Dat's your sins a-fallin'
into hell." Den, quicker'n I can tell, he reached out his hand
ag'in, so kinder soft and tender, and closed me up, and didn't
leave a rent or a scar or a sore place in my heart, and he sez
to me, "Son, dy sins, which is many, is forgiben dee." Den
I knowed I'd been born ag'in; dat old things was passed
away, and all things had become new. Happified was I.
From de risin' ob de sun to de goin' down ob de same dat
day, it 'peared like I was in heben, a-standin' on de sea ob
glass, wid de harp ob God in my hand, and golden slippers
on my feet, singin' de song ob Moses and de Lamb.

"'From dat day I'se been surer dat I'se borned ag'in dan I
am dat I was borned de fust time; for I can't nowise remember my fust birth, but de second I'll remember all eternity,
and never cease to praise de Lamb dat redeemed me.

"'Dat's my experience. Some folks don't believe it, but I
knows it, for it's what I'se tasted and seen.'

"Now I dare say that my readers, having listened to this
extraordinary story, will conclude that any one capable of

such highly wrought enthusiasm as this would have very little sober sense or solid judgment for the ordinary affairs of the church of Christ. On the contrary, Moses, becoming a deacon in a colored church not long after my first acquaintance with him, has used the office so well, and gained for himself such a good degree, that by general consent he is now regarded as a very pillar and stay among his brethren. His good judgment in managing the affairs of God's house has constantly surprised me; even more have I been impressed with his fine discernment of evangelical truth, and his deep insight into the problems of Christian life and experience. Certainly he must have been profoundly taught of the Spirit; and I can say sincerely that I am always spiritually refreshed by my wayside conversations with him, and that if I should ever be in great affliction or darkness of mind, I can think of no one to whom I should more readily turn for consolation than to black Moses.

"But now to the sidewalk discourse.

"'Have you any special religious interest in your church?' I asked Moses, after his few words of hearty greeting on the occasion referred to.

"'No room for any interest,' he replied; 'de church is so lumbered up wid fairs and festibals and jollifications dat de Sperit's got no chance to work among us. Leastwise dat's my solemn 'pinion, dough some sez I'se heady and setful. But I'se sick of it, sah! I goes to church Sunday, after prayin' to be in de Sperit on de Lord's day, and de fust thing de minister gets up and reads a long program of de worldly doin's and goin's for de week—de music and de supper and de gramatic readings and what not; twenty-five cents admission, and all must come. I tell ye, I kicks ag'in' it, sah, and will long's I hab bref in my body.'

"'What do you mean by saying that you kick against it?' I asked.

" ' I rebukes it, sah, in de name ob de Lord.   Last Sunday I spoke out in meetin' and said, " Breddren, what's ye been redeemed for and brought into de church?   Didn't de Lord tell you dat you'se to be de light ob de world and de salt ob de earth?   Well, when I sees how much time some ob you gibs to fairs and festibals, and den you can't come to de prayer-meetin' 'cause you'se so busy, I sez, if you ever was de Lord's true salt, you've lost your flavor, and if you don't look out you'll be cast out and trodden underfoot ob men." '

" ' But, Brother Moses,' I asked, wishing to draw out further wisdom from this deep fountain, ' don't you think these things are necessary for making the church attractive to the masses and inviting to the young? '

" ' No, sah!' he replied, with great warmth; 'no, sah! Christians is de salt ob de world, and dey is put into de world to preserve it from corruption.   But some's got de idee dat you must bring de corruption into de church so's to preserve de salt, as dough de gospel is goin' to die out unless it's sugared and seasoned wid carnal 'musements.   Dat's de pop'lar notion.   But I kicks ag'in' it, sah.'

" ' Yes; but people say there is no harm in a social gathering and a plain supper, and a little music and reading for entertaining the people,' I continued.

" ' Well, dat's de question,' replied Moses.   ' I takes de Scriptures for my standp'int ob faith and practice, and I hab searched in vain to find where de 'postles and elders ever got up suppers of turkey and chickens and sandwiches and cold tongue, and den invited de breddren to come to church and eat 'em at twenty-five cents a head.   No, brudder; 'musements in de church is unsanctifying, howsomever folks may think 'bout it.   We had a festibal in our meetin'-house two weeks back.   I looks in a few minutes, and sees de crowds dere and de doin's.   Fust de pianny and de fiddle strikes up; and sez I, " Take off de 'straint, and how long 'fore dis whole

company'd be a-dancin' and a-waltzin' in de house ob God?"
Den dey had de guess-cake and de waffles, and waffled off a
calica quilt to de one dat drawed de prize; and sez I, "What's
dis but eddicatin' people to gamblin' and lotteries?" Den de
gramatic reader comes on, all dressed up wid ribbons an' fur-
belows, an' when I seed her rollin' her eyes an' p'intin' her
fingers, sez I ag'in, "What's dis but jus' nussin' our young 'uns
for de stage and de theater?" I tell you, I kicks ag'in' it,
sah, and allers shall.

"'Well, next night was prayer-meetin'; only twenty out,
an' all as mum as if de Lord had never opened deir mouths,
and when I warns em 'bout it dey sez, "Brudder Moses, de
Sperit didn't move us." And sez I, "De Sperit moved ye fas'
'nough last evenin' at de festibal, but I'se 'fraid 'twas de
sperit dat works in de children of disobedience." Brudder, I
reads it dat dey dat's goin' to wear de crown must bear de
cross; but what's we doin' in dese days but 'bolishin' de cross
and puttin' eatin' and drinkin' and 'musement and 'dulgence
in de place ob it? And whar's it goin' to end?'

"Here Moses pointed furtively to the residence in front of
which we were standing, and in a confidential tone said, 'De
folks dat libs here was once 'fessors ob religion, but I reckon
dey's backslid, for dey don't hab no prayers in de family now,
and dey's all taken up wid theaters and card-playin' and balls
and parties. O brudder, I has great sorrer and trabail ob soul
when I sees how de debbil prowls round and steals de Lord's
sheep right out ob his fold.'

"'Don't you think, Moses,' I asked, 'that the devil works
harder to lead Christians astray than he does to destroy the
people of the world?'

"'Don't I thinks? I knows it, sah. Why d'ye s'pose I
works and tugs and sweats beatin' dese carpets and doin' dese
chores? 'Tain't de dollar dat's in my pocket dat I'se workin'
for; I'se got dat already. It's de dollars dat's in my employ-

er's pocket dat I'se workin' for. So if de Lord has a real shure-'nuff saint—one dat's plain stamped wid de image and 'scription ob de King, and shines like a new silver dollar—de debbil, he'll rise up early and sit up late to get hold ob dat one. But your 'bandoned sinners and your high-steppin' ones, dat's all taken up wid deir moralisms and self-righteousness, he doesn't trouble himself 'bout; he knows he's got dem already.'

"Here our report of the sidewalk discussion might properly end, but it would be an injustice to Moses to leave the impression that he is only a sour and censorious critic, who takes satisfaction in pointing out the faults of Christians. On the contrary, with an indescribable pathos and tenderness, he thus concluded his talk: 'Well, brudder, I'se prayin' 'bout it night and day. It's 'cause de Lord's children don't think, dat dey does so. You remember how he sez, "My people don't consider." Well, I'se been on de way now nigh on to forty years, and it's been my 'sperience dat a day's considerin's worth more'n a year's workin'; 'cause when we takes a day for considerin' now and den, we get's 'quainted wid de Lord, and finds out his secrets, and de Lord tells us jus' what he's doin' and what he's a-goin' to do. And, brudder, he tells me in my soul I'se goin' to see a great outpourin' ob de Sperit afore I dies. Den when Christians gets deir tongues afire, as dey did on de day ob Pentecost, how our dross will be burned up, and what a cracklin' dere will be in de hay, wood, and stubble we'se buildin' into our churches in dese days! But, brudder, 'twon't come easy. We'se got to get low before de Lord, and be ob one 'cord and in one place. Trouble is now dat ebery one's ob a different 'cord; one wants one thing, and 'nother wants 'nother. But when we gets where we all wants de same thing, so we's satisfied to lib all our days on a crust ob bread if we can only hab de Lord and de fullness ob his Sperit, den he'll come down like rain on de mown grass; and dat day's a-comin', brudder!'

"Reader, Moses is a real character, and not a myth. He was born in slavery, and if he is able to read it is only a recent acquirement. But his mind is saturated with the Scripture as he has caught its phraseology from the rude preachers of his race. May it not be that he is one of the 'babes' to whom the Father has revealed some things which he has 'hid from the wise and prudent'?"

II

The pulpit of this colored church being at one time vacant, various probationers were asked to supply. The stanchly conservative deacon took a great interest in the candidates who came from time to time, and rigidly tested their orthodoxy and "pulpit style." Of one, who took with the people because of a popular narrative quality in his sermon, he complained on the ground that he was "too fond of retailing antidotes." Finally he secured a brother from South Carolina, sound, hearty, and suitable in every respect. The pastor and committee from the white church were invited up to pass judgment upon him. Coming in a little late, they found the whole gathering swaying back and forth in an ecstasy of religious excitement. The preacher, with hair kinky as astrakhan wool and a face like polished teak-wood, had worked them to a pitch of unusual fervor by his thrilling eloquence. It was a veritable plantation homily untainted by sobering New England influences.

The text was drawn from the Eighty-seventh Psalm: "And of Zion it shall be said, This and that man was born in her." When the visitors entered, the preacher was maintaining that, wherever a man's home might happen to be, his spiritual birthplace was of necessity in Zion, the joy of the earth. "Let us go to de city ob Charleston," he went on to say, "an', hubberin' ober dat great an' wicked city, let us shout down to de Lord's chillern, 'Whar war yer born?' an' dey will holler back, 'We'se born in Zion.' An' den let us go on to Richmond an' ask de breddren dere, 'Whar war yer born?' an' dey will say too, 'We'se born in Zion.'" So he passed on from city to city up the Atlantic seaboard until there were none left to question. The appeal was then carried to Greenland, and the Christians "libbin' in dat benighted lan'" were asked, "Whar war yer born?" and returned the same unfailing answer. "An' now, breddren," he continued, "let us go to de north pole, an' twinin' our legs round de pole, let us lift up our voices and cry, 'Whar war yer born?'" The congregation was now keyed to the highest tension. Women were clutching the seats, men were swaying in tremulous excitement, as the rhythmic allegory proceeded.

The visiting committee looked on in astonishment from the rear of the church. It was felt that the preacher had perforce reached the end of his journey. Not at all. After pausing a moment to recover breath, he continued, "Breddren, *let us go on to de east pole.*" Up to this point Gordon had sat as impassive as a statue of Memnon, the twinkle of his eye alone suggesting his appreciation of the scene; but the last flight was too much for that self-restraint which had, among his people, passed into a proverb. He broke out into uncontrollable and agonizing explosions of laughter.

There were many other black stories of a similar character. He used to recall with amusement the testimony of a freshly converted brother in the same mission. This man had formerly been a devotee of the ball-room, and confessed that, even in his renewed state, whenever his ears caught the strident note of bow on fiddle his unregenerate feet would begin to move, "like de unthinking horse rushing into battle." Gordon would tell, too, of one who, commenting on the power of the gospel, remarked that it was able "to make the immoral moral, the intemperate temperate, and the industrious *dustrious.*" With the negro preachers of reconstruction days, whose chief ambition seemed to be to found " universities " in the " black belt," with generous powers for conferring degrees, he had in his early ministry large experience. His own church was wealthy, and well known for its quick response to appeals for help. Every few months a shining-faced darky with huge glazed bag would call at his house and talk eloquently on the promising prospects of a new college or on the great needs of the particular region where his people were putting up a church building. One of these, with an ingenuous fervor which immediately corrected the bad impression his mistake might otherwise have conveyed, declared himself to be " in a deplorable state of mendacity." * And another, when required by a committee-man with some sharpness to give the reason why colored collectors for feeble institutions invariably made for the Clarendon Street Church, answered archly, " When we goes shootin', sah, we allus goes whar de ducks is." It may be added that this retort touched the hearts of the committee to the extent of a substantial subscription.

III

Of the quaint experiences incidental to every pastor's life Gordon had his full share. Marriages always recall to a minister's family much that is amusing. Silk handkerchiefs and walking-sticks were to many whom he married, like the cowry shells of African tribes, a convenient legal tender with which to pay the customary wedding-fee. Once he received a fifty-cent piece, out of which he was asked to " take what he thought right." The fact that in seven cases out of ten he made over the fee to the bride was deeply appreciated by many. This so impressed one whom he married that he returned in a day or two with a friend and suggested that the

* i.e., mendancy.

minister might like to pay the latter's fare to New York, whither he had been unexpectedly summoned. At funerals, too, the grotesque often entered unbidden, as when a bereaved husband requested Dr. Gordon to give out the doxology while the friends were assembling.

In visiting among the poor, the pitiful and the droll were commingled now and then in a startling way. One poor creature, in relating the various misfortunes which had befallen her, declared that some years before she had been "struck with lightnin'." "I went to the cupboard when I realized what had happened," she continued, "and took a strong emetic. After I had thrown up the electric fluid I soon recovered."

During the revival of '77 the after-meetings were held, as has been mentioned, in the Clarendon Street Church. One evening Gordon was called to the rear of the church by an Irishman, who acknowledged that he was seeking light, but who refused to talk with any save the pastor. "I want to see Dr. Garrdon. I'm goin' to give him the priferince," he reiterated again and again. The two talked together some time. Finally the son of Erin, who had been an outrageous drunkard, declared himself converted. He was not seen again for nearly a year. One smiling day in June, however, he turned up at the pastor's house in best clothes and happiest vein. This time there was another with him. He related how he had found work in the country as a coachman, how he had stood without drinking for a twelvemonth, and how he had won the heart of the cook in his master's establishment. "Shure an' we talked over the question of parsons atwixt us," he continued, "and decided to give Dr. Garrdon the priferince." But unfortunately "Dr. Garrdon" was away and was not to return till evening. It was agreed that the betrothed should separate till later and visit among their respective friends. The decision was, alas! fatal. The "fri'nds"

of the groom were of a dubious, dangerous sort, and before
he left them for the minister's home he had spent his all and
changed his best clothes at the pawnbroker's for others of a
very doubtful respectability.   The wedding was now out of
the question.   He determined, however, to keep his engagement.   It so happened that when he called Gordon himself
went to the door.   The battered, half-sober figure on the steps
greeted him with his whole serio-comic story, and then added
that, though he had " fri'nds " in the city who unquestionably
would lend him enough to get back to his work, he had decided, in placing his loan, " to give Dr. Garrdon the priferince,
as he knew him to be a ginerous, free man."

There can be little question that the unfriendly treatment
which prophecy often receives at the hands of Christians is
half due to the eccentricities of those strange folk who cherish a
special delight for fantastic interpretations.   One of these, a
correspondent from the far West, was accustomed to write
Dr. Gordon the most extravagantly long and perversely irrational letters on the Apocalypse.   These he sent in the
largest-size government envelops, every inch of which would
be covered with titles and degrees.

Of a visit received from another of this ilk, Gordon
often spoke with amusement.   On entering the parlor one
morning, he was startled by the peremptory question, " Do
you believe this Book? " which accompanied the vigorous
shaking of a Bagster Bible in front of his face.

" I think I do," was the quiet reply.

" Do you believe it from cover to cover? " inquired the
stranger again.

" Yes."

" From Genesis to Revelation? "

" I do."

" Then we can proceed to business."   After a pause the

visitor continued abruptly, " Who are the two witnesses in Revelation xi. ? "

" I am not sure, though I have my own opinion," replied Gordon.

" They are," retorted the other, with great positiveness, " myself and Mr. Moody."

This statement was indeed startling, but the request which followed was even more so. " Now," said he, " I will tell you what I am here for. I want you to call a meeting to ordain me for the ministry."

" But why don't you get those who are acquainted with you to do this for you—some one in your own town who knows your history and your qualifications? " returned Dr. Gordon.

" Well, to tell the truth," he replied, in a confidential tone, " they say in W——, where I come from, that I am not quite level-headed; but I am."

" Yes," answered Gordon, encouragingly.

" Yes; I learned some time ago that my head has two poles, one positive, the other negative. Now every morning, when I get up, I go to the glass and, putting my hands to my head " (which he proceeded to do by way of illustration), " I bring those poles into proper balance. That makes me level-headed for the day."

With this explanation, and with a few words of regret that Dr. Gordon did not see fit to induct him into the ministry, he seized his hat, made for the door, and disappeared.

IV

It may not be out of place to record here the following interesting experience :

" Opening my mail one morning," writes Dr. Gordon, " I found a most earnest appeal from a poor student in whom I

had for some time taken much interest.   He detailed the circumstances by which, in spite of his utmost endeavors, he had
been brought into rare straits; debts for board and books
severely pressing him until he was utterly discouraged.   He
was extremely reluctant to ask aid, and only wrote now, he
said, to tell me how earnestly he had besought the Lord for
deliverance and to request my prayers in his behalf.   It was
only a little sum that he needed to help him out of his di-
lemma—fifty dollars—but it was a great sum for a poor
student, and he was now asking the Lord to send it.   Having read his letter with real sympathy, I continued opening
my mail, when, to my surprise, the next letter whose seal I
broke was from a wealthy gentleman, expressing great thankfulness for a service I had rendered him a few days before,
and inclosing a check of fifty dollars, which he begged me to
accept as a token of his gratitude.   Instantly I perceived that
the poor student's prayers were heard—that the second letter
contained the answer to the first; and, indorsing the check, I
sent it by return mail to the young man, with my congratu-
lations for his speedy deliverance.   The noon mail of the
same day brought another letter of the same sort from another
college.   A young colored man, full of faith and earnest desire
to fit himself for useful service in the Lord's work, had made
himself known to me some months before; and as he had, by
his earnest piety and diligent scholarship, approved himself
to his teacher, I had done what I could to help him.   He
now wrote, telling a pathetic story of his struggles, how spar-
ingly he had lived, how he had failed in getting help from expected sources, and how now, having reached the end of the
term, he was in debt and had nothing to pay.   He too had
called earnestly upon the Lord, but as yet no help had come.
To show me how prudently he had lived he inclosed a list
of his expenditures, which demonstrated clearly enough how
poorly he had fared.   Toward night I was at the telegraph

office writing a despatch to the poor student to say that I would be responsible for one half of the amount needed provided he could raise the other half from Mr. W——. But what his street number was I could not remember; neither could I recall just the amount needed. So I went back to the house to find his letter in order to get the exact address. On my way I called at a certain place to pay a bill—*thirty-seven dollars and fifty cents.* I had written a check for the sum, and as I passed it in to the bookkeeper, he turned his book to look up the account, and said, 'This bill is paid, sir; you do not owe us anything.' 'Who paid it?' I inquired. 'I cannot say; only I know that it was settled several weeks ago.' And so saying he handed back my check. I took it, quite surprised to find myself so much better off than I expected, and returned to my house to find the poor student's letter. Referring to it, I found that, in adding up his little list of debts, it came to just *thirty-seven dollars and fifty cents.* The Lord had provided the exact amount even to the cents. I had only to indorse the Lord's check again and send it forward.

" Mark you, it was not my prayers that were answered, for I had not been moved especially to pray for these young men, not being aware of the necessity. It was not my money; the Lord provided the exact funds in each instance; but I have told you literally what happened. Does not the Lord know how to provide?"

A strange incident occurred in the vestry of Dr. Gordon's church shortly before his death. He was standing after meeting, conversing with a few friends, when the sexton stepped up to tell him that some one in the lobby insisted on seeing him immediately. Going out in response to the call, he was accosted by a man with harsh, deep-cut features and a blotched face, who demanded money for a night's lodging in a rough, peremptory tone. Dr. Gordon replied gently that he would help him, and took out his pencil to write an order. This seemed, however, only to embitter the stranger. He broke out in violent abuse of society and of the church, denouncing God as responsible for his poverty and for the miserable estate into which he had fallen. In the course of this outburst he disclosed the fact that he had been that day discharged from prison after serving a long sentence for theft.

After several vain attempts to quiet him, Gordon desisted altogether, thinking that the man's excitement would soon subside. Meanwhile another had entered the hallway and stood listening intently. When the former paused for a moment's breath, the new-comer stepped forward and, placing his hand on his shoulder, began telling him slowly and minutely the story of the crucifixion. He described in detail the choosing of Barabbas, the procession to Golgotha, the mockery of the soldiers.

Then he spoke of the malefactors. "They nailed him between two thieves," said he. "One of them abused him and cursed him; the other repented, was forgiven, and received the promise of the eternal companionship of Jesus." He stopped and asked slowly, "Do you know who that man was?"

"No," retorted the other, his harsh tone softening somewhat with curiosity; "I never heard."

"Well," said he, with emotion, "it was I. For years I lived the life of a thief and outcast; for years I broke the laws of God and man. Finally I was caught and put in jail over in Charlestown. There I stayed month after month. In the quiet of my cell I saw a face, sad, tear-stained, looking at me with beseeching eyes. It followed me out of prison; it met me in a little mission down-town; it constrained me, and I yielded.

"I cried out, 'Remember me, Lord Jesus, when thou comest in thy kingdom.' Immediately the promise of Paradise came to my heart.

" I was that malefactor! "

There was a moment of perfect stillness. Then the stranger said in a low voice, " Yes, and I was the other."

Then he went out.

CHAPTER XVII

" CHRIST FOR THE WORLD "

The significance of the modern missionary movement—Misapprehensions concerning it—Dr. Gordon's work for this cause—The International Conference of Missions in London—The Scotch campaign—Chairman of the Executive Committee, A. B. M. U.—Personal relations with missionar.es

"HISTORY," says Schäffle, "moves on the axis of religion." This truth is rarely recognized while history is making, but is always apparent when the record is completed and filed away in libraries. Most men to-day agree that the present century is one of preëminence. Yet its claim to distinction lies, according to their thinking, in its career of political, institutional, and scientific development. The men of to-morrow, however, we venture to predict, will consider as its most noteworthy feature its religious unfoldings. For the first time in the history of man religion appears to be losing its local, national, and ethnic character, and to be entering upon a universal phase. The faiths of the ancient world were for the family and for the state. Outsiders who had no share in the sacred fire were barbarians, without claims and beyond the pale of sympathy and fellowship. Judaism itself was as exclusive as the religions of the hearth. But when the apostles announced the breaking down of the middle wall of partition, and proclaimed the unity of Greek and Scythian, of bond and free, a new era opened. Nevertheless, far from being a pro-

duct of the age, the new evangel was centuries in advance of
the age's comprehension, as is clearly seen by the lapse from
it which followed, and which has made of ecclesiastical history
a vast parenthesis of error, a terrible deflection from the intent, teaching, and commands of Jesus and of Paul. This
hiatus—inscrutably permitted of God—endured from the days
of the apostles to the period of modern Protestant missions,
which began with the disembarkation of Carey at Calcutta in
1793.

If, as the author of "Ecce Homo" tells us, the missionary
impulse is the test of a standing or falling church, the church
of fifteen centuries was essentially decadent. For during
this whole dark interim her responsibility toward the remote
and pagan peoples of the earth seems to have been almost
completely forgotten or ignored. The work of Anskar and
Boniface and Ulfilas and Columba and John Eliot and Lullius
is indeed memorable; yet it was not in the least characteristic
of the age. Evangelism was discouraged on the ground of
the unworthiness of the heathen. Turk and Saracen and
Moor were enemies to destroy, not possible converts and
brethren in the commonwealth of faith. Whenever proselytism was entered upon it was the proselytism of the sword, as
when Charlemagne drove the followers of Wittekind into the
cold baptismal waters of the Elbe, or when the Jews were
compelled to church-going on Holy Cross days at Rome.

We might naturally have looked for some general evangelistic impulse at the Reformation did we not remember that
the Calvinists along the dikes of Holland and inside the forti-
fications of La Rochelle, as also the Puritans watching for the
galleons of the Armada off the misty channel headlands, were
engaged in a struggle for existence which gave little time for
considering the needs of the dark peoples without in the
world's penumbra. Even Luther, with all his light, held to
the curiously inverted theory that, for the bringing back of

Christ, evangelical religion must cease from off the earth,* while his successors, as soon as they were released in some measure from fear of the Romish wolf, plunged into interminable quarrels over polity and the metaphysics of theology — questions which proved as fatal to the missionary motive as problems of criticism are in some quarters to-day. Xavier and Ricci and Ruggieri, the missionaries of the counter-reformation in the East, compounded with heathenism to such an extent as to nullify most of the essentials of Christian teaching, and finally indulged in fatal political intrigue, which resulted in their expulsion. Their brethren in Canada, Jogues and Brébeuf, likewise carried on what was, after all, rather an heroic propaganda of Romanism than a preaching of Christianity.

With the stirrings in the nonconformist churches of England in the last years of the eighteenth century a new epoch opened. Since the days of Carey, of Martyn, of Judson, of Gützlaff, of Heber, the missionary movement has swept on, decade by decade, gaining in scope and tidal propulsion, until it has, in our day, reached the most remote parts of the earth. After eighteen centuries of confined and limited existence, Christianity is becoming cosmopolitan. It is destroying and superseding all other forms of religious belief. It is the last type of faith which is to appear upon this earth. We have indeed reached a stupendous crisis in the world's religious life, the issue of which must be either the glorification of Christianity or the final death of religion. Successors there can be none. This gives to our time a religious significance far exceeding that of either apostolic or Reformation era.

* " Another hundred years and all will be over. The gospel is despised. Asia and Africa have no gospel. In Europe, Greeks, Italians, Spaniards, Hungarians, French, English, and Poles have none, either. The small electorate of Saxony will not hinder the end." (Quoted in Froude's " Luther," p. 54.)

The world-wide spread of Christianity implies, of course, the enunciation and popularization of an unapproached and unassailable moral ideal and system. It means, further, the unification of the race through the agency of a common faith and a common hope. It means the establishment of one moral type among Anglo-Saxons, Sikhs, Slavs, Hunanese, and Basutos. The establishment of such a type will constitute a final argument for the truth of Christianity beside which the *apologiæ* of book-writers and creed-makers, as well as the efforts of those who seek to commend Christianity by paring away its supernaturalism and by assimilating it to " progressive " opinion, will seem the veriest trifling.

The modern missionary movement is, then, an undertaking admirable and important beyond all, even in our age of multitudinous activities. It is without question unprecedented as an example of elaborate, persevering, and extensive voluntary effort. It offers, too, illustrations of faith and of obedience equal to any. What a suicidal plunge is that into the vast yellow ocean of eastern Asia! What an apparently impossible undertaking this of evangelizing four hundred millions of the most materialized people on earth! What misgivings must the brave, determined march into the night and gloom of the Dark Continent not awake! And to all the seemingly insurmountable difficulties abroad are added the continuous, persistent ridicule and misrepresentation of a secularized Christendom. The wisdom of God is still the foolishness of men. Christianity in its phase of world-wide expansion is as completely misunderstood as it was in the days of its inception. Many have dwelt upon the blindness of the world at large to the extent and importance of religious phenomena in the first centuries of this era. One of the most brilliant of living historians has said :

" That the greatest religious change in the history of mankind should have taken place under the eyes of a brilliant galaxy of philosophers and historians who were profoundly conscious of the decomposition around them; that all these writers should have utterly failed to predict the issue of the movement they were observing; and that during the space of three centuries they should have treated as simply contemptible an agency which all men must now admit to have been, for good or evil, the most powerful moral lever that has ever been applied to the affairs of men, are facts well worthy of meditation in every period of religious transition." *

And yet they are facts which have a very close counterpart to-day. The contempt with which Tacitus spoke of "auctor nominis ejus," in the famous passage in the "Annals," is brother to the scorn which breathes through every utterance of the London "Times" and of the New York "Post" when missions are under consideration, and is not unsuggestive of the spirit which many Christians, as, for example, Charles Kingsley in certain scurrilous pages of "Alton Locke," have at times indulged. If this is true of Kingsley, what shall we say of the vilification which club-men, Gymkhana idlers, globe-trotters, and correspondents turn ceaselessly upon the representatives of Jesus among the heathen? The carnal mind is indeed enmity against God. Nay, more, it is stupidly bat-like in its vision of spiritual things and in its interpretation of history. While minimizing or ignoring the patent results of missionary labor in India, in Uganda, in Japan, in Polynesia, and elsewhere—the schools, the hospitals, the opium refuges, the leper asylums, the zenana enterprises, the rescue work, the prison-gate efforts, the great native Christian conferences, the innumerable self-supporting native Christian churches—it remembers to forget the almost geologic deliberateness with which fundamental religious changes occur. It forgets the dim eons which have shaped and moulded and bound the followers of Vishnu and Siva; it forgets, too, the nine centuries

* W. E. H. Lecky, "European Morals," vol. i., p. 359.

which it took to subdue Japan to Buddhism, and demands
from the hands of a few awakened Christians cataclysmal
results in mere decades.

Yet, if neither the sublimity of project involved in the movement for a universal Christendom nor a knowledge of accomplished result nor a sense of historic proportion were present, one would think that the remarkable concurrence of
events which marks the present era would provoke attention
and lead to a conviction of the import of the situation.   For
not only has the return to Bible study, so characteristic of our
time, led to an emphatic reassertion of Christ's missionary in-
junctions, not only has the reawakened life of the churches
prepared the way for missionary enterprise, and not only has
the increment of wealth for the prosecution of such work fallen
to Protestant hands; our century has also witnessed those
great political changes which were the condition precedent to
a world evangelization.   It has seen an enlargement of the
moenia mundi by the exploration of all remote and hitherto
unknown parts of the earth.   It has seen those regions brought
to our doors by the extensive use of steam as a mode of motion.
It has seen the opening to commerce and to missionary operations of countries isolated, dormant, and closed against foreigners.   It has witnessed the uninterrupted passage of control
over dark-skinned races from the hands of the Latin nations
and from the influence of intolerant clericalism.   It has witnessed the decay of papalism and of persecution in Catholic
countries.   It has witnessed the founding and growth to titanic
power of new Protestant states in America and Australasia.
It has, beyond all, witnessed the advance, decade by decade,
of the British raj throughout the earth—the growth of a new
Roma imperialis with proconsuls and pretors able to protect
the representatives of Protestant Christendom in their work.
The great God who hangs out nightly the stars in heaven does
so not merely because they serve as lamps for us.   Neither is

he shaping contemporary history solely with reference to British pride and " British interests." The " weary Titan, with deaf ears and labor-dimmed eyes," as Matthew Arnold called this great cosmopolitan power,

> " Bearing on shoulders immense,
>   Atlantean, the load
>   Of the too vast orb of his fate,"

is, all unknown to himself, the serf of God preparing for and protecting his sons in their work.

Those, therefore, who see in these almost cosmic movements no unity of divine purpose, but merely a multiplication of the complications of international politics, have indeed seen a great light, but have not heard the voice.   To Lucian Jesus was but a "crucified sophist," and his followers outcast fanatics.   To the world at large modern missions are estimated in much the same fashion.   It is not to be expected that those who are so oblivious to this convergence of the currents of history should regard with either interest or patience the testimony of Scripture as to the importance of evangelistic developments.   That these constitute, according to Jesus' own words,* the condition of his return to earth in power, is something of which, doubtless, they do not know, or know only to mock.   If this is really so, the final estimate of those engaged in this witnessing will be very different from that now current.

It is from this point of view that the task of writing Dr. Gordon's life has been undertaken.   Were it not for the fact that he was one of the very foremost figures of his day in America in the agitation for a world-wide propaganda of Christianity, his career would not, perhaps, be of such distinc-

* " And this gospel of the kingdom shall be preached in the whole world for a testimony unto all the nations; and then shall the end come." (Matt. xxiv. 14.)

tion as to require particular record. He would be remembered as a useful pastor, a gifted preacher, a friend of the poor, and a man of exalted saintliness. His labors, however, in behalf of missions were, during the last decade of his life, incessant; they constituted his absorbing interest, his inspiring enthusiasm. In journeyings often, in labors of missionary tours, in labors of conventions, in labors of committees, as coeditor of the leading American missionary review, as author of missionary literature, as pastor of a church unsurpassed in missionary efforts, as the executive head of the denominational missionary organization, as founder of a training-school for missionaries, he toiled to the full measure of his strength. Even after his death—suggestive, indeed, of faithfulness to the end!—there was found in his ulster pocket an appeal in behalf of the little blind girls of Canton who live in the slavery of enforced immorality!

The year 1888 was marked by greater activity in this line than any previous. The London conference gave a new impulse, the campaign in Scotland new opportunities, and his election to the position of chairman of the Executive Committee of the American Baptist Missionary Union new responsibilities. In the seven years of life which remained to him his best work for this cause was accomplished.

The great Centenary Conference on Foreign Missions, convened in London, June, 1888, holds, even in these days of memorable conventions, a place of preëminent interest. It was a gathering in the best sense ecumenical. Every Protestant missionary society in the world gave to it its adherence. Every evangelical church having any agency for the extension of the Redeemer's kingdom was represented. Distinguished missionaries from abroad—Hudson Taylor, Bishop Crowther, John Wilkinson, Dr. Post, Murray Mitchell—gave to the gatherings the results of years of observation and experience. There were laymen, too, friends of missions, whose names command attention in the East as well as in the West—Sir William Muir, Sir Monier Williams, Sir Richard Temple, Sir W. W. Hunter, General Phayre, Sir Robert Cust, and Lord Northbrooke, the ex-viceroy of India. There were promoters of missions present like Messrs. Stock, Broomhall, and Guinness. The Vatican Council of '70 was the last and complete expression of Romanism. The Chicago Parliament of Religions of '93—that strange gathering of religious and irreligious miscellanea—embodied, directly or by implication, the essentials of "liberalism." The London International Missionary Conference of '88 exhibited to the world Christianity in its purest, best, and most useful phase. The spirit of the gathering was beyond criticism. From beginning to end there was no friction, notwithstanding the variety of denominational interests represented. The divisions of Protestantism, so much dwelt upon, seemed to have disappeared. Dr. Gordon, who, though speaking only occasionally, was listened to with marked interest, said very pertinently, after contrasting this spirit of comity with the spurious "unity" so often demanded:

"We have a Bible that is one, but that has been translated into at least three hundred languages. Now remember that the old church, that shed rivers of blood to prevent one church of Christ Jesus being translated into various sects, also shed rivers of blood to prevent the Word of God being translated into various languages. That church is just as opposed to a polyform Christianity as it is to a polyglot Bible. But we have both.

"Are we not, then, to look for a reunion of the church? I cannot dwell on this point long, but will simply say, Yes; I 'beseech you, brethren, by the coming of our Lord Jesus Christ, and *our gathering together unto him*.' That will be a reunion of Christendom, a reunion in which there will be included nothing 'that defileth, or worketh abomination, or maketh a lie.'"

The problems discussed were of great variety and delicacy. As an executive in the management of extended missionary interests, Dr. Gordon listened with absorbed attention; the reports from the fields filled him with delighted enthusiasm. He could think only of the great review which closed our Civil War as veteran after veteran came to the front and related his struggles and victories in Africa, in Asia, or in the islands of the Pacific. He was introduced to a Moravian brother, "a man of humble bearing and broken English." The remembrances of Herrnhut welled up into his eyes and rolled out on his cheeks as he grasped his hand. In the auxiliary meetings following the conference—at Mr. Guinness's East London Institute, at Association Hall, and at Mildmay—he was listened to by great throngs. He preached, too, in the streets and parks of London without interference. At the Mildmay Conference he enjoyed the fellowship of the choicest spirits of British Christianity. With brimming eyes did he listen to the wonderful expositions of Hebrews by Adolph Saphir. With brimming eyes was his own beautiful address on " Union with Christ " received.

The conferences being over, he went to Paris to look into the work of the McAll Mission. His addresses at the various halls had, according to the testimony of an eye-witness, a powerfully moving effect on the audiences of French men and women. While speaking in Paris, an urgent message reached him from representatives of the Scotch churches, who had heard him in London, begging him to address a series of meetings which had been arranged in Edinburgh for July 14– 17th. These dates were chosen in order to reach the university students before their dispersion for the vacation. At the cost of complete alteration of plan, he left for Scotland with Dr. Pierson. The meetings in Edinburgh were of great power. The large Synod Hall was filled to its utmost capacity. As the meetings progressed it was clear that the tide was rising.

Before the conference was over an appeal was drawn up importuning Dr. Gordon and Dr. Pierson to make a tour of the principal cities and towns of Scotland in behalf of the missionary interests of Scotch churches. This was adopted with fervor, two thousand people rising *en masse* to express their approbation as soon as the letter had been read. Then followed a laborious but fruitful missionary campaign. Largely attended meetings were held in Edinburgh, Oban, Nairn, Elgin, Inverness, Aberdeen, Strathpeffer, Dundee, and elsewhere. Everywhere the American ministers were received with enthusiasm; everywhere their words made a deep impression. Gordon's allusion to his Scotch name and ancestry excited warm response. "We are getting much enjoyment, too, along with this unexpected service into which we have been drawn by the importunity of our Scotch friends," he wrote. On a lovely day he visited Iona, the center from which wide-reaching missionary impulses radiated in medieval times. The day at this shrine he counted one of the most inspiring of his life, and ever after St. Columba shared with Brainerd and Carey in his heart's affection.

On his return to America he was elected to the honorable and onerous position of chairman of the Executive Committee of the American Baptist Missionary Union. He had already served as a member of this committee for more than seventeen years. In his new capacity he was to guide its deliberations for six years more. A minute passed by his associates at his death, after adverting upon "the advantages which the prestige of his honored and growing name brought to the Union," remarked:

"But the value of his incumbency was enhanced by the unvarying courtesy of his demeanor, the combined dignity and affability of his bearing toward his associates, the clear knowledge and sound judgment which he brought to the elucidation of the questions involved in our work—questions always grave and often intricate and perplexing—the patience, the faith, the mingled moderation and energy, and the untiring industry of his service."

This work was the most taxing in which he engaged; nevertheless none was nearer his heart. For he was no perfunctory official who dismissed from his thought the whole business of the committee as soon as the meetings adjourned. No one on the foreign field but could at any time appeal to him for the most intelligent sympathy in his labors. "The best prayer-book is a map of the world," he said once. The denominational mission stations in Burmah, in Africa, in China, were collects in this prayer-book to which he often turned. "Instead of praying for the Lord's blessing upon our mission fields and upon our missionary brethren in general, let us get a list of their names and take some one of them before the throne of God each day. Let us make ourselves so far acquainted with their circumstances of trial or success that we shall have definite petitions or thanksgivings to make for them. Let the missionaries be reminded to send home specific requests for prayer, and let them be taken up for definite remembrance at our monthly meetings. For ourselves, we have found great blessing and profit in going through the missionary list day after day. The heartfelt solicitude of the apostle to the Gentiles nowhere comes out more manifestly than in the frequent recurrence of that saying, 'Without ceasing I make mention of you always in my prayers.'"

He was, furthermore, constantly writing letters of encouragement to lonely and isolated missionaries. One of these remarks, "In intellectual appreciation and heart experience of the profoundest truths of the gospel, I owe to A. J. Gordon a debt next to that I owe the apostles. I deem him the beloved apostle, the John of our generation." He then goes on to say, "His fatherly interest touched my life in many ways and when I most needed a touch divine. When alone with my wife in the mountains of Assam, I received from him ' In Christ' and ' The Twofold Life,' with the autograph and the love of the author on the fly-leaf of each. Words can never tell what these two books were to us in that mountain fastness." Another writes, " I feel the Congo Mission has met a great loss in his death. Oh, that some one might be raised up to enter into the sympathies and hold the confidence of the missionaries as he did! I remember writing, at the suggestion of Brother Hoste, for a chapel at Lukunga, though we had little faith in asking. The promise of help which the following letter gives was redeemed to the full:

" ' MY DEAR BROTHER: Your letter is just received, and I am rejoiced to hear that you are well and hopeful. Dear, devoted Brother Hoste, of whom all speak with such admiration and affection, certainly ought to have a chapel. I will talk it up and see what can be done. Our prayers are much toward you and your great, dark field, where the open sore of the world is awaiting the healing of the great Physician. Your position is an enviable one considering the rewards which belong to it from the Master, but I do not forget also the hardships and trials which belong to it. These may the Lord give you grace to bear. . . .' "

At another time an iron chapel was needed at Banza Manteke. He took the matter up, raised the money in his own .church, and cabled the order for its immediate construction. When the Congo Mission was first assumed by his society, complications arose which interrupted the channels of supply to those in Africa. In this crisis he himself guaranteed a shipment of provisions on order at Bywaters in London. No wonder that, as another wrote from another quarter of the world, " we looked to him as to an elder brother, one to whom we could go for advice in critical junctures, upon whose confidence and prayer we could rely. . . . For a whole night I have been weeping his departure."

CHAPTER XVIII

ON THE CONDUCT OF MISSIONS

Missionary administration—On " witnessing " as the church's chief function—Education vs. Evangelization—Government grants to mission
schools—Philadelphia address on "Decentralization"

WITHOUT doubt Dr. Gordon's conviction of the immi-
nence of Christ's return affected his advice on matters
of administration. " He believed," wrote one of his associates on the board, " that some of the types of mission policy
prevailing were formed without due regard to what he thought
a preliminary stage of missionary operation, and that this view
of the present dispensation as final practically nullified any
expectation of the Lord's return. With many people the
advent of civilization and a broad view of mission work are
practically identical. Not so with Dr. Gordon. He believed
that the gospel was to be preached in a profound sense ' as
a witness,' as a provisional stage of effort, and that to turn
aside to various forms of higher education and to other semi-
secular methods of work was to minimize the chief function
of the church of Christ in this age. He entertained, however,
no superficial or shallow view of what that witness included.
He believed that the word ' witness,' as used in the New
Testament, is descriptive of the profoundest form of human
effort possible to the Christian—effort endowed with the very
power and energy and wisdom of the Holy Ghost. His conception of the witness embraced the idea of witnessing churches
and institutions. He believed that many forms of quasi-mis-
sionary enterprise were representative of a partial departure

from apostolic standards and New Testament conceptions of evangelizing the world."* He was not, however, unmindful of the representative character of his office or of the constituency behind him which dissented from this view. He sought accordingly to emphasize those phases of mission work which are necessarily acceptable to all. Evangelism he considered beyond all the proper and pressing work of the Union. Primary education, too, he felt to be a legitimate function, in that Protestantism and illiteracy cannot coexist. But the higher education ought, he contended, to be a development of the life of the native church. Its superimposition by the home board he considered untimely in view of the black masses of the unevangelized. With the policy of educating heathen from the contributions of American Christians he would have nothing to do. He questioned whether, in any large degree, conversions followed as a result of the extensive educational propaganda which is carried on in India and elsewhere. And, apart from considerations of expediency, he denied to it the spiritual and essentially Christian note which should characterize missionary operations. He compared the missionary professor who devotes his days to teaching Brahman lads English literature and algebra and physics, that in a Christian atmosphere they may be attracted to Christian truth, to the sacramentarian who hales the multitude into "the church" that they may by its intermediary influence be saved.

"Has this dispensation of teaching," he asks, "after all, proved really helpful in preparing the heathen mind to receive the Word of life? No more, probably, than a gymnasium in

---

* "The work distinctly appointed for this present time is the gathering of the *ecclesia*, the called out. Not that we would question for a moment the ultimate conversion of the world. When ' that which is in part shall be done away,' and when ` that which is perfect is come,' then indeed shall our Lord Jesus have dominion from sea to sea, and from the river unto the ends of the earth." (Article "Education and Missions," A. J. Gordon, "Missionary Review," December, 1893.)

the basement of an American church, with its curriculum of dumb-bells and vaulting-bars, has conduced to a change of heart in the young men who have entered therein. The tendency is inevitable for these preparatives to become substitutes. Education, by all means! But in the school of grace the law seems to be, not 'know in order that you may believe,' but 'believe in order that you may know.' Culture, when set forward as a forerunner of Christ, has constantly failed to become such, because it lacks the humility to say, 'He it is who, coming after me, is preferred before me, whose shoe-latchet I am not worthy to unloose.' It being true, according to our Lord's own words, that the Father hath 'hid these things from the wise and prudent, and revealed them unto babes,' it cannot be the missionary's business to make men wise and prudent in order that they may receive the gospel, but rather to tell the wise and prudent that, except they repent and become as little children, they shall in no wise enter into the kingdom of heaven."

To the custom of receiving government grants for mission schools he was likewise heartily opposed. He felt that there was an insidious danger in this bond between church and state. He clearly saw that there can hardly be a conscience other than the nonconformist conscience, since state religion tends, by a natural gravitation, to become the organ of expression for officialism, and therefore for the majority, for the controlling element in the state, and for the almost invariable opponents of reform opinion. He had seen how, on the mission field, the government grant had often dulled the moral sense of missionaries, making them wabble and trim and flutter like a pigeon whose brain has been partly removed.*

---

* As, for example, in the case of the Anglican bishop and clergy of Calcutta, who testified recently in favor of the continuance of the state opium trade, and certain missionaries in the last Decennial Conference at Bombay, who deprecated agitation against licensed vice in the Anglo-Indian army.

"The stipend rarely fails," he wrote, "to assert its authority over the stipendiary; subsidies are almost certain, sooner or later, to subsidize. Therefore let missions be on their guard against the encumbrance of state aid. . . . To give secular teaching in exchange for government grants may be an honest transaction, but is the missionary of the cross commissioned for such a business? As a matter of fact, the missionary societies of free churches and established churches alike have fallen into the habit of receiving government grants in aid on the foreign field. The system of secular education among our missions is largely related to this usage. The wrong principle —alliance of missions with the state—has led to what many regard as a wrong result. It was through this principle, gradually and almost imperceptibly adopted, that the early church, from being 'more than conqueror,' became more than conquered, since, instead of Christianizing paganism, her Christianity was paganized. The law of the kingdom of heaven is not the law of the kingdom of earth. The world's motto is, 'In union there is strength;' the church's motto is, 'In separation there is strength.'"

For many years Dr. Gordon represented the board at the May meetings of the denomination, voicing as spokesman its appeals for greater activity, and presenting the results of the year's work to its constituency. His addresses constituted a striking feature of the yearly gatherings. "Always unique in character, they were given without apparent self-consciousness, without the least effort to make a great impression. They were the overflow of his mind and heart respecting the biblical conception of missions and the obligations of the servants of Christ to pour out their lives in the very spirit of their Lord himself in behalf of the most abandoned and abject races of the earth. There was a quiet, awe-inspiring majesty about them that gave them a character entirely their own. Their moral and spiritual force was always invincible. As a rule, Dr. Gordon, in his public addresses, rarely adverted to the details of policy or to his own special views. His appeal on these occasions was to those instincts and convictions which are common to all Christian minds. He held his audience to the profoundest yet most simple and primary obligations." *

The address at Philadelphia in 1893 was one of exceptional power. One hundred years of mission work had been finished. The future, with all its hopes, its anxieties, its responsibilities, was opening a new volume for the record of new enterprises, of new dangers, of new victories. The moment was of a solemnity and import which Gordon clearly realized. For nearly two hours he held an audience of four thousand people in the Academy of Music, unfolding to them the conclusions of twenty years' experience, pointing out the lines which the program of the new years must follow, dwelling on the portentous needs of the world, and stimulating his hearers to better things by the recital of the triumphs of self-sacrifice and of missionary heroism. " I wanted to say more in regard to the work of the Moravian missionaries," he said afterward, with a perceptible tremor in his voice, " but I could not trust myself." For on that day his heart was full!

A part only of that address can we quote here, the part which deals with the policy of decentralization in missionary administration :

" I am to speak to-night of the missionary outlook. Need I say how much depends upon an intelligent apprehension of our past, in order to an intelligent forecast of our future? The century of missions is closing; and what inspirations, what resources, what preparations, what opportunities, has this century brought to us! At the beginning of the century there were only two or three missionary societies in all Protestant Christendom; now there are upward of one hundred such societies, whose representatives are preaching the gospel

* Dr. H. C. Mabie.

to every nation under heaven.   Then less than fifty versions
of the Scriptures comprised the entire work of Bible translation since the days of the apostles ; now the Word of God has
been translated into more than two hundred and eighty languages, and the whole Bible made accessible to nine tenths
of the human race.   In the beginning of the century £13 2s.
6d. was cast into the treasury, at the house of Widow Wallace
at Kettering, for inaugurating the enterprise of modern missions ; at the close of the century the societies which have
sprung from that humble beginning are contributing eleven
million dollars annually for evangelizing the heathen.   A
hundred years ago women's missionary societies were unknown ; to-day there are nearly thirty such societies in America alone, with twenty-five thousand auxiliaries, contributing
a million and three fourths dollars annually for spreading the
gospel.   At the beginning of the century, though the doors
of several of the heathen nations stood ajar, hardly one had
been securely opened ; now every nation under heaven is to
such degree accessible that missionaries of the cross have
entered in.   Well may we write the word ' opportunity ' over
the closing decade of this nineteenth century ; and well may
we be admonished that opportunity is but another name for
importunity, as though God were beseeching us by every open
door to open our hearts and to open our hands and to open
our purses, that we may worthily meet the crisis of missions
which is upon us.

" Now, measuring our fidelity on the scale of our opportunity, what estimate do we reach?   The field is the world, and
the whole world is accessible ; and in all the world we have
at the present time about seven thousand missionaries.   But
the same constituency which has seven thousand missionaries
in the foreign field has a hundred and twenty-seven thousand
ordained ministers laboring at home.   In parishes of Great

Britain and America there are repeated instances of two or three ordained preachers to the thousand and two thousand souls; while it is estimated that every ordained foreign missionary has a parish of three hundred thousand souls. Does this look as though the Shepherd and Bishop of souls were bearing rule in the diocese of the world, and receiving loyal obedience from those who are under him?

"Again, the wealth of Protestant Christians has increased so enormously during the century that the evangelical Christians of the United States are credited with possessing *thirteen billions of dollars*. But do they possess this wealth, or are they possessed by it? is the question which must be raised when I tell you that these same Christians contribute annually only twenty-five cents per capita for foreign missions, and that this contribution is computed to be but one thirty-second part of one per cent. of their wealth.

"In spite of the meagerness of our contributions of men and money, missionaries have won marvelous triumphs. The converts from heathenism and their families are estimated at *three millions*—a result for which we should thank God and take courage. But, according to the statistics of Mr. Johnstone, in his 'Century of Missions,' the gain in heathen and Mohammedan population has been seventy times greater than this. Considering, then, that of earth's one thousand four hundred millions of population a thousand millions are yet destitute of any saving knowledge of Christ; and considering, moreover, that every success already won constitutes a new call for laborers and contributions and evangelical zeal, is it not clear that the demand upon us in the closing decade of this century is greater than ever before? And what shall be our answer to this demand? In replying to this question, I may disarm prejudice by saying that I repeat what many of our wisest men thought at the beginning of the century, and what more think at the close, when I give this threefold challenge: churches to the front, reserves to the front, pastors to the front!

"First, in regard to the duty of our churches. In a very able article in a recent number of the 'British and Foreign Evangelical Review,' I find this somewhat startling statement: 'The churches of Great Britain have never as yet made foreign missions a part of their work. The great missionary societies in England are all outside the churches, which, as churches, have nothing to do with their management or maintenance. It is true the money comes from members of the churches, and church-members are the managers of the societies; but all that the churches do is to manifest a benevolent neutrality or to bestow a benevolent patronage. Missions to the heathen are not made the work of the churches.' This statement is just as applicable to America as to Great Britain. As churches we are not directly participating in the great work of foreign missions, though we are doing so by representation and by delegation. And yet I sincerely believe that our divinely given polity commits us to such participation. 'For ye, brethren, became followers [*imitators*] of the churches of God which in Judea are in Christ Jesus,' says the apostle. I have no doubt that the church at Antioch is our inspired model as a missionary church as truly as a gospel church. That church, under the immediate guidance of the Holy Spirit, set apart and sent forth its own members as missionaries of the cross. And I have the strongest conviction that, if every church would do the same to-day, we could multiply our missionary activity a thousandfold.

"'But single churches would be unable to undertake such a work,' it may be said. 'How many do you count me for?' asked the Macedonian general, as his soldiers expressed their fear of going into battle against great odds. 'How many do you count me for?' asks the Holy Ghost, who still abides in the church with his undivided presence and his undiminished power.   If it were not for this last consideration I would not broach this subject at this time.   Christ, in the person of the Holy Spirit, dwells in every church in the fullness of his presence.   'Where two or three are gathered in my name, there am I in the midst of them,' is the Magna Charta of the local church.   Christ is not divided; he has not distributed himself among his churches, giving a part of himself to each, so that only by a union of all the churches can we secure the presence of the whole Christ.

"Herein is the immense difference between spiritual force and physical force.   You can obtain a hundred horse-power by harnessing a hundred horses into one team; but you cannot secure a hundred church-power by uniting a hundred churches into one society; and for this reason: by separate church action that sense of weakness and dependence is promoted by which Christians are driven to take hold on God; by united church action that sense of denominational strength is nourished by which Christians are led to take hold of one another.   My brethren, need I tell you that responsibility is the mother of activity—that necessity is the spring of prevailing prayer?   Therefore I affirm that the greatest problem which we have to solve is that of putting the weight of spiritual obligation, which belongs to every church and to every Christian, upon every church and upon every Christian.   And I believe that our divinely appointed church polity was ordained for this very purpose, and if rightly carried out can effect it as no presbyterian or episcopal government can do. By a wonderful arrangement of natural law the atmosphere presses with a weight of fifteen pounds to the square inch on every human body.   Unite a thousand people in one body and you do not relieve the pressure by a single ounce from any single individual.   Would that the same law held good in regard to the weight of moral and spiritual responsibility!

But, as a matter of fact, organization and association tend to take off the pressure from the local churches and from the individual Christians, and our vast machinery of secretarial agencies has been invented in order to restore this pressure as best we can.

"President Wayland, speaking on this subject more than forty years ago, predicted, with the wisest missionary statesmanship, that the tendency among us would be more and more for churches to turn over their missionary obligation to societies, for societies to turn it over to boards, for boards to delegate it to executive committees, and executive committees to secretaries; so that, in the last result, the chief responsibility for the great work would come upon the shoulders of a dozen men. As one who has been honored for twenty years to stand under this burden at the center, I can say that I do not desire to see an ounce of it lifted; but it would be a new era for missions if the same pressure could rest upon every local church which rests upon the favored twelve men at the center. Nor do I for a moment plead that our noble Missionary Union should be set aside or its present functions curtailed. Without such organizations the great missionary movement could not, humanly speaking, have been inaugurated. As in the building of railroads there must be a combination of labor and capital, so here the organized union and coöperation of all our churches was needful. But, the railroad being completed, it is adapted for private traffic as well as for public transport. Such was evidently the thought of the fathers and founders of the Missionary Union, as shown in the sixteenth article of our constitution, which requires the Executive Committee to 'afford such aid and encouragement as may be suitable to such individuals, churches, or local associations of Baptist churches as may prefer to support missionaries of their own appointment.'

"If we could only come to this—that each church would

take up missionary work directly, making the Union its commission house for the transaction of its business, its banking house for transmitting funds, and its Bible and publishing house for supplying literature—who doubts that we might do vastly more than we are now doing?

"Do you accuse me of being an idealist, going back to a remote Antioch for an example instead of considering the changed circumstances and conditions in which we are living? I reply that it is the *actual* which has awakened my interest in this question rather than the ideal—the exhibition of what has really been accomplished where churches have undertaken direct missionary work.

"By universal consent, Moravian missions hold a unique place among the evangelizing agencies of the world. When I remind you that the Moravian Brethren send one out of every sixty of their members to the foreign field, that they are credited with raising ten dollars per member annually for foreign missions, and that their success has been such that they have three times as many communicants on the foreign field as in the home churches, you will admit that they deserve the peerless honor which has been accorded to them by the historians of missions. What is the secret of this astonishing preëminence among all the missionary enterprises of Christendom? I believe that this secret is told in a single sentence, which I take from their own official declaration. That declaration says, '*There is never a church among the Brethren without a mission to the heathen; and there is never a mission of the Brethren which is not the direct affair of the church.*' In other words, while all other Protestant bodies carry on missions through societies, the Moravian Church is its own and only missionary society. Dr. Warneck, of Germany, a very high authority on the subject of foreign missions, believes that this fact furnishes the real secret of the unique position and the unparalleled success of Moravian missions. Is not here a question, then, deserving the most serious and unprejudiced consideration?   Our great societies were needed for pioneering the modern missionary enterprise, and they would still be needed if every local church were to take up missions for itself —needed for conducting and perpetuating the work.   For, though the church, as the body of Christ, is complete in itself and can develop no new organs, it can create for itself the tools and implements of its spiritual husbandry.   Such exactly are missionary boards.   But we need constantly to be reminded that our strength is not in tools, but in life; not in outward organization, but in the indwelling Spirit of God.

"With our exaggerated confidence in the power of association, I imagine some one asking impatiently, 'Do you mean to imply that one church acting alone can do one one-hundredth part of what a hundred can do acting through an organized society?'   Giving the answer of history, I might truly say that a single church, acting in union with the Holy Spirit and in supreme dependence on his power, can do as much as a hundred churches depending on the power of organization.

"I make good this affirmation.   Pastor Harms, of Germany, because he could get no sympathy from men in his missionary idea, was constrained to turn his own peasant church of Hermannsburg into a missionary society.   He was appalled at the greatness of the undertaking; and he tells us in graphic language how, in the crisis of his life, he prayed far into the night that God would anoint him for the mighty enterprise.   At midnight he rose from his knees and said, 'Forward, now, in God's name,' and from that moment he never faltered.   And what was the result?   His church of poor artisans and farmers took up the work in prayerful co-operation with their pastor; and at the end of forty years they had put into the foreign field more than three hundred and fifty missionaries, supporting them in their work, and building a ship for transporting them to and from the field; and they had nearly fourteen thousand living communicants whom they had won from heathenism. Is there one of our great mission-ary societies, with a constituency of thousands of churches, which can surpass for its first forty years the record of this single missionary church? The experience of Pastor Gossner and his Bethlehem Church in Berlin is hardly less wonderful. He sent out and maintained one hundred and forty-one mis-sionaries—two hundred, including the wives of those married —who did a work among the heathen second to none.

"It may be said that these are exceptional men. They were so only in this, that they believed implicitly in the im-manence of the Holy Spirit in the church, in the unlimited power which they may have who depend upon him and who throw themselves unreservedly upon him. I believe such ex-amples as these are given us as divine object-lessons for re-calling us to primitive missionary methods, reminding us how much greater is consecration than organization; how much mightier the personal responsibility which compels us to take hold on God, than the association which leads us to take hold on one another. I repeat it, then, the greatest problem which confronts us for the opening century is that of distributing the missionary responsibility which has become congested in the official centers. As touching the duty of giving and of pray-ing and of going, this is the question of questions.

"If an obligation of half a million annually resting on our executive board only registers twenty-five cents a year on the individual pocket-book, does it not prove the necessity for a transference of pressure? Think how some insignificant church enterprise, like the purchase of a new organ or the hiring of an incomprehensible soprano, unlooses the purse-strings. Oh, if Christians would only lift for the needs of a perishing world as they lift to supply the luxuries of their own church worship, what should we not see accomplished!

"And praying, like giving, needs the pressure of direct obligation to sustain it.   If, somehow, the life of the missionary could be bound up with the life of the local church, so that his success should be their success or his failure their failure, what an impulse it would give to their intercessions!   Prayer is the last thing which should be put into a joint-stock company in which we invest general supplications for all men, and from which we take out only general dividends with the church universal.   I believe that God designed to lay the burden of the whole world upon every church, that every church might thus find out that it has a whole Christ with whom to bear that burden.   Then would it not only pray and give, but it would go and send of its own instead of depending on a central bureau to attend to all this.

"This, then, is the problem to be solved.   If my suggestion toward its solution seems visionary and impracticable, depending for its demonstration upon examples borrowed from remote times and places, I strongly insist that it is most practicable.   I think you must acknowledge the vast inequality of the pressure, and the *possibility* at least of correcting this inequality, when I tell you that I know of a single church—by no means wealthy, but which has begun the enterprise of supporting its own missionaries and otherwise coming under the most immediate responsibility for the foreign work—whose contributions last year equaled the combined gifts of either one of three New England States with their hundreds of local churches.   At all events, what I have suggested is a harmless endeavor toward the solution of a difficult problem; and I pray that if any church or pastor should be moved in loyal fellowship with our Missionary Union to take up this plan, he may not be frowned upon as an innovator. . . .

"And, finally, how imperative is the summons for pastors at home to enter with whole-souled consecration into the work of foreign missions!   Until the great body of ministers do this, making foreign missions their chief business, and investing all their capital in the business—time and money and energy and influence—the mighty missionary impulse which is now called for will not be gained.   I believe that we have now reached a crisis, and that, with worldliness and rationalism coming in like a flood on the one hand, and missionary enthusiasm moving out like a flood on the other, we must inevitably be carried in one of the two directions.   I say worldliness and rationalism.   These are but the two names of one and the same thing.   Rationalism is worldliness on its Godward side, as worldliness is rationalism on its earthward side.   As invariably as pietism has been the mother of missions at every rebirth, so invariably has rationalism stood ready to destroy the young child as soon as it has been born.   As certainly as the great commission was sounded anew in the ears of our fathers a hundred years ago, so certainly is it sounding anew in our ears to-day.   We may well tremble to think what had been the result had William Carey's brethren silenced his missionary appeal, as at first they tried to do.   But, by the providence of God, they listened, consented, and coöperated, and the result is that the English-speaking race has become the missionary army of the world.

" But let us remember that there were Careys before Carey. More than a hundred years before his day, Baron von Weltz had sought to rouse the German Protestant church to its duty of renewed obedience to the great commission.   In what pathetic, almost frantic appeals he voiced his conviction, surrendering his title and his wealth, and offering himself to go to any part of the world if only his brethren would take up the work of giving the gospel to the heathen!   But his cry was silenced, Lutheran clergymen and university professors uniting to suppress him as a dreamer and a fanatic ; and so, with broken heart, he turned from his church and his country, saying in spirit, ' Behold, your house is left desolate,' and went forth to fill a solitary missionary grave in a foreign field.   Is it accidental that such an age of dreary rationalism should have followed this rejected opportunity in Germany? a rationalism relieved, indeed, by the holy lives and teaching of a little company of Pietists, like Francke and Spener, who were hated and denounced as bitterly as Von Weltz had been. Is it an accident that Germany, instead of being the chief fountain of missionary influence, as it might have been had it not rejected its opportunity, has become in some sense a missionary field, the co-religionists of Carey now supporting missionaries and evangelists in the heart of the Lutheran Church in order to win back the people to an evangelical faith in Christ? Let us be afraid of lost missionary opportunities! Such a one may be just before us. The church which is not a missionary church will be a missing church during the next fifty years, its candle of consecration put out, if not its candlestick removed out of its place. As ministers and churches of Jesus Christ, our self-preservation is conditioned on our obedience to the great commission. Now it is preach or perish! evangelize or fossilize! be a saving church, with girded loins and burning lamp, carrying a lost world on the heart day and night; or be a secularized church, lying on the heart of this present evil world, and allowing it to gird you and carry you whithersoever it will. Which shall it be? "

CHAPTER XIX

AS MAKING MANY RICH

The faith element in missions—The Clarendon Street Church as a missionary church—Its training in giving

IT will be readily believed that the voice which rang out with these sentiments in the churches and in the great gatherings of the denomination did not fail to advocate in the meetings of the Executive Committee a policy of continuous advance. We have seen with what earnestness Dr. Gordon went over the country in behalf of the Congo Mission. Every other forward movement had likewise his unhesitating support. This was not bravado or an irresponsible recklessness, though it often seemed so to the timid. It was an enthusiasm of faith conscious of the opportunities which a humble coöperation with God in his work opens up.

"Is Christ the chief treasurer who supplies the missionary funds?" he asked in an article on "The Faith Element in Missions." "Practically there is a very wide difference of opinion upon this point. 'And Prudence sat over against the treasury, watching the expenditures, to see that Faith did not overdraw her account,' would fairly state the financial method of many missionary committees. 'Faith in the work of preaching the gospel, indeed, but in administering the missionary exchequer sound business principles, if you please.' So we have often heard it, and we do not dispute the wisdom of the saying.

"But here we are conducting the King's business, let it be

remembered, and in its transactions are no overdrafts of faith ever allowable? May the promises of God never be taken as collateral in this business? Is the Lord's servant forbidden to hypothecate the bonds of the everlasting covenant as a security for a missionary contract when he has no funds in the bank? The enterprise of missions is peculiarly the Lord's work, and as such has guarantors and guaranties back of any that are human.

"The paradox, 'Verum est quia impossibile,' which Tertullian uttered concerning doctrine, it is time for us boldly to apply to action, saying, 'It is practicable because it is impossible;' for, under the dispensation of the Spirit, our ability is no longe. the measure of our responsibility. 'The things which are impossible with men are possible with God,' and therefore possible for us who have been united to God through faith. Since the Holy Ghost has been given, it is not sufficient for the servant to say to his Master, 'I am doing as well as I can,' for now he is bound to do better than he can. Should a New York merchant summon his commercial agent in Boston to come to him as quickly as possible, would he be satisfied if that agent were to arrive at the end of a week, footsore and weary from walking the entire distance, with the excuse, 'I came as quickly as I could'? With swift steamer or lightning express at his disposal, would he not be bound to come more quickly than he could? And so, with the power of Christ as our resource, and his riches in glory as our endowment, we are called upon to undertake what of ourselves we have neither the strength nor the funds to accomplish.

"We have watched with the deepest interest an experiment of enlargement which has come under our own observation. A missionary treasury, taxed to the utmost for years to meet the demands upon it, was assessed at one stroke an extra fifty thousand dollars annually for a new work which the providence of God seemed to enjoin. Seven years have passed since the undertaking, and yet the treasury has kept just as full through all this period, notwithstanding the extra draft, as during the seven years previous. Certainly this outcome does not seem like a divine admonition not to do so again, but rather like a loud invitation to repeat the experiment upon the first new call. And now, when the bugle is sounding for an advance along the entire line, we do well to mark the significance of such experiments. Our Lord does not say, 'Be it unto you according to your funds,' but, 'Be it unto you according to your faith.' If he sees that we trust him for large missionary undertakings, he will trust us with large missionary remittances. If, on the contrary, we demand great things of God as a condition of attempting great things for God, we shall be disappointed; for that is not believing, but bargaining. 'Said I not unto thee, that, if thou wouldest believe, thou shouldest see the glory of God?' (John xi. 40.) Shall we reverse this order, and believe only according as we have seen that glory? If so, he will give us little credit for our faith. Most significantly is it written, 'Many believed on his name because they saw the miracles which he did; but Jesus did not believe in them.' (John ii. 23, vide Greek.)"

This was the theory which, in the administration of missionary interests, Dr. Gordon advocated. As a pastor of a local church supporting and contributing to the executive board, he proceeded upon similar lines. The faith element became, as the spiritual life of pastor and church progressed, the dominating factor in this ministration. In the early years of his pastorate it was customary to appoint collectors, who went about once a year soliciting for the missionary fund. A friendly rivalry always existed among these. To secure more than any other collector gave one a pleasant prestige among the friends in the church. The regular church contributions were made once a month. The amounts given were relatively small, the proportions contributed to outside missions and charities being often not half the current expenses of the church.

Soon after Gordon became pastor he set about to develop deeper convictions of responsibility in this direction. Systematic giving was urged. "Milk a cow every other day, and you will be sure to dry her up. How much more certainly will a church be dried up by infrequent giving!" he once remarked. Weekly collections were advocated, but this was felt by many to be too radical a step. "It will drive people away," was the commonly expressed opinion. And so for many years the old system lingered on. The pastor did not, however, relax his efforts to create new standards and new ideals of giving. In a series of sermons on the subject delivered in the early years, he said:

"Let a decree go out from the Lord's day that every week shall be taxed, and you will soon find that your business hours have received a wonderful consecration. Instead of looking back upon your six working-days as a band of marauders, each making way into the irrevocable past with its plunder of time and energy and devotion, you will see each of them marching up to pay its tribute to him who is Lord of the Sabbath.

"Thus the Lord's day to the Christian will be a kind of summary and epitome of his week-days. Instead of being a periodic exception, a fragment of holy time interjected between certain portions of secular time, it ought to be the culmination of all his week, the flower of his days, that has drawn all their finest juices into itself. Business robbing God, a ledger purloining the attention that belongs of right to the Bible, work trenching on the rights of worship in family or private—all this is to be regretted and mourned over. But if, when Sunday comes round, it puts the climax on this fraud of holy things, compelling God to say, 'Ye have robbed me in tithes and offerings,' our case is truly pitiable. For it is to indorse and, as it were, reiterate our six days' remissness by a seventh day's defalcation.

"What are we to do, then? Lay by in store each Sabbath a deposit for the Lord. Then see if you do not get your heart into your Sundays. See if you do not get dividends of grace that you never knew of as falling due on that day. See if your whole worship is not pervaded with a new spirit and power thenceforth.

"How thoroughly this rule, if observed, would fix in us the habit of a thoughtful consideration of God's mercies! How profoundly would it discipline our inward spirit to the truth that we are only pensioners of our Father and almoners of his bounty! The Lord's day worship would be more sincere, more hearty, more chastened, if we came to it always from a little sanctuary at home, where we had settled in quiet medi- tation the claims of God upon us and apportioned out our sacrifice for him. It would turn our charity into orderly and systematic service for the Lord who bought us instead of leav- ing it to be, what it so often is, the unripe fruit of emotion or the heartless price which we render to the demands of custom or respectability.

"I would, therefore, that we could bring ourselves to a lit- eral and whole-hearted conformity to this apostolic rule, 'Upon the first day of the week let every one of you lay by at home [this the words mean literally] as God hath prospered him.' Here is a kind of family devotion, an act of private and household worship, in preparation for the service of God's house. If it were habitual with us it would, I am sure, settle all our difficulties in regard to this department of our Christian service. The calm hour of retrospection on the Lord's day morning, wherein all the mercies of the week should be made to pass before the memory; the mind that has been busy for itself now sitting for God at the receipt of custom and taking tribute from all the week-day blessings; gratitude summing up the account and directing the obedient worshiper how much to carry with him to the sanctuary—if this were our method, there would be great inequality in our contributions, indeed, since the degrees of human prosperity are infinitely various; but there would be perfect adjustment of charity to necessity, since the returns would be according to God's providence and not according to man's caprice. In that providence, summing up all its variations, there is a perfect equilibrium between man's ability to give and man's necessity of receiving."

As the years passed on, and as the needs and opportunities of foreign work became more deeply impressed upon him, he labored with increased zeal to educate his people in giving and to stimulate their self-denial. He would make special appeals, the strain of which upon himself was to the last degree taxing. He urged immediate giving, placing in strong contrast post-mortem and present-day benevolence. " Is it not distinctly affirmed in Scripture that we must all appear before the judgment-seat of Christ, that *every one may receive the deeds done in his body?* " he would say. " Why, then, should Christians so industriously plan that their best deeds should be done after they get out of the body? Is there any promise of recompense for this *extra corpus* benevolence? And, after all, these benevolences of the dead hand are usually nullified. By a strange irony of custom we call a man's legacy his 'will'; it is really too frequently an ingenious contrivance for getting one's will defeated."

He urged his people, too, to limit to the lowest figure possible the expenditures on their own worship. " Ecclesiastical luxuries " always irritated him. " If the angels are invisible spectators of the church," he said, "what must their impression of our sanctuary self-indulgence not be! Can we not easily imagine them shutting their ears to these voluptuous strains and holding their noses at these sickening odors of Easter flowers, and eagerly searching through the whole elaborate scene that they may, perchance, 'rejoice over one sinner' bowing in the dust of repentance?'" Neither did he stop here. Many times he notified the standing committee of the church that he did not need or ask for the salary which he received, and urged them finally to give him no fixed amount, but whatever the people might choose. This was never done; yet his personal contributions to missions were so frequent and so large as to lead virtually to the same result. "If it be asked, 'How about costly ministers?'" he said once, when speaking on church administration, "we will not wince under the question. 'Even so hath the Lord ordained that they which preach the gospel should live of the gospel.' But this can signify no more than a humble and modest support. It gives no warrant for sumptuous salaries or palatial parsonages or the accumulation of clerical fortunes. Is not the teaching of ecclesiastical history sufficiently solemn on this point? And are there not tendencies visible among the ministry in our great cities which should occasion deep heart-searching? Like priest, like people! We have no doubt that our missionary contributions would soon reach the high-water mark if in every pulpit the Christ-like humility of becoming poor in order to make many rich should reach the low-water mark."

Year by year the contributions of the church reached higher points in spite of the fact that the proportion of wealthy members was steadily declining. In the last five years remarkable results in this line were attained. There had been a cumulative education which was now yielding its fruits. Giving was, furthermore, made by both pastor and people the subject of special prayer. Direct appeals, with all that they implied of exhausting anxiety, were a thing of the past. "I am tempted never to beg a cent for God again, but rather to spend my energy in getting Christians spiritualized, assured that they will then become liberalized," he wrote; and again: "Experts in such matters say that a bottle of wine that cannot throw out its own cork is rarely good for much. Certainly a Christian's prayers and gifts and testimonies are of little value if they do not come forth by the effervescence of his own inward spiritual joy. For one, I am tired of using the pulpit corkscrew to draw out of Christians the offerings and prayers and service which, to be of real value, ought to be spontaneous. I shall continue to pray and persuade and plead, but I shall not come begging you to do your duty. 'My people shall be willing in the day of my power,' says the Lord."

Statements were made of the needs of fields. Missionaries and Christian workers were constantly invited to present their causes. When large contributions were required, the situation would be presented and the people urged to go to their homes and consider prayerfully their personal accountability. Sometimes several weeks intervened before the collection was taken, in order that the full import and responsibility might be felt, and that the giving might not be prompted by a mere impulse or by an unhealthy, feverish enthusiasm. The results were extraordinary. Money came often from wholly unexpected sources. Thus when the contribution for the Centenary Missionary Fund was made (a contribution which amounted to the aggregate benevolent contributions of the first four years of Gordon's pastorate), a gift of five hundred dollars was sent in by one unconnected with the church or denomination and wholly unknown to the members.* The outside gifts of the

* " I am glad to get the good tidings of you contained in your letter and circular. Especially do I rejoice to know of your interest in the great theme—the indwelling of the Holy Spirit. I am now more and more persuaded that the greatest things are possible if only we have his power resting upon us. I have seen such a demonstration in. my church last year as I never witnessed before. We met morning after morning in the early year simply to pray for the power of the Holy Ghost. We were looking for a revival. When I made my plea for foreign missions, I astonished my conservative brethren by asking ten thousand dollars this

church, chiefly to missions, amounted from 1890 to 1895 to nearly eighty-five thousand dollars. The influence of this ex- ample upon the Baptist churches at large was, according to the testimony of the Executive Board, very great and very salutary.

year for our contribution. Only a few wealthy men among us, and they not likely to do largely. But when the collection was gathered twenty thousand dollars came, nobody asked, no solicitation made. It was sim- ply a great impulse of the Spirit, and the astonishment of all still continues. Now is coming a gracious ingathering of souls."

CHAPTER XX

Establishment of the Boston Missionary Training-school—Administration
on faith principles—The assault on the school—Dr. Gordon's reply
—" Short-cut methods "

IN the winter of '89 a new agency was started for the fur-
therance of evangelistic work throughout the earth. In
various ways Dr. Gordon had been made conscious of the
stirrings which were profoundly moving men in the common
walks of life to missionary service. He had noticed also, with
sorrow, the deficit of laborers for certain difficult fields.

"In Africa," he wrote in a letter, "we nearly forfeited our
opportunity for want of men. I determined, therefore, to do
what I might to find them for that field. We have learned
what such men can do from the example of——, who has
been in Africa three years and has proved a master missionary. The sum of my wisdom on this point is what I have
learned at the Missionary Board. I think of those whom we
hesitated over and at first rejected because of a want of the
qualifications which we considered of first importance. And
then to see how God has rebuked us by showing how wonderfully he could use them! I must speak in confidence, but
that is the history of three within my memory, every one of
whom now stands as a confessed leader in his field. I think
that I, for one, have learned the lesson, 'What God has
cleansed, call not thou common or unclean.' The experience

of years has demonstrated that there are scores of men, from thirty to forty years of age, who hear the call to missionary service at home or abroad. What shall be done for such? This is a question over which I am more sad than hopeful. It is not easy to persuade them that they may do acceptable service for the Lord, and besides this, there is the humiliation of the 'short-cut' stigma now on so many lips. Altogether, it is hard to inspire them with confidence. Well, may the Lord direct us all into the perfect knowledge of his will, and make us ready to do that will as it shall be revealed to us. . . ."

After much prayer and long consideration, the Boston Missionary Training-school was opened in the old Bowdoin Square Church. Its aim was to exercise men and women in practical religious work in the neglected parts of the city, and to furnish them with a thoroughly biblical training. For this project there were high precedents. In a volume published later * Dr. Gordon described· the extraordinary work accomplished on these lines by Pastors Harms and Gossner. The results which attended the labors of these pioneers doubtless constitute an important plea justificatory, if such is required, for the policy of providing, as Gordon phrased it, "plain men with a plain outfit." "It is the sacrilege of Christianity," so he writes, "that the church has so often undertaken to manufacture missionaries *by priestly ordination or by literary training.* The prerogative of furnishing the ministry for his own church is sublimely accorded to Christ alone. It is his office to give the various orders of the ministry, ours to ask for them and to receive and recognize them when sent." To furnish preparation for those who were thus burdened with a divine call—the laymen desirous of doing evangelistic work, whom the seminaries seem hardly to care to train, the women who hoped to undertake zenana work abroad or slum work at home, the Christian engaged during the day at ledger or in

* " The Holy Spirit in Missions."

shop, who might wish to obtain evenings a systematic knowledge of the Bible, the candidate for the foreign field of advanced age and slight resources—in short, to supplement the work and to enlarge the constituency of the seminary by establishing a sort of seminary extension, this enterprise was cautiously and humbly launched.

The move was made not without much hesitation. Indeed, it would never have been made at all except from a feeling of divine constraint. A burden of this character is not assumed lightly by a man whose hands are full. That Gordon considered it the Lord's work is evident from the distinct way in which, as the condition precedent to his own participation in it, he required of Him the supply of all its pecuniary needs. To those of the committee who brought out at the first meeting little subscription books with the purpose of soliciting funds, he gave a point-blank refusal. He "declined once for all to make the Lord Jesus a pauper," and refused to allow any connected with the undertaking to "wait in rich men's counting-rooms, hat in hand," for subscriptions to the Lord's work. In a letter engaging an instructor he wrote, "*Of course* we begin without funds, depending on the Lord for help; but we shall try to look after our fellow-helpers."

In continuous, strenuous, unremitting prayer, however, there was no slackening; and the prayers were not unhonored. From the inception of the enterprise to the present time its needs have been invariably provided for. To recount the numerous incidents illustrating the reality—the concrete, definite, proving reality—of answer to prayer, would be here impossible. Money was sent from entirely unexpected quarters. On one occasion, for example, a large wooden box came by express from a back town in Indiana—evidently from one who did not venture to trust the banks or the government to transmit his funds—containing a great, bulky roll of one- and two-dollar bills, perhaps the frugal saving of years. Again, an envelop was handed the treasurer by an unknown person, which was found on opening to contain four one-hundred dollar bills. The donor has not been seen since. At another time, when the needs of the school were unusually pressing, Dr. Gordon was in his study asking of the Lord some token of his watch-care and of his continued provision. On reaching home he found that one hundred and fifty dollars had been left by a stranger, one who, as it was afterward learned, had been healed in answer to prayer, and who was now determined to give even out of poverty to the important work of preparing men and women for a missionary life.

Such instances—and there are many others in the outline handed to the writer—are not unique. They are the natural sequence of the prayer of faith the world over. Like cause has produced like effects in the work of Müller, of Spurgeon, of Guinness, of Simpson, of Christlieb, of Hudson Taylor, of Gordon. If the Vine is interested in the life of the branch, it must be even more so in the prosperity of the fruit. It is not supposable that He would refuse to it the life-giving sap through the agency of which it can alone be filled and developed. "How long do you expect to carry on this work?" was frequently asked. "Until the Lord forgets to supply its needs," was the unfailing answer. And the Lord never forgot. We all remember Sancho Panza, hanging desperately from the window all the night long, his toes within three inches of the ground, his forehead beaded with perspiration, in abject terror of the supposed abyss beneath. A parable, truly, of most Christians, and a type of the conduct of many Christian institutions! Here was one, however, who had dropped and had found beneath him the great round globe of God's care.

The new work was not begun without serious trial and opposition. Hardly were the doors of the unobtrusive and modest institute opened before the assault began. Cold controversies, like cold dishes, leave so disagreeable a taste that

one would willingly pass them by. Yet there is a lesson in the
very unaccountableness of the storm of criticism which followed.
In the church to which both critics and criticized belonged
there is supposed to be complete freedom of action. The
ideal of the statesman, local self-government, is here, as hardly
elsewhere, fully attained. Yet this happy absence of a central authority is a standing temptation to men of a pontifical
spirit to assert themselves and to adopt the principle, *Ubi Petrus
ibi ecclesia*, substituting, consciously or not, their own names
for Peter's. This is especially true of those who are intrusted
with the management of the denominational press. The ex-
cathedra utterance is heard quite as loudly from behind the
roll-top desk of the editor as from the recesses of an ecumenical council. Baron Bunsen, so his biographer tells us, was
wont to have by his bedside a candle-extinguisher wrought in
the shape of a Jesuit padre, who very properly and significantly, we may imagine, rejoiced in his function of putting out
lights. The editors of certain religious weeklies would have
made equally suggestive figures. What was worse, in the present case Dr. Gordon's assailants seem to have been very much
of the disposition of John Lilburn, the Puritan, of whom it was
said that, if he could get no one to fight with him, he would
set the John against the Lilburn and so precipitate a quarrel.

Now Gordon was wont to say, in speaking of the training
of humble men for Christian work, that " he preferred a little
man with a great gospel to great men with a little gospel."
Whatever the reason—whether the worship of our American
fetish, education, or that temper of mind which stickles for
the conventional method and for a lawn-tied uniformity, as of
bobbins in a cotton-mill ; whether it was the spirit which accepts
nothing unless " hammered on its own anvil " and having
its own die, will take no coin save that with the image and
superscription of an accepted system—whatever the cause at
bottom, it is certain that these great men of the press did furi-

ously assail the champion of the " little man." To realize the
bitterness with which the school was attacked one has only to
turn back the files of the New York " Examiner " to the winter of '89. " The short-cut plan," a characterization peculiarly pleasing to these critics, was denounced as " a method
fraught with grave perils to our denomination." It was
questioned whether such schools " could be established without both brains and money and a great deal of both." It was
doubted whether " the strong common sense of the Baptist
laity, from whom the money was to come, could be brought
to support " this novelty. It was claimed " that the new
school could do a great deal of harm, and that the sooner denominational opinion was decisively expressed against it, and
its abandonment secured, the better for every cause that
Baptists have at heart." " The Bowdoin Square craze " was
denounced as " a movement for reversing educational qualifications among the Baptists, and as an accusation of incompe-
tence against our seminaries." The demand for " half-educated
but self-confident men " was ridiculed, and finally (indicating
perhaps the real animus of the attack) the doctrine of the ever
imminent return of the Lord Jesus derided as the mainspring
of this piece of educational fanaticism.

No direct reply was made to these attacks at first. A sym-
posium, however, was arranged between the opponents of the
school and Francis Wayland, who, as the father of higher
education among the Baptists, would perhaps be listened to
with respect. A clever appeal was thus made to denominational precedents. From the neutral position of moderator
Gordon could, without participating directly in the discussion,
enjoy the sight of the denominational Nestor rebutting the
aspersions of the editors and discomfiting the " young professor of divinity who has proposed an assignment of our
effects, though as yet we have incurred no debts, and who has
named the parties to act ' as reversionary heirs.' "

The contrasted views were ranged in deadly parallel down a column or more of blanket-sheet. We have indicated the positions taken by the complainants. The reverent, spiritual, kindly, and yet shrewd and far-seeing defense which President Wayland makes of a varied ministry and of the mission of the unprivileged as workers in the kingdom of God we cannot here quote at length. It suffices to say that it rebuked those children of the Sorbonne who in America and in our day are so strongly emphasizing mere ecclesiastical standing. He declared that a refusal to employ "*every laborer*" was "equivalent to abandoning the effort to evangelize the world." He objected "to giving to education a place not authorized by Jesus Christ, thus establishing a ministerial caste." He declared that if it were true that a Baptist is "not to preach the gospel without years of heathen learning, or if he does that he is nothing but a backwoodsman of whom every one ought to be ashamed, *we are dead and plucked up by the roots.*" And finally says, "Of those called by God to the ministry some may not be by nature adapted to the prosecution of a regular course of study. Many others are too old. Some are men with families. Only a portion are of an age and under conditions which will allow them to undertake what is called a regular training for the ministry; that is, two or three years in an academy, four years in college, and three years in a seminary. Therefore theological training should be so adapted as to give the greatest assistance to each of these various classes. Let each take what he can, and then the seminary is at rest."

It was characteristic of Gordon to turn attention from himself and his work and to avoid controversy in this admirable and satisfactory way. It was equally characteristic of him, when a friend was ungenerously and unjustly attacked, to enter the lists in his behalf. For when "the chorus of indolent reviewers" turned on Mr. Guinness, the reply from Gordon's pen was immediate. No one who reads it will question to whom belonged, in this instance, that perennial advantage which the courteous and quick-witted have in every controversy.

SHORT-CUT METHODS

" They were indignant at the assumptions of this man, who, without having attended a *beth-ha midrash* (house of instruction), and without being able to show up a *horaah* (certificate of ordination), had ventured to become a teacher."—Delitzsch's " A Day in Capernaum."

" The ' Examiner's ' recent editorial on ' new short-cut methods seems to demand a word of reply. A dislike of controversy has restrained us hitherto. But since this article has been followed by two others equally misleading and injurious in their implications, we now take in hand to set forth the whole matter.

" Early in the year, Dr. Guinness, of London, became my guest. I found that he was deeply burdened for Africa, literally bearing it on his heart night and day with tears. As the founder of the Congo Mission, he longs that we should go in and possess our heritage on that great ' Baptist river.' Our mission there is confessedly the most prosperous of any in the region, fifty in a month having been baptized during the last year at one of the stations, where there is now a church of four hundred baptized believers. And yet, when Dr. Guinness, who planted this mission at such cost of life and money, and who five years ago gave it to us, arrived here, we had not sent to that field a single native *American* ordained missionary, for the reason that we had sought in vain for such to go. Without a word of criticism of this fact, he began to visit our theological schools and colleges, white and colored, to beg for reinforcements. All this he did at his own expense, holding missionary meetings almost daily, during the summer months, and working nights on the Scriptures, so that, by the aid of an African boy whom he kept with him, he translated the entire Epistle to the Romans into the Congo dialect, in order to help on the work of our missionaries.   I am sure that he did all this from the most disinterested motives, and with the sole desire to forward the work that lies nearest his heart.   I am therefore the more sorry that the 'Examiner' should seek to create prejudice against him by slurring him as 'a Plymouth Brother' who is attempting to shape our missionary policies.   The simple fact is that he is not a Plymouth Brother, and never was; but a Baptist minister, for twenty years a member of Rev. Archibald Brown's church in East London, who, in addition to his great labors for the foreign field, has constantly worked as an evangelist in that wretched region of the great metropolis, and as the result of his labors has gathered and organized two or three flourishing Baptist churches.

" I am equally sorry that the scare of premillenarianism should be raised in this connection.   If the writer belongs to this school in obedience to what he believes to be the literal teaching of Scripture, he considers himself neither better nor worse than his Baptist fathers, many of whom have held this view.   Indeed, it is interesting to recall that one of Mr. Spurgeon's predecessors in the ministry, Benjamin Keach, was put in the pillory for several days on the two charges of Anabaptism and premillenarianism.   But it was a lord chief justice of the Episcopal Church who inflicted this humiliation on a Baptist pastor, and it furnishes no precedent for a Baptist paper's attempting the same thing on Baptist pastors of to-day.   As touching the question of missions, premillennialists maintain nothing peculiar except that during this dispensation the doctrine of 'election according to grace' holds true, and that the scriptural promises concerning world-wide conversion are to be completely fulfilled only in the next or millennial age. And is it possible that any of our denominational papers have become so Arminianized that they must be constantly deriding consistent Calvinists for holding this doctrine of election, as though it were some novel article of faith? But let it be remembered that, in connection with the subject under consideration, no one has raised this question except the 'Examiner,' and no one has intended to do so.

"How can we secure more missionaries? Dr. Guinness, seeing the earnest, soul-saving work going on constantly under the ministry of Pastor Deming in the Bowdoin Square Tabernacle, suggested to him and myself that we open in that church and in the adjoining buildings 'a recruiting-station for lay missionary workers.' The enterprise was designed to give practical experience in evangelistic work, and a course of systematic biblical study. So far from intending to interfere with any higher schools of biblical learning, or to encourage a short cut into the ministry, we undertook the work solely for the benefit of such as could not by any possibility avail themselves of these advantages. In our prospectus this sentence occurs: 'All students whose gifts and age warrant them in taking full college and seminary courses of study will be strenuously encouraged to do so.' It will thus be seen that the 'Examiner' has raised a false issue, and has undertaken to set us by the ears with those with whom there can be no controversy. The applicants for admission have come from the carpenter's bench, from the painter's pot, from the tailor's shop, some of them confessing to a desire which had burdened them for years to give themselves to foreign missionary service, but seeing no chance till this door opened. They are all poor, and have undertaken, while engaged in study, to work for their board in such places as the Tabernacle Employment Office may furnish them. With the superb opportunities for higher culture which our denominational colleges and schools afford, is it quite gracious to grudge these poor men this very humble opportunity for instruction in the Word of God?

" But will it do to encourage such candidates for missionary service ?   We have three or four precedents to which we can appeal for an answer, and in every instance the result has been satisfactory.   A member of my own church, for example, was sent to India by the Executive Committee of the Union as a lay missionary on half the usual pay.   He had absolutely no theological training except that received by the Spirit's work in his heart.   Yet, after five years of most self-denying service, his co-laborers have asked for his ordination, one of them, in a letter to his pastor, acknowledging that in intelligent zeal and in practical success he has proved himself not a whit behind the very chiefest of missionaries on that field.   This example, seconded by others eminently satisfactory, suggests that, by inviting such men as this to enter missionary service, we may do much more than we are doing to meet the great emergency which is upon us.

" The question raised, therefore, by all the training-schools referred to in this connection is simply this : ' Shall earnest men and women who hear the call to missionary service, but whose age and circumstances absolutely bar them from obtaining any higher education, be helped to such biblical preparation as a few pastors, out of their very meager store, may give them, and then be sent forth, provided always that there are missionary boards willing to employ them ? '   This last question is declared by one of the most eminent missionary secretaries of this country to be one that is now confronting every great missionary society.   And it might have modulated the ' Examiner's ' outburst of sarcasm against ' Boanerges Jones and Chrysostom Smith,' with their ' aggravated attack of big head ' in presuming to undertake the work of saving souls without college or seminary preparation, to have known that the conservative Church Missionary Society of England is the first board to settle this question, having recently resolved to call out and put into the field a large body of lay workers, who shall consent to go on a limited salary, no other preparation being insisted upon than a simple knowledge of the way of salvation as revealed in Scripture.

"This whole outcry against an uneducated ministry we hold to be not a mark of genuine culture, but of intellectual snobbishness. The following sentence, from a recent article in the 'Independent,' by Professor Samuel I. Curtiss, on the late Professor Christlieb, is instructive in this connection:

"'Perhaps,' says Professor Curtiss, 'he was the only theological professor in a German university who has ever knelt in a prayer-meeting. He was accustomed to meet with a small circle of earnest evangelical Christians in the Scotch-Irish church in Bonn. After the death of the pastor, Dr. Graham, he purchased the church and the house connected with it as a place for training evangelists. It was called the Johanneum. It was his earnest desire to raise up godly young men who should engage in evangelistic work in Germany. In his later years, in connection with more abstemious habits in the use of wine and cigars (!), he became a premillenarian in his theological views.'

"The 'Johanneum' here referred to was started for precisely the purpose of which we have been speaking. Professor Christlieb sorrowfully recognized the fact that the German clergy, with all their high culture, were utterly failing to reach the lower classes, especially in the great cities. Therefore he conceived the idea of calling into the service plain men— artisans, clerks, and laborers—who, with a simple knowledge of Scripture, might be able to address these people in their own dialect. He gave himself to the work of raising up such a class, teaching theology in the university, and at the same time humbling himself to instruct in the Bible these lay workers. His work was met with the same conservative frown which has been turned on less pretentious efforts in this country. The feeling raised against this movement in Germany was such that Christlieb was obliged to appeal to America and England for help in training and sending out these lay evangelists. I had the honor to serve as one of the American committee for receiving and transmitting funds, and I had by this means considerable opportunity to learn something of the blessed and soul-saving results of this much-despised work.

"Let it be clearly understood, in fine, that this undertaking is not for promoting any 'new ministerial short cut,' as the 'Examiner' affirms, but is an humble effort, undertaken without funds and without any intention of seeking an endowment, to enlist for lay missionary service men and women who otherwise might not find their way to the field. If the word 'recruiting-station' be kept in mind, none will be misled. Those of us engaged in this enterprise propose, in our missionary addresses and evangelistic tours and by correspondence, to appeal for volunteers for the foreign work; as we secure such, to test them by a year's experience in city mission work, and if we find those whose age and circumstances warrant them in going to college or seminary, to help them in their way thither; to others we will give the best practical and biblical instruction we can."

The interpretation of the new movement as antagonistic to higher theological education was as false as uncalled for. That the founder of the school was as friendly as ever to the seminaries can be easily seen from the following letter. Its real import is made more clear when it is known how largely the financial weight of his own enterprise pressed upon him, and how busily his pen wrought in those days to earn money for continuing the modest work which was being so acrimoniously criticized. For during the first year more than eight hundred dollars of his own salary was turned over to the school, and in succeeding years all the proceeds from copyrights and articles, as well as his entire income as coeditor of the " Missionary Review."

" December 17, 1890.

" *To Professor Charles R. Brown :*

" . . . In regard to your appeal for Newton, I have been waiting for a favorable time to invite you and Burton to present the matter.   In the crisis in the affairs of the Missionary Union — a debt of one hundred and fifty thousand dollars being inevitable unless immediate help is forthcoming — I have thrown my church into the breach.   We are raising an extra five to ten thousand dollars before January 1st.   After that, or before the end of the year at least, I will try to give the matter attention.   I wish to be put down for fifty dollars myself, and hope to continue the same yearly.   I trust the work on the hill is greatly prospering."

The attack on the school served to advertise it.   Students began to come in from all parts of the country.   Contributions to its support followed.   One lady wrote to the head of the school that she had read the " Examiner " articles, and that, though she had no knowledge of the working of the new project, was sure it must be a " good thing," else the " Examiner " would never have assailed it.   She sent in the letter a large check and in each succeeding year gave generously toward current expenses.   Later results richly repaid the investments of time and labor.   Prayer and self-sacrifice are justified of their children.   Graduates of the school are now working in all parts of the globe — in Algeria, in China, in India, on the Congo, in Barbadoes, in Oklahoma, and in the Soudan.   Many have become efficient and prized city missionaries and pastors.   One has charge of a chapel car and has founded a hundred or more new churches since he began his work.   Of the apostolic labors of those who have fallen in Africa and elsewhere, we might speak at length.*   Suffice it to say that they died for the testimony of Jesus after much toil and suffering, and that their praise is on all lips.   Of the summer work of students in the destitute parts of Maine and among the hills of Vermont and New Hampshire we have spoken elsewhere.   The letters which come back from the graduates are full of gratitude and affection for the school, for the instructors, and for the founder.   Finally, the numerous institutions of a like character which have sprung up all over the country constitute a reinforcing justification for the establishment of the Boston Missionary Training-school.   They point to a recognition of the need of such schools, and of the adequate way in which the need was here satisfied.

* David Miller in the Soudan; Richard Jones, Banza Manteke, Free State of Congo; and Idalette Mills, Barbadoes.

CHAPTER XXI

THE PREACHER AND THE PULPIT

Dr. Gordon as a preacher—His view of what the pulpit should be—Power in illustration—Examples

"THE mutes," said a recent French critic of the pulpit, "are on all the violins of God." Preaching has become too often in our city churches an art where it should be an enthusiasm. It ripples from a type-written manuscript; it ought to pour from a bursting heart. It suggests not the mountain cataracts, but the linden-lined canals of Holland. It is of Bossuet, not of Savonarola. Faultily faultless in finish and style, it recalls the sophist lecturing on ethics to the Roman ladies of the Antonines in some private amphitheater of marble; it should rather bring up a prophet in leopard-skin to whom a message from God is intrusted. Ah, yes, the mutes are indeed on the violins. The old word "repent" is heard rarely save in undertone. The horror of sin has not taken hold as it must and will. The mighty rushing wind sweeps not yet over these fine-twisted, taut strings of silver.

Whatever the character of Dr. Gordon's preaching in the earlier days, there was in him in the years of maturity little of the court preacher. He proclaimed without flinching the helplessness of man, the impotence of the unrenewed will, the destiny of sorrow and punishment to which the unconverted are drifting. And where the knife probed the ointment followed. For, while there was no abatement of stern truths, there was in his preaching, as in the gospels, no want of tenderness. As the Etruscans were wont to whip their slaves to the note of flutes, so did the preacher lay bare sin, yet with much gracious invitation and pointing away to the Lamb of God. Controversy he shunned as a canker. "Prophesying against the prophets of Israel that prophesy" would have been arduous work indeed to one so absorbed in holding up the perfect Christ before men. Self-advertisement never suggested itself to him; he was but a wire to transmit currents.

The best estimate of any preacher is apt to be his own estimate of what the pulpit should be. In the present case we have much information. The advice to ministers, the criticisms, favorable and unfavorable, on the development of the contemporary pulpit, and the suggestions and remarks and observations on the whole subject of the ministry of the Word which Dr. Gordon left behind, would, if collected, constitute almost material enough for a text-book on homiletics—a text-book which, from the point of view of apostolic preaching, would be fairly classical. In reading these over we see, as it were, the fresh types from which the message has been struck. The man himself rises before us, massive in delivery, earnest in appeal, from whose lips rivers of living water flow continually. Here is unconscious self-portraiture.

Let us look, then, at the ideal which this preacher of God's truth set before him. The notes which we quote first, on "The Homiletic Habit," are indeed suggestive to those familiar with the absorbed look, the abstracted, meditative face of his week-days. Tauler was wont to draw his cap over his eyes that the violets might not disturb his introspections; Gordon likewise lived much within the veil.

I

"In one of Professor Shedd's admirable chapters on 'Homiletics' we find the phrase, 'homiletic habit,' as descriptive of that mental mood which in ministers is most conducive to easy and successful preparation for the pulpit. We like the term and commend it to our brethren as exceedingly suggestive. The method by which the vast majority of sermons are produced is anything but easy and natural. Many are the result of the most painful retchings and strainings of the brain. Many are the issue of mere spasmodic throes of the intellect. Many have only a galvanic life, the heart having really given nothing of its own emotions for their inspiration. How few are part and parcel of the preacher's daily life—a piece cut from the texture of his habitual experience !

"Now it would be a grand thing if preachers could only live in their sermons. Milton declares that to be a poet one must make his whole life an heroic poem, and it is equally clear that to be a true preacher one must make his whole life a gospel sermon. It is a good thing to be able to find sermons in stones, but better to be able to find them in one's own heart. And he is a wise preacher who keeps his mind so filled with the seeds of Scripture, with the fruitful and springing germs of pious studies and meditations and experiences, that it readily yields the weekly harvest, and does not compel him to spend his time in gathering exotics from a foreign soil. The thoughts of other men can never be truly appropriated except they have been first planted and reproduced in our own experiences. Fervor a century old is poor leaven for a sermon of to-day. Unction fried out of the lore of some old divine is thin anointing for the discourse of the living preacher. These things must be peculiarly one's own in order to possess any real value. They must be the outcome of a genuine experience—the product and commodity of an habitual mental and spiritual discipline.

"Hence the importance of keeping the mind and heart toned up with respect both to fervor and activity in order that the preacher may be able to bring forth freshly and readily the living message.

" There is an almost universal habit among ministers of letting down and unbending after the fatigues and pressure of the Lord's day.   This is well, provided it does not result in disorganization and demoralization.   But if the preacher in attempting to rest disbands his Sabbath thoughts and gives furlough to his holier frames and feelings so that several days are requisite to get them back into rank and file again for producing a sermon, his rest has been really a serious loss.   Let a minister be Mondayish on Monday provided he does not thereby incapacitate himself for being Sundayish on the other days of the week—those days over which the work and worship of the approaching Sunday must always project themselves, and for the labors of which the strength and tone acquired upon the preceding Sunday should be always prudently economized.   The minister can ill afford to let his fires go out and his mental machinery come to a dead standstill for a day.   If he does, when he returns to work he will find much of the time which ought to be wholly used in producing demanded for the mere work of starting up again.   Having lost his preaching mood, he finds it exceedingly difficult to get it back again ; for a mood is not like a colt turned out to pasture that can be caught and bridled at will, but a very illusory and often refractory thing.   And so, having to preach of necessity, he finds himself forced up to an unwelcome and ungenial task in the preparation of his discourses, instead of finding in this process of composition a grateful vent for the outflow and overflow of his resources and a joyful exercise of ready and spontaneously acting powers.

" Preaching ought to be ' a mode of self,' to use Dr. Alexander's striking phrase—the exhibition of one's own religious life and experience. . . .   To be obliged to borrow a character to preach in is worse than being obliged to borrow a sermon to preach.   The latter is literary plagiarism, and the former moral plagiarism, which is worse.   Yet who that preaches has not been at times painfully conscious of his two personalities? Who does not feel that the perfect harmonizing of the two, the complete blending of the two into a consistent and inseparable unity, is the greatest attainment for the work of the ministry? Nothing is stronger or more inexorable than habit. Blessed is the man to whom the duties, the spirit, the aim, and the example of the ministry have become a habit and no longer a painfully acquired exception. The best commentary on the whole subject may be found in the recent saying of Canon Wilberforce concerning his father—that 'in his later years he gave up preparing sermons, and simply prepared himself.'"

II

In the next few extracts polemical and sensational preaching is deprecated:

"A Christian is the most powerful evidence of Christianity, and an infidel is the most potent factor of infidelity. Let the man of God do his utmost to conquer the man of no God, and skepticism will go inevitably. We have not the impertinence to call a halt in the war upon abstraction—so many hundred embattled theologians discharging their logic guns at agnosticism, positivism, atheism, and what not—but we may be pardoned for inviting a fresh assault upon agnostics and atheists, not in any martial attitude, but on our knees. If the thousand pulpits and churches in our land would concentrate their prayers, their faith, and their tender persuasions upon such skeptics as come within their range, what inroads would be made upon unbelief within a few years!

"'Brethren,' writes James, 'if any of you do err from the truth, and one convert him; let him know, that he which converteth the sinner from the error of his way shall save a soul from death, and shall hide a multitude of sins.' And shall we reverse the method, and first aim at the multitude of sins, battling with the whole brood of doubts and denials and liberalities and speculations in hope that, having slain these, we may arrive at last at the sinner who harbors them, to turn him from the error of his way and save his soul from death?   No; the sinner converted, the multitude of sins will be swept away; the doubter won, his doubts will vanish into air.   God's warfare does not set us first to reduce the circumvallation of doubt and unbelief, but to capture at once and completely the citadel of the heart.   Is it not true that most of the attacks on skepticism are made from a fondness for intellectual tournaments, or at least for the *gaudium spolii*, the joy of victory, which the contests may afford?   Were the real purpose to win over the unbeliever, there would be often more self-denial than self-gratification in the undertaking.   *Let us lay down the cudgel and take up the cross.*   The beginning of strife is as when one letteth out water; therefore leave off contention and take up prayer and pleading, that it may be as when one letteth out tears."

III

"One of the most fatal errors of the time is that ministers undertake to be feeders of men instead of fishers of men. One cannot be fed upon the gospel until he has been renewed. But what if a preacher with a crowd of unconverted hearers before him makes it his chief aim to feed them, instead of dropping the gospel hook among them, and holding it there until upon its barbed point somebody is pricked in the heart and led to cry out, 'What must I do to be saved?' and so be caught for Christ?   Feeding the fish may be very exciting business, but it is very profitless.   Bait with no hook on it, bait consisting of popular hits at the faults and inconsistencies of the church, keen thrusts at the stupid bigotry of the old musty creeds, sharp innuendoes about sanctimonious deacons and hypocritical professors—what a stir and excitement and flash of exhilaration will follow when a handful is thrown out! By it how many fish will be caught? Nay; 'I will make you fishers,' not feeders, 'of men.' Catch the fish first and bring them into a regenerated life; then they will have a relish for the solid and substantial food of Scripture truth, and we shall not have to feed them on the bait of popular novelty and bits of sensationalism. . . .

"But let us not forget that we are sent to save men, not to destroy them; to win them, not to wound them. And, therefore, what glory is it that we have won a reputation for keenness in rebuke, for brilliancy in pulpit repartee, for pungency in hitting off the faults and foibles of our brethren? It is a short road to popularity, indeed. Let it be known that a minister on next Sunday is going to give a hot, spicy discourse on the crookedness of deacons and the shallowness of Christians in general, and it will be sure to call out a large attendance. The popularity of some of our most noted preachers has been largely due to their ingenuity in this direction. But this is not our calling as Christians. It is for us to set forth the beauty and excellency of Jesus Christ, and not to exhibit the follies and blemishes of human nature. In either case we shall be unconsciously assimilated to the image of that on which we dwell. 'I do not allow myself to look at a bad picture,' said Sir Peter Lely, the artist, 'for if I do my brush is certain to take a hint from it.' Caricaturists of human nature likewise come at last to present very bad specimens of human nature in their own character. They learn unconsciously to personate their own pictures and to exemplify their own exaggerations. Take now and then a sorrowful look at human nature, but for one look in this direction take ten toward the perfect Christ and hold him up steadily and faithfully, and all the while you will be growing into the same image from glory to glory."

IV

Compactness, humility, unwearied reiteration of the truth, unction, the preëminent use of the Word, the avoidance of speculative preaching, the commingling of the sterner truths of the gospel with the more pleasing in due proportion, are inculcated in the extracts which follow:

" That is an admirable and witty homiletic maxim, ' Do not make too many heads to your sermon, lest you may not be able to find ears for them all!' Indeed, having the ears already at hand, how many a minister by his long sword of intolerable prolixity wantonly repeats the offense of Peter upon the servant of the high priest ! Brevity is not only the soul of wit, but the soul of wisdom for the preacher. . . .

" Self-seeking corrupts everything and turns even the Lord's work into a means of self-promotion. How often the minister quenches the Spirit by trying to shine! How often the soul-winner goes out of the pulpit because the great preacher has come in! . . .

" What is considered a fault in rhetoric is a virtue in testimony, viz., repetition, saying the same thing again and again till it has fairly worn a hole in men's indifference and let the light in.

" The Lord would not have told Simon to put up his sword if it had been the sword of the Spirit that he was wielding. The sword of the Spirit lays open the heart, while the sword of the flesh only cuts off the ears. Now there has been a long succession of Petrine apostles, valiant swordsmen of the faith, whose principal ministerial trophies are severed ears, and not converted hearts; who have preached with such two-edged severity as to alienate their hearers when they should have won them. The Lord has not called us to be theological gladiators, to win applause from the crowd by our skill in cutting and slashing. . . .

"We are God's witnesses, not his logicians sent to argue men into the kingdom of heaven. We are not God's debaters, sent to discuss theology with men, and to convince them of the truth of Christianity. If this were so, we might well be afraid of getting worsted; for the world is full of good logicians and skilled debaters—men that are more than a match for us on that ground. We, on the contrary, as Christ's servants, are simply to bear witness year in and year out, using the Word of God, and not our own. Our success will not depend upon our acuteness or our eloquence or our skill, but upon God's Spirit, that accompanies and energizes that Word. It takes a strong muscle to throw a hand-ball so that it shall strike a hard blow; but a child can fire a rifle-ball effectively, since the propelling power is in the powder and not in the muscle. So it takes a strong man to use an argument effectively; but a babe in Christ can use a text of Scripture with prevailing force, since it is not by might nor by power, but by God's Spirit, that the text is impelled. 'The power of a word,' says Emerson, 'depends upon the power of the man that stands behind it.' But the power of God's Word depends upon the power of the Spirit that stands behind it, its inspirer and its abiding energizer. . . .

"The sincere milk of the Word may be dispensed from the pulpit, yet given out so frigidly and unfeelingly as to make it very hard to receive. In Siberia the milkmen sometimes deliver their milk in chunks, not in quarts, it being frozen solid and thus carried about to the customers. Alas! is not this the way many pulpits deliver the milk of the Word? It is the pure article, sound, orthodox, and unadulterated, but it is frozen into logical formularies and hardened and chilled by excessive reasonings. Let us so preach, O men of God, that our sermons shall not have to be thawed before they can be digested. . . .

"Use nourishments instead of stimulants in your efforts to

bring up the spiritual tone of the church.   By stimulants we
mean frantic appeals, severe denunciations, stinging rebuke.
These rouse for the single day on which they are employed,
but their effect is exhausted before the week is over, and the
application must be repeated the next Sunday, and so on
week after week.   By nourishment we mean the Scriptures
unfolded, expounded, and steadily applied. 'The words that
I speak unto you, they are spirit, and they are life.' . . .

"Feet shod, not with the preparation of the gospel of peace,
but with conjecture, tracking an experiment, running in the
way of some unexplored 'perhaps'—these can leave no path
for sin-blinded and truant souls to walk in. . . .

"Two chemical elements which are very mild and innocu-
ous in themselves often have prodigious energy when combined.
So it is with love and truth.   Those who preach love alone
are often the weakest and most ineffective witnesses for Christ ;
those who preach the truth alone not infrequently demonstrate
the impotence of a soulless orthodoxy.   But the truth in love is
vital, penetrating, and has the dynamic force which we seek. . . .

"The highest reach of genius comes far short of the lowest
degree of inspiration.   To electrify a hearer is one thing ; to
bring a hearer prostrate at the feet of Jesus, quite another. . . ."

In power of illustration Dr. Gordon had few equals in the
contemporary pulpit.   His comparisons were always vivid,
always, to use a fine French phrase, "palpitating with actuality."   They had a power of instantaneous illumination, making clear at once any abstruseness in thought which it might
be necessary to light up.   Never were they haled in for their
own sake.   "Distinguished guests," he was wont to say, "we
may introduce with as extended formality as we choose, but
we do not introduce our servants.   They fulfil their office
best by coming in quietly and unheralded, performing their
proper duty, and then retiring.   Illustrations are the preacher's

servants. Their elaborate presentation to the audience tends to lift them out of their proper subordination, as though they came to be ministered unto instead of to minister."

These illustrations were not raised, as turnips or roses, by careful cultivation. They were plucked by the wayside, and had all the freshness and artlessness of wild flowers. Returning one day from a fishing excursion—the only one, we believe, since boyhood in which he ever took part, and which was, naturally enough, ill fated in its results—he ran across a lad with a long string of black bass. He announced his own poor luck and asked the reason therefor. "I guess yer didn't keep out of sight," was the appropriate answer, which was used to explain in the next Sunday's sermon why some ministers made so few converts. At another time, in passing through the woods, he noticed two trees which had rubbed the one against the other and had then grown together. Shortly afterward he was called upon to speak at the Mildmay Conference in London. At the end of his address he recalled the fact of the crossed trees and used it in the following exquisite and perfect illustration :

"And now I must close. In the part of New England where I spend my summer holidays I have seen a parable of nature which sets forth what I have said. It is an example of natural grafting. Two little saplings grew up side by side. Through the action of the wind they crossed each other. By and by the bark of each became wounded and the sap began to mingle until, in some still day, they became united together. This process went on more and more, and by and by they were firmly compacted. Then the stronger began to absorb the life of the weaker. It grew larger and larger, while the other grew smaller and smaller, withering and declining till it finally dropped away and disappeared. And now there are two trunks at the bottom and only one at the top. Death has taken away the one ; life has triumphed in the other.

" There was a time when you and Jesus Christ met. The wounds of your penitent heart began to knit up with the wounds of his broken heart, and you were united to Christ. Where are you now? Are the two lives running parallel, or has the word been accomplished in you, ' He must increase, but I must decrease '? Has that old life been growing less and less and less ? More and more have you been mortifying it until at last it seems almost to have disappeared? Blessed are you if such is the case. Then can you say, ' I live; yet not I, but Christ liveth in me: and the life which I now live in the flesh I live, not of myself, but by the faith of the Son of God, who loved me, and gave himself for me. Henceforth for me to live is Christ.' "

Biography furnished constant illustrations. Now it would be the story of Ziska's skin stretched over a drumhead, leading the Utraquists to victory; now the heroic tale of some early saint or of some Reformation martyr. We recall the thrilling power with which the story of John Coleridge Patterson's death was used in a missionary meeting in Philadelphia. The isle on the distant horizon, unvisited and unexplored, was first described. Then came the story of the departure, the voyage over the still water, the landing, the attack upon Patterson, the flight back to the canoe, and the return with the dead missionary's body pierced with five wounds and covered with palm-leaves. The application of the incident followed. This earth, a little isle in the infinite, was pictured, and the yearning of the Lord Jesus for its blessing. He too put out through the seas of space; he too landed on an errand of grace; he too was rejected and slain; he too was laid away in grave-clothes with five bleeding wounds. The stillness was intense as the preacher passed from point to point through the whole series of touching correspondences, and as he urged the duty of Christians in the task of completing the missionary work of the Lord Jesus on earth, as the successors of Patterson on the lonely Melanesian isle had finished his.

With this power of illustration went along an extraordinary scripturalness. His mind had become saturated with biblical phraseology by the long years of patient meditation on the Word. He held the Bible, so to speak, in solution; he was completely assimilated to it in word and in thought. His illustrative gifts were to him as a second language by which he could interpret his meaning at will. His skill at translation back and forth from the vernacular to the Scripture equivalent gave him the power of a third tongue. Thus he was trilingual in his exposition, using, as it might happen, his own vigorous Saxon dialect, the mellow diction of the Bible saturated with tender associations, or the picturesque idiom of illustrative anecdote.

In the pages which follow there are collected a few fine and pregnant characterizations and some quaintly apposite illustrations, together with a number of examples of beautifully discriminating exposition. Perhaps in years to come these and many which have appeared elsewhere will be referred to and quoted as the Puritan divines of former days were quoted by him.

" ' Ye became *followers of us and of the Lord.*' Not of us alone, but of us and of the Lord. We are to imitate good men, but all the time we must look beyond them to the Lord himself. If you examine a school-boy's copy-book you will find that the writing grows worse and worse as you go down the page. Why? Because in the first line he looked only at the master's copy. Ever after that he looked more or less at his own reproduction of it. Look at human models, but follow them ever back to the divine original. Christ's example stands at the head of the page; all that comes after is more or less imperfect. Let us look to it, therefore, diligently, lest, by our faulty example, we become dissenters from our own creed."

"In the order of divine providence, the Lord needs the action of our will just as much as we need the action of his will. In the old-fashioned watch there are the mainspring and the hair-spring. The hair-spring does not move the mainspring, but is moved by it; and yet the mainspring depends on the hair-spring to take off the power that was stored up in it. By tick after tick of this little spring the motion that was coiled up in the great central spring is released and communicated to the machinery. So we say our will does not move God's will; it is moved by it. At the same time God's will is dependent on the submission and choice of our will in order that he may bless us and give us the things that we need."

"It costs our government just as much to uniform a well-dressed recruit as it does a ragged one. In either case the recruit must put off his citizen's dress and put on the army blue; and so it is not worth while for a volunteer to spend his labor and pains to get a new suit to enlist in. There is likewise no necessity for a sinner's waiting to get a better moral garb, a more respectable wardrobe of frames and feelings, before he may come to Christ."

"I saw a sign-painter take a dish of gold-dust and pour it over the board upon which he was working; but when he turned the board over all of it seemed to slide off. But no, not all; the lines where his brush had been drawn a few moments before with the adhesive preparation, these caught the glittering particles and held them firm. So, thought I, must the teachers of God now do. They must pour the golden sand of the gospel over the whole congregation; and if it seems to slide off and get no hold upon their hearts, they must know that many a one who has been touched with the preparing grace of the Holy Spirit will catch and hold fast the Word of life, and so the Word shall not return to God void."

" The audacity of unbelief is the secret of its attractiveness
to many minds. The act of walking on a rope stretched over
Niagara does not differ materially, as a physical performance,
from that of walking on a brick pavement; yet the latter is so
sober and common an act that it attracts no attention, while
the former from its very peril and hardihood will draw hundreds to witness it. And so the feats of those who walk on
the perilous edge of truth, the ventures of those who play
with falsehood and hang suspended over the vortex of unbelief, with just sufficient hold on faith to keep them from falling
in, are always vastly more diverting than the proceedings of
those who pursue an orderly and even way of truth and orthodoxy."

" Some people seem to think that if they can pack the gospel away into a sound and orthodox creed it is perfectly safe.
It is a sort of canned fruit of Christianity, hermetically sealed
and correctly labeled, which will keep for years without decay.
An extravagant reliance has been placed, therefore, on confessions of faith as the preservatives of a pure gospel. But
the heart is greater than the creed; and if the heart is wrong
it will very soon corrupt the creed and interline it with its own
heresies. Hence the wise injunction of the apostle, ' Holding
the mystery of the faith *in a pure conscience.*' "

" It is a sad fact that evil is far more infectious than good.
Disease is contagious; health is not. If an invalid could only
catch the robust healthfulness of the one who sits next him in
the street-car as readily as a well man catches the cholera or
the smallpox from his traveling companion, what a happy circumstance it would be! Instead of quarantines for isolating
disease we should have hospitals for propagating health. We
should vaccinate men with the contagion of sound lungs and
pure blood. But alas! while it is very easy for evil commu-

nications to corrupt good manners, it is very difficult for good communications to correct bad manners. Puritan Manton says, 'Ears of corn do not catch our clothes and hang about them, but thorns and burs do.' Very true. And how the burs of avarice and the thorns of worldliness catch upon the garments of the church as she passes along Therefore it is necessary that we should pick off these burs every night when we come home from walking through this present evil world. Be sure it is not the function of the pulpit to paint these burs so that they shall look like roses, to blunt these thorns so that they shall cease to wound the conscience."

"When you carry a manuscript to the printer for him to put into type, he says to you, 'In a few days I will send you a proof.' He makes the proof by laying a sheet of paper on his types and taking an impression of them. Now the ordinances are proofs of Christ, the facsimile of the death and resurrection; and creeds are proofs of Christ, the duplicate copy, if they are correct, of his Word and doctrine."

"*Experimental religion*, as it used to be called, has an immense advantage over philosophical and sacramental religion at this point. One can go into court on an experience, but who cares to hear one swear on a syllogism or a tradition? To have come into direct personal contact with Christ in regeneration enables believers to say, with John, 'that which we have looked upon and our hands have handled of the Word of life.' Unanswerable confession. That which we have handled with our hands is very warm and vital; that which has been handed to us by priestly hands gets strangely cooled and devitalized in coming through the long reaches of tactual succession. We have a living Christ made ever present to us through the Holy Spirit; and we cannot afford to receive our grace through lessened and circuitous channels when such pro-

vision has been made for obtaining it immediately by the touch
of a personal and appropriating faith. The Chinese worshiper,
in praying to his ancestors, believes that if he makes known
his petition to his dead father, and he in turn to his father till
the remotest ancestor is reached, the latter will hand it over
to God. This, it will be perceived, is sacerdotalism with the
current reversed. Poor Chinaman! Poor sacramentarian!
How faint the echo of those intercessions, how feeble the
impact of that grace, which has come through such interminable routes!"

"Pascal says very beautifully, 'Jesus let only his wounds
be touched after his resurrection. Hereby I perceive that we
can now be united to Christ only through his sufferings.'
Yes; now only through his atonement which those sufferings
have purchased. It is not the life of Christ lived before the
crucifixion by which we are to be saved, but the life of the
risen and glorified Christ. 'Henceforth I know no man after
the flesh,' says Paul: 'yea, though I have known Christ after
the flesh, yet now I know him no more.' Many to-day are
trying to imitate the earthly life of Christ; many others are
trying to be saved by imitating the death of Christ. The
world is pretty nearly divided between these two classes, those
who are seeking salvation by copying Christ's life, and those
who are seeking salvation by copying his death, the one looking for peace by self-morality and the other by self-mortifica-
tion. One of our missionaries relates the terrible suffering of
a heathen whom he found. So many years he had lived with
his body immersed in water; so many years he had swung on
hooks piercing through his flesh—a horrible record of studied
barbarities inflicted on the body. He was simply trying to
make peace with God through his wounds. Here, in this little
meeting of the disciples, is the most significant answer to such
blind yearnings of our poor humanity—the risen Lord stand-

ing before the world and saying, 'Peace be unto you,' and then showing the wounds in his body by which he has purchased that peace.   No longer are we called to make peace with God, since the Scriptures declare that Christ has made peace by his cross.   The gospel which we preach now to the world is not *Make peace*,' but '*Take peace*.' . . .   Choirs of angels—all the orchestra of heaven—singing, ' Peace on earth, good will to men,' are nothing compared with this little sermon within the closed doors.   ' Peace be unto you'; 'and when he had so said he showed them his hands and his side.'   Here was the handwriting of redemption deeply engraved in his flesh ; here was the title-deed of pardon written in his risen body.   The wounds of Christ are an eternal and unanswerable reply to all accusations of conscience.

"We are aware, however, that men will not look to Christ's wounds for healing until their hearts have been wounded for sin.   This, then, is the first requisite—that our hearts be melted for our sins.   We say *melted*.   David said, ' A broken and a contrite heart, O God, thou wilt not despise.'   The law of God by the hammer of affliction or by the smitings of judgment may break the heart.   But broken ice is just as cold as solid ice.   And we have seen worldly hearts all shattered and bruised to pieces by calamity, yet remaining as frigid as an iceberg.   We do not undervalue law work in preaching, but oh! it is grace work that melts.   And the wounds of Christ are just as powerful to melt the heart as to heal it."

"What a solemn expression is this, ' Making the cross of Christ of none effect '!   No power or might of man can sweep the stars from the sky or blot the sun from the heavens or efface the splendid landscape ; but one wound in the eye can destroy the sight and make all those things as though they were not.   So the atonement of Christ can never pass into eclipse or cease to be a fact ; but there is such a thing as the eclipse of faith—unbelief filming the soul so that the cross and atonement of Christ shall become a great blank—vacant, lifeless, meaningless. O eyes that are becoming dim, but not with age; blinded, but not with tears; hard of seeing, but not with use—hear the Lord speaking from heaven, 'Anoint thine eyes with eye-salve, that thou mayest see.' It is not that God has need to do greater things for us, but that we should open our eyes and see what he has done."

"I have been struck in observing the various attempts to explain a certain phrase that Paul uses—'In all these things we are more than conquerors.' Yet how simple it is when taken in its connection. He sums up all the things he is enduring—the sword, peril, nakedness, dying all the day long for Christ, led daily like a sheep to the slaughter; and then he says, 'In all these things we are more than conquerors.' How? Plainly thus. The man who is victorious through victory is a conqueror; but he who is victorious through defeat is more than conqueror."

"Many persons prefer not to know their whole duty lest they should be obliged to do it. We read the other day of a rich miser who was afflicted with cataracts on both his eyes. He applied to an eminent surgeon to remove them, and after examination was told that it could be done. 'But what will it cost?' was his anxious question. 'One hundred dollars for each eye,' was the answer. The miser thought of his money and then thought of his blindness, and said, 'I will have one eye restored; that will be enough to enable me to see to count my money, and I can save the expense of having the other operated on.' 'O Lord, open thou mine eyes, that I may behold wondrous things out of thy law,' cries the true Christian. But the half-and-half Christian wants only one eye opened. He likes to have the minister preach conversion strongly, because he has been converted himself and believes in it; but he does not like to have him preach consecration, for that implies laying himself and all his wealth on God's altar, and he is not ready for that.   In other words, he deliberately chooses a one-eyed religion—that which sees Christ as Saviour but ignores him as sanctifier.   But is Christ divided?   Can we halve him by our partial faith, so that he can be our Saviour who delivers us from the penalty of our sins, and not be our Master who commands our obedience?   We do not think so.   We cannot be saved without Christ's cross, and we cannot be sanctified and made meet for the kingdom of heaven without our own cross.   'Except a man take up his cross daily, and follow after me, he cannot be my disciple.'   To begin to be a Christian is an easy thing, but to *be* a Christian, in all the length and breadth of meaning involved in that word, this costs a battle—a battle with self, a battle with sin, a battle with the world, a battle with the evil one."

In a gracious article on "The Names of Scripture" he says: "None will have their names stricken off because of their waywardness and wanderings.   On the contrary, these will be the oftener mentioned, as the straying sheep hears its name called more frequently than the one which keeps close to the flock.   Did you ever think to listen and hear Jesus, the Good Shepherd, call his sheep by their names?   'Simon, Simon, behold, Satan hath desired to have you, that he may sift you as wheat: but I have prayed for thee.'   'Martha, Martha, thou art careful and troubled about many things: but one thing is needful.'   'Saul, Saul, why persecutest thou me?'"

"Speech is that which especially reveals the flavor or quality of the man.   It may sometimes feign sanctity, to be sure, when it is wanting in the life; and it may seek to make itself redolent with a borrowed grace, as the tippler disguises his breath with spices and perfumes; but the illusion cannot be long maintained. 'Thy speech bewrayeth thee,' is a saying of universal application. One cannot live sinfully and talk holily, live impurely and talk cleanly, live selfishly and talk generously. 'Show me your tongue,' says the doctor, as the first demand of the patient. Here is the most favorable point for a diagnosis. And the truest diagnosis of the soul can be made in the same way by examining the tongue to see what kind of a deposit and coloring the thoughts and desires have left there. Therefore, of those who are constituted the salt of the earth we are not surprised to find the requirements made, 'Let your speech be always with grace, seasoned with salt.' Well shall we mark the words. We are not told to let our speech *be salt* entirely, totally. To take a whole mouthful of salt will choke one and turn his stomach. We may in spiritual things disgust and repel men by a too raw and excessive and unmixed use of religious conversation. A pious but very refined and sensitive minister recently declared that the greatest provocation to anger and intemperate speech that he had ever encountered was in the conduct of a rough and boisterous Christian, who used to shout at him across the street or in the cars or wherever he chanced to meet him, 'Well, brother, how's your soul?' It was difficult, no doubt, for him always to answer the salutation with grace; and the reason is obvious. This man's speech was not delicately seasoned with salt, and so was nauseous and intolerable when it might, if fitly seasoned, have proved refreshing. It is a great art to temper one's Christian conversation exactly to the occasion."

"The life of Jesus gave us the inspiration of example; the cross of Jesus kindled the inspiration of love; the resurrection of Jesus begot the inspiration of hope; but the ascension of Jesus gave the inspiration of direct power."

" 'Blessed be the Lord God of Israel; for he hath *visited* and redeemed his people,' is a significant note in the prophecy of his birth. Four times in the gospels is our Lord's advent to earth spoken of as a visit. But it was a visit which never for a moment looked toward a permanent abiding. At his birth he was laid in a borrowed manger; at his burial he was laid in a borrowed tomb because he owned no foot of earth; and between the cradle and the grave was a sojourn in which the Son of man had not where to lay his head. The mountain-top whither he constantly withdrew to commune with his Father was the nearest to his home. And hence there is a strange, pathetic meaning in that saying, 'And every one went to his own house. Jesus went into the Mount of Olives.' "

" Covering sin is allowable if only the sin is another's, not ours. 'He that covereth his sins shall not prosper,' but 'Charity covereth a multitude of sins,' the faults and flaws and imperfections of others."

" Many have been the kinds of bread that have been devised to meet the cravings of the perverted appetites which everywhere prevail. Bread of intellect and bread of imagination; bread of art and culture, and bread of doubt and denial; bread half baked in which gospel and science, faith and philosophy, have been kneaded together in an impossible mixture; and poisoned bread, which is the sheerest infidelity, sent forth with the stamp of some pulpit on it. Of the two things which are distressing to look upon to-day, one knows not which is the more distressing, the great multitude which cares nothing for the bread of life, or the other multitude which feeds on the bread of death and is satisfied with it."

" The uplifted gaze without the outstretched hands tends to make one visionary; the outstretched hands without the upward look tend to make one weary."

" It is not the fleshly heart alone that has a right ventricle and a left ventricle. The spiritual heart is divided in the same way, and the great majority of Christians assign one compartment of the heart to self, and leave the other side to Christ. That is half-heartedness in service."

" Persecution, indeed, like everything else which the Lord has blessed and sanctified, has been counterfeited by his great enemy. Many a man who glories in tribulation is really glory-ing in his own shame, his fancied crown of martyrdom being only a fool's cap which signalizes his preëminent self-deception. The ritualist setting up in the church his half-heathen ceremo-nials, and complaining of the discipline that sets him aside from the ministry ; the rationalist crucifying the faith of Christ with the nails of his unsanctified logic, and then, because God's true servants hold off from him, counting it persecution —what have these to do with wearing the crown of Christ's rejection? "

" Never shall I forget a scene which I witnessed in yonder cemetery. There was one solitary mourner bearing an only child to burial. I stood by his side and offered the last prayer, and then he shut the lid of the casket and locked it, and, put-ting the key into his pocket, turned away. Instantly I seemed to hear from the garden of God, where Jesus is, the words, ' Why weepest thou? Fear not; for I am he that liveth and was dead, and behold, I am alive forevermore, and have the keys of death and of the grave.' That father could turn the key that shut in his child, but not the key that opened the door back to life; but Jesus has the key that openeth."

CHAPTER XXII

ERRANT MAN AND THE INERRANT BOOK

Dr. Gordon's theology—The Bible and inspiration—Estimate of human
nature

THE text was for Dr. Gordon not the winding horn of the
chase to signal the start across the moors of rhetoric and
through the tangled woods of theology ; rather was it the inscription above an entrance opening into the Word of God.   Scripture he compared to the dissected map.   To find the complete
statement of truth it is needful to hunt through chapter after
chapter, book after book, and to combine the scattered parts.
The concordance, he said, is, after all, the best commentary.
" In Scripture single words, like blazed trees in a forest, are
sure guides through the labyrinth of revelation. ' Lamb,'
' blood,' ' faith,' ' forgiveness,' ' peace '—these are God's words ;
and whoever will take one of them and trace it through the
Bible, threading together on this single word, as on a cord, the
various texts where it occurs, will find both a wondrous con-
tinuity and a wondrous unity thereby established."

It is hardly necessary to say that to the Bible he accorded
a place of solitary and unapproachable preëminence.   With
those who stand ready to degrade it to the ranks, stripping
from it the sword of the Spirit, and sending it down to march
with Shakespeare, Plato, and the raw conscripts of heart and
brain, he never argued.   The sensitized film photographs
more than the eye can detect.   The prepared heart sees more
than the acutest critic.   " There is a finer sense than the scien-

tific, a more delicate touch than the exegetical. It is written, and cannot be altered, 'The natural man receiveth not the things of the Spirit of God : for they are foolishness unto him : neither can he know them, because they are spiritually discerned.' The Bible repeatedly suffers violence, and the violent seek to take it by force. But the Holy Spirit alone holds the key to it. He only knows the combination of faith and study by which it can be unlocked, and all its hidden treasures of wisdom and knowledge appropriated."

As to modern Old Testament criticism, he doubtless felt, as do many others, that, though it may be as scientific as paleontology, it is also as lifeless and as dry. He thought it a new scholasticism as wearisome as that of Aquinas or of Duns Scotus, as far removed, too, from the method of Jesus. On the other hand, he was not ready to make a *casus belli* of theories concerning "priestly writers" and "redactors." The time is short. Speculation soon dies out if not fed with the oil of controversy. Fruitfulness is more important than an abstract accuracy. The way of light is not paved with lexicons, but with self-denials and faithful testimonies. He shut the door behind him, therefore, leaving the sanhedrim of critics and conservatives to wrangle and bicker, and passed out into the world of the needy and the sorrowing. "'Take and eat in simplicity the bread as you have it before you,'" he said, quoting Bengel, "'and be not disturbed if you find in it now and then a grit of the millstone.' In reading some of the lucubrations of the higher criticism, it seems as though it had deliberately selected the grit and ignored the grain. Let such as like this way grind their teeth on biblical criticism ; but such as prefer food to fault-finding will eat the grain of the Word."

And again : "Upon the much-mooted question of 'inerrancy' we do not presume to enter. But we do express the wish that our higher critics were as ready to test their own inerrancy by Scripture as to test the Scripture's inerrancy by their own.

"We can conceive of nothing better than Bengel's rule for searching the Word of God with profit: ' *Te totum applica ad textum; rem totam applica ad te.*' ('Apply thyself wholly to the text; apply the subject wholly to thyself.') Subjective criticism was never so urgently needed as now; and we might even copy with profit the example of some of our Puritan fathers, who used to spend hours on their knees before the open Bible, praying, 'Search me, O God, and know my heart: try me, and know my thoughts: and see if there be any wicked way in me, and lead me in the way everlasting.'

"On the contrary, has not the *te totum* application to the text of Scripture been vastly overdone in our day? 'Truly light is sweet, and a pleasant thing it is for the eyes to behold the sun,' and unquestionably very useful scientific ends are promoted by the spectroscope, which unbraids the sunbeams, assorts their rays, and assigns them to their various sources. But this is not the process which makes the flowers grow, and the grain ripen, and the orchards bring forth their fruit. Many who are engaged in practical Christian work believe that the principal use of Scripture is for regeneration and spiritual nutrition; that its words are 'spirit and life,' and as such are as certain, if received and cherished in the heart, to produce transformed and holy characters as the wheat grain to beget the wheat harvest. Why not occupy ourselves, therefore, principally with sowing the seed of the Word broadcast among men? And as to our personal use of Scripture, is it not better that we use the Bible as a search-light for illuminating our understanding than to use our understanding as a search-warrant for discovering whether some error or contradiction may not be hiding in the nooks and crannies of its history or chronology?

"An errant Bible is exactly what is demanded by errant youth. To a 'man beholding his natural face in the glass'

of Scripture it is a vast relief to be assured, on scientific authority, that the glass is perchance considerably convexed, so
that the sinful self seen therein, which has often been so trouble-
some, after all, may have been greatly exaggerated. Our plea
is not, however, for war on the critics, but for watch over ourselves—that we let no day pass in the new year in which we do
not turn the light of Scripture upon our lives, subject our hearts
to its searching inquisition, and rejoice to be found out by it concerning those sins of which we have been willingly ignorant."

This reverential regard for the Bible pervaded his whole
teaching and gave to his theological opinions an anchorage in
days of drift and uncertainty. We remember reading in a
Boston newspaper a report of one of his sermons made by a
young woman from the Harvard Annex, who prefaced her
column with a brief description of the church and of its pastor. Her remarks on the well-filled house and hearty congregational worship were appreciative and commendatory. Of
the sermon she observed that one could scarce have believed
that any progress had been made in theology since the days
of Jonathan Edwards if the words of the speaker could be
used as a test. Ah well! what she heard there was truly
older than Edwards, older than Calvin, older than Augustine,
older even than Paul. It came from the heart of Jesus himself. "Back to Christ," was the cry and aim of the preacher.
The soul of man was to him not a common inn for nondescript
and vagrant theories, but a home for the perpetual residence
of God's Spirit. In "progressive theology," therefore, he took
little interest. "'Advanced thought,'" he used to say, "is very
aptly characterized by the Revised Version: 'He that goeth
on and abideth not in the truth is not of God.' We can go
on and outstrip the Word of God, but such advances are at
our peril. Almost better lag behind the truth than outrun it.
Best of all is it to walk in the truth."

The common term of opprobrium with which opinions of

this sort are stigmatized in Boston is "narrowness." "Broad" and "narrow" are at best vaguely relative terms, and ordinarily mere ungracious epithets bandied by partizans. For it should be marked that the test of "liberalism" is as purely personal as that of heresy in the middle ages. If you agree with me you are "broad"; if not, "narrow." Properly used, however, these adjectives concern not belief, but temper, animus, and manner of presentation. Thus most of us would agree that the man who wrote the thirteenth of First Corinthians, "that pæan to charity," was more of a liberal, spite of his Calvinism, than many who bear the name. The honest, just, and pertinent characterizations of doctrine are not "broad" and "narrow," but "true" and "false." So we have "broad" men advocating false doctrine and "narrow" men maintaining the truth. Now, while exception might be freely taken to the interpretation of Christianity set forth weekly from the pulpit of the Clarendon Street Church, of the courtesy of the preacher, the generosity, the liberalism (in its uncorrupted sense), there could be no question. "It is," confessed one of his opponents, "more of a delight to me to hear Dr. Gordon speak what is not according to my mind than to listen to any other man discourse on that which I like and agree with."

Gordon himself would have said that the test by which the truth or falsity of his opinions was to be determined was that of scripturalness or unscripturalness. The test of experience and of history, however, in all important particulars reinforces the teaching of the New Testament. The axiom with which he started was the corruption of man and the hopelessness of all attempts at self-recovery. The human heart is, in his opinion, an incorrigible recidivist. Its fallings are incessant. It is at ever-recurring intervals remanded by the judge, conscience, to the punishment of remorse, to the lonely cell of despair. Men without Christ are, as the contagion-smitten crews on those Baltic vessels in the days of the black death, dead, dying, drifting. In themselves there is no hope, no salvation, no escape.

"The simple fact is," he writes, "that we are in a fallen condition by nature; yes, worse than fallen, we are in a burdened condition. We bear the weight of inherited transgression in our bodies and souls. Every man carries his father and his grandfather on his back. People sneer at the doctrine of original sin, but let them look at the facts of human life and be silent. Hawthorne in his 'Note-book,' published after his death, says, 'I have been reading Bunyan's "Pilgrim's Progress." What a strange figure Christian cuts, going through the country with the burden on his back! I wonder what he has in his pack?' Had the great novelist no dealings with his own conscience that he should ask such a question? Had he had no observation of human life not to mark how men come into the world weighted down with hereditary tendencies toward wrong-doing, under which they stagger to the grave?"

This doctrine of the exceeding sinfulness of man is the *pons asinorum* of both theology and experience. It is the one certainty of which it is allowable to speak with dogmatic positiveness. To say that "men are by nature and from the beginning sons of God," that "there is nothing in Christianity which has not its roots in human nature," and that "reverence for our own human nature is the only salvation from brutal vice and every false belief," is to declare one's self unsophisticated, unaccountably blind, a prophet, if not of the deceit of one's heart, at least of the sightlessness of one's eyes.* In the "era

---

* How can men preach thus? Probably because their minds dwell upon the convergence of worldly Christians and respectable worldlings into one group, where classification is as difficult as of those diatoms and desmids which scientists at one time declare vegetation and at another animal life. There is no mistaking a milch cow for a beech-tree, however. Neither should there be any difficulty in discriminating between unspeakable Turks and ineffable saints. They cannot both be "sons of God."

of good feeling " in which Gordon lived the distinctions between good and bad, the regenerate and the sullenly and ob-
stinately evil, were commonly slighted. The world was declared
to be growing hourly better, the flesh proclaimed to be in no
need of renovation, and the devil ridiculed as a figment of the
imagination vanishing at the cock-crowing of science. " Ruin
and redemption," he was wont to say, " are the two poles of
evangelical theology ; but it cannot be denied that to-day and
in Boston orthodoxy is at both poles considerably flattened."
The sentimental theory of " universal sonship" was mingled
with the teaching of Jesus, as santonin powder is mixed with
food, resulting in a strange color-blindness which made the
whole earth appear beautifully but falsely rose-hued. In this
Pelagian teaching, as Amiel says, " the specifically Christian
accent is lost. Christianity becomes a religion of dignity, not
of humility. Penitence, the struggles of weakness, find no
place in it. Holiness and mysticism evaporate, the law is
effaced, and faith is made a poor, dull thing." *

" Life is deeper than faith, and death is deeper than denial.
Heterodoxy, generally speaking, is simply spiritual death translated into a creed. If the men who are now promoting the
new theology—a counter-reformation destined to bury every
church it touches in helpless spiritual death—had been engaged
for years in the hand-to-hand labor of bringing the unconverted to Christ, we believe that such a movement would have
been impossible." So Gordon wrote of those martyrs " of the
chair," the Andover professors, in the days of the Andover
controversy. It was doubtless his work among outcasts and
drunkards which saved him from the incorrigible optimism in
regard to man's nature current, and which enabled him to
preach Christ crucified with such steadfastness and tenderness.
The following extracts illustrate his evangelicism and exemplify
the fervor and power of its presentation :

* " Journal Intime," p. 115.

" Liberalism is the religion of human nature. It does not make stern and rigid claims on men. It does not hold them up to strong convictions on such subjects as sin and retribution and the need of regeneration. Hence when men get careless and easy-going in their opinions they drift into what is called liberalism as inevitably as water runs downhill. You never find men backsliding into orthodoxy; you never find men drifting into high Calvinism; and you never will till you find water running uphill and iron floating upward in the air. On the contrary, one has to climb to get into this kind of faith, trampling on pride and self-esteem, and holding himself rigidly up to that conviction which is hardest to receive, that human nature is naturally depraved and needs regeneration, and that God is righteously holy and must punish sin. If one gets tired of believing this he has only to shut his eyes and slide, and by the simple gravitation of human nature he lands among the liberals as certainly as a stone loosed from the mountain-side lands in the valley."

" We have sometimes turned up a flat stone in a field just to see the nameless brood of hideous insects that would be found there, and to see them rushing in every direction to hide themselves from the sun that was poured in upon them. So if the shield of respectability were suddenly removed, if the sanction of false custom were lifted, if human palliations and excuses were for a moment taken away, and our hearts were left naked and open before him with whom we have to do, what a hurrying and hiding there would be from the face of him that sitteth on the throne! what a shrinking away of secret sins— of enmity and jealousy and falsehood and impurity! So in these days of shallow theology there is nothing so needful as that we should have times of thorough self-examination in which we should try to see the worst there is in us. We ought now and then to take out a search-warrant for our own hearts, and, when we find what evil there is in us, to say, 'Strike, Lord, for I deserve the worst. I will not evade, I will not palliate, I will not contend; I will bear the indignation of the Lord, because I have sinned against him.'"

"One can no more compel his heart to love that to which he is disinclined than he can change the law of gravitation so that it shall lift him up instead of holding him down. But if you have a new heart the law of your spiritual gravitation will be changed so that you will be attracted heavenward instead of earthward. 'Be of good cheer: I have overcome the world,' says Jesus. But why should I be of good cheer on that account? If the world has overcome me so that I lie bruised and bleeding beneath its feet, it is no comfort for another to say to me, 'Be of good courage; for though you have fallen, I stand upright; and though you have been defeated by sin, I have conquered sin.' It would only deepen my chagrin and discouragement instead of giving new courage. But in the Epistle of John we have a text which supplements this: 'This is the victory that overcometh the world, even our faith.' Does this mean that having faith in yourself enables you to overcome the world? No. And yet this is all the gospel that many have for the helpless sinner. They would go to the poor victim of lust and intemperance, who lies utterly defeated and despairing, and who cries, 'Oh that I could get away from myself, for I am my own worst enemy,' and they would say to him, 'Have faith in yourself.' As well tell a drowning man to lay hold of his right hand in order to rescue himself when both the right hand and the left belong to the same sinking body. No! 'this is the victory that overcometh the world, even our faith'—the faith that fastens to Christ, the great overcomer for us, and appropriates his victory and makes it our own."

" I go into my garden after a terrific storm and find that my grape-vine, which for years had climbed into the sunlight and basked in its beams, has fallen down, its leaves all torn and its boughs bespattered with mud.   And I begin to talk to my vine : ' O vine, thou needest to be pruned and enriched. I must pour ashes about thy roots and pour water above thee to cause thee to revive, and then thou wilt lift thyself into the light and warmth.'   Then I do my best at pruning and enriching, but each day as I walk into my garden I see the vine lying there.   It stretches up its tendrils, indeed, like supplicating fingers to the sky ; but because it can find nothing upon which to lay hold it still creeps on the ground.

" Suppose, instead of talking any more to my vine, I build a trellis upon which it can lift itself up to the sunlight?   Ah, that is Christ's method.   He casts a glance of pity upon us and says, not simply, ' I am from above ; ye are from beneath. No man can come to me except the Father draw him ;' but listen : ' I have loved thee with an everlasting love : therefore with loving-kindness have I drawn thee,' says Jehovah.   But how, O Father?   ' I have drawn thee with the cords of love, and with the bands of a man.'   But what love and what man? I will tell you.   ' This is my beloved Son ; hear ye him,' and the Son says, ' I, if I be lifted up, will draw all men unto me.' The cross is the divine trellis for lifting men's affections to God.   The heart that was striving in vain to love the Father, and was only falling back to earth beaten and baffled after each effort, finds at last its firm support.   ' The preaching of the cross is to them that perish, foolishness ; but unto us which are saved, it is the power of God.' "

" ' *If any man preach any other gospel unto you than that ye have received, let him be accursed.*'   This makes very serious business of the ministry—serious in view of the fact that we have no more choice as to what kind of gospel we will preach than as to what kind of money we will use to pay our debts. There never was a time when 'another gospel' had such free course and was so glorified among us as now. It is not so much open infidelity as fictitious Christianity that we have to fear—a gospel which uses all the phrases and exercises all the seeming fervors of the true faith, but is as unlike it as lead is to gold. Indeed, I may say that to-day liberalism has, for the most part, left off contending and taken up counterfeiting. One of the most artful methods of issuing spurious currency is to take a gold coin, bore into it and dig out the great bulk of the gold, and then fill up the cavity with lead. The face of the coin remains intact, but the heart has been hollowed out.

"So the most dangerous theology in circulation among us to-day is an evangelicalism which keeps most of the phrases of orthodoxy, and yet is utterly void of the vital substance thereof. 'Atonement! Yes, indeed,' says this other gospel. 'Jesus Christ is the martyr-man of the race, one in whom the enthusiasm of humanity kindled to such intensity that it consumed the heart from which it proceeded, giving the most splendid example of self-sacrifice which the world has ever seen. Not that in his death he bore the curse of a violated law! Such an idea spoils the poetry and pathos of his martyrdom, needlessly embarrassing it with the theology of substitution and vicarious satisfaction for human guilt, thereby keeping alive the old "offense of the cross." Divinity of Christ! Yes; with all the heart let it be believed; and since by his incarnation Christ became our kinsman according to the flesh, let us rejoice in "the essential divinity of human nature" also.' Thus, whereas in a former generation the contention was for bringing Christ down to the level of our common humanity, now it is for lifting up our common humanity to the level of Christ. And so is brought in that most deadly doctrine of broad Christianity, that 'all men by nature are sons of God,' a doctrine proclaimed among us with such alluring eloquence that thousands of uninstructed souls imagine they hear the ring of the true gospel coin in what is really only the prolonged resonance of an old Pelagian heresy.

" We fully affirm that this doctrine is not only contradicted by all Scripture, but disproved by all human experience. '*As many as received him*, to them gave he power to become the sons of God, even to them that believe on his name: *which were born, not of blood, nor of the will of the flesh, nor of the will of man, but of God.*' Here is sonship to God, but it is predicated solely on the ground of the new birth, the solemn necessity of which, as announced by our Lord, bears witness to the depravity, not to the divinity, of human nature. Can we brave it out with God, still maintaining in the face of explicit Scripture that without repentance and without regeneration . . . men are the children of God? Such a doctrine Milton rightly traces not to Christ, but to the prince of fallen angels, whom he makes to say:

> " ' The son of God I am, or was,
>   And if I was I am ; relation holds
>   All men are sons of God.' "

CHAPTER XXIII

EVOLUTION, OR THE APPEARING?

"Progress"—Review of Drummond's "A City without a Church"—The coming of Christ—Eschatology—The Roman Antichrist—The restoration of Israel—The resurrection

CLOSELY allied to this view of man's moral incompetency stands the doctrine of the hopeless inability of the race to attain social redemption. The vaunt of "progress"* is but the echo of the boast of self-righteousness. Both heresies have their common source in the self-esteem of the human heart. They are "the counterfeit presentment of two brothers," the face and obverse of the same false coin. Those who preach the dignity and goodness of man generally minimize the appalling corruption of society, and explain that tragedy, human history, as if it were a pleasant drama proceeding through five acts to a delightful dénouement.

This was not Gordon's attitude. He believed that the present age was evil and would remain so unto the end. "Jesus

---

* To quote Amiel once more: "The plea justificatory of progress has a criterion that is quantitative, that is to say, purely exterior (having regard to the wealth of life), and not qualitative (the goodness of life). Always the same tendency to take the appearance for the thing, the form for the substance, the law for the essence; always the same absence of moral personality, the same obtuseness of conscience, which has never recognized sin present in the will, which places evil outside of man, moralizes from outside, and transforms to its own liking the whole lesson of history." ("Journal Intime," p. 60.)

did not say," he wrote, "'This is the best world that was ever made; things are growing better and better; there is ten times more happiness than sorrow on the earth. Only live on the sunny side of the house and keep your curtains lifted and you will be all right.' No such optimistic vaporing as this! But, 'In the world ye shall have tribulation. Let not your heart be troubled. I go to prepare a place for you'—a place of deliverance. Ah, that is what we long for—deliverance from the world's great crushing machine, with its wheels of war and famine and pestilence and earthquake and alcohol grinding men to powder by millions every year. To be able to see God behind all this satanic discord, and to believe in him spite of all this titanic cruelty of the elements, is not always an easy thing. . . . Let us not imagine that we are now reigning with Christ on earth or that the kingdom of God has been set up in the world. The church's earthly career during the present age is, like her Lord's, a career of exile rather than of exaltation, of rejection rather than of rule, of cross-bearing rather than of scepter-bearing."

The permanency and sovereignty of evil during the present age was one of his deepest convictions. The poor we have with us always, but there are others too—their oppressors, and the continuous, unending army of sin. The historical orbit of our planet is no more than its astronomical orbit an upward spiral. Mankind passes century after century through like phases of sin and through the same experiences of moral wretchedness. Only he that hangeth the stars on nothing and holdeth the earth as a very little thing can and will deflect its course finally to higher planes.

The progress which seems to be making in certain periods of the world's history Gordon felt to be external and formal, a mere coating of the surface hiding perilous depths. The present age he believed to be an age of election. Its ultimate purposes are purely disciplinary. Human society is the earth in which the plant grows.　What happens to it is immaterial, except in so far as its development is tributary to the church of Christ.　It may be vastly improved, enriched with the blood of a dozen revolutions and a score of liberation wars; it may be weeded of numberless noxious and parasitical growths; it may be cleared of innumerable stones of stumbling and rocks of offense.　But the great Gardener is thinking not of his plot, but of the transcendently beautiful flower, the church of Christ, which he is raising on it with tender interest and solicitude. Like the Japanese florist, who often spends fifty months on a single chrysanthemum bush, he is laying out on it the care and nurture of millenniums.　The church and the world stand in eternal contrast on the pages of the New Testament.　Any attempt to make the one coterminous with the other will result, as in the past, in corrupting the church down to the level of the world and in the reduction of its religio-thermal line to the cold temperature of secularism.

That Christianity has modified, in a greater or less degree, the world's life, and that it will continue so to do, he of course never questioned.　"The patient sunbeam brooding over the buried seed till it draws out the hidden germ which it contains is all the time warming the surrounding atmosphere."　But this resul is to be considered as entirely subsidiary to the purposes of God in the present age.　"Civilization is not regeneration.　Civilization puts Christianity into the world; regeneration takes man out of the world.　Civilization attempts to diffuse God's life and truth among men; regeneration separates men unto God.　The one process is pervasive; the other elective.　The one makes men better citizens of earth; the other makes them citizens of heaven."　The blessing which the world receives from the church is thus collateral, for the latter is not destined in this dispensation to establish its ideals as recognized statutes for the control of mankind.　Its position is to the mass of men now, as ever since the day of the crucifixion, that of an unwelcome and rejected witness to unappreciated truth.

This insistence on the Paulo-Calvinist formula, as opposed to what might be called the formula of Rousseau, found expression in a criticism of Professor Henry Drummond's " A City without a Church," so cogent, so just, and so scriptural withal that we cannot refrain from quoting it at length.   It is an admirable reply to those who are so taken up with social programs as to forget the program of the ages and the promise of Christ's appearing, and who, like our first parents in Blanco White's sonnet, are, in their keen interest in grasshopper, tree, and leaf which the sun reveals, wholly unconscious of the starry possibilities which it conceals.

"The theology of the Broad Church is emphatically an Elysian theology, at whose fountains those who have been embittered by the rigorous teaching of the former or Puritan age drink and forget their sorrows.   Its preaching is as idyllic as that was dogmatic ; and, so far from any suspicion of a paradise lost, it constantly assures us that, if man ever fell at all, he must have fallen upward, judging by his present goodly estate.

"Now we are not called to choose between optimism and pessimism in religion.   The mischief comes of just this choosing ; the magnifying of the hopeful elements in Christianity and in common life, to the utter ignoring of the dark and dreadful facts, and vice versa.   Indeed, some one has reminded us that, etymologically, heresy signifies a dividing or choosing—the selecting of one extreme of Christian truth to the utter ignoring of the other extreme.   And one need only glance through the history of dogma to observe how many of the great heresies have been exaggerated half-truths instead of absolute falsehoods.   A true theology will certainly be both pessimistic and optimistic ; for it will contain within its scope the doctrine of a paradise lost, with all the dreadful consequences past and present issuing from man's fall; and also the doctrine of a paradise regained, wherein shall be no more sin and no more death.

"We remember listening not long since to a sermon from the honored Bishop of Massachusetts, who has just passed away—noble man and eloquent preacher, but, as one of his eulogists has claimed, 'a Broad-churchman without apology.' 'We know that the Son of God has come,' was the text. As he went on in its unfolding, there was the rush of impassioned thought and fervent speech so characteristic of the speaker, bearing the great congregation irresistibly onward to the end. But when the sermon was completed one hearer began to reflect in silent amazement upon what had been said. The sum of it was this, that the King's Son had been sent to visit an outlying province of the kingdom; that at the tidings of his expected coming the whole people were filled with glad expectation; that his arrival was signaled by an outburst of popular acclamation, in which the people said one to another, 'The King's Son honors us with a visit. He is our prince; we are brothers. Let his coming give a new sense of our d vine sonship, a new impulse to our universal brotherhood.' It was a fascinating picture, and painted with a brush dipped without reserve in 'the enthusiasm of humanity.' To an eminent preacher of the new school, who was afterward expressing his admiration to us, we replied, 'Yes; but, as a matter of fact, when the King's Son came, did not the citizens hate him, and send a message after him, saying, "We will not have this man to reign over us"? Did they not say, "This is the heir: come, let us kill him"?'

"'Very true,' replied my friend; 'but you must remember that the preacher is an idealist.'

"And this is the point of the whole matter. We are bound to be realists in the pulpit, since we live in a world of real sinners in danger of real judgment—a judgment resting on the awful but real fact that men have rejected the Son of God, whom the Father sent into this world for their salvation. Idealism in poetry and in romance, if you please, but not in the sermon. Not that one should be a pessimist in preaching any more than an optimist; he should, above all else, be a *truthist*. And he is the best friend of humanity who rouses men from their self-complacent dreams, and confronts them with the hard facts of real life and revealed truth.

"We doubt if any Broad Church preacher has yet measured up to the superlative optimism of Professor Henry Drummond. One of his latest discourses lies before us as we write entitled 'A City without a Church,' based on the words of Revelation, 'I John saw the holy city, New Jerusalem, coming down from God out of heaven.' In what does the professor find the realization of this lofty vision? Listen: 'This city, then, which John saw, is none other than your city, the place where you live, as it might be, and as you are to help to make it. It is London, Berlin, New York, Paris, Melbourne, Calcutta,' etc. In a word, the dream is that by sanitation, by drainage, by ventilation, by education, the municipality where we reside is to be transfigured into a veritable city of God on earth. The part that we are to have in effecting this metropolitan evolution is very glowingly set forth. 'Begin with the paper on the walls: make that beautiful; with the air: keep it fresh; with the very drains: make them sweet; with the furniture: see that it is honest. Abolish whatsoever worketh abomination in food, in drink, in luxury, in books, in art; whatsoever worketh a lie in conversation, in social intercourse, in correspondence, in domestic life.' All very admirable; but it is the possible evolution of New York, with its unspeakable Tammany rule above and its Stygian pool of nameless sin beneath, into a Jerusalem the Golden which staggers our imagination.

"And this is what is dreamed of by the preacher: 'What

John saw, we may fairly take it, was the future of all cities. . . .
It was the dream of a new social order, a regenerate humanity,
a purified society, an actual transformation of the cities of the
world into cities of God.'   Now we would not criticize the
amiable philanthropy by which this transformation is proposed
to be effected.   But why not tell exactly what John did see?
If it is worth while to take a text, why not expound it fairly in
its relation to context and connection?   First, John saw the
earthly city, the metropolis of Christendom, as commentators
have generally held, 'Babylon the great,' which has 'become
the habitation of devils, and the hold of every foul spirit, and
a cage of every unclean and hateful bird,' which has made
'all nations to drink of the wine of the wrath of her fornica-
tion.'   But this city, so far from showing any upward development, goes down with a crash under the accumulated
weight of her own abominations.

"And John saw an angel who cried mightily with a strong
voice, saying, 'Babylon the great is fallen, is fallen!'   What
a text is here for one who would preach to the cities of the
nineteenth century!   What an enforcement would be given
to it by citing the long array of sister cities, from Sodom and
Gomorrah to Pompeii and Herculaneum, which have sunk in
like manner beneath the wrath of God against their accumulated sins!   And what a tremendous force the preacher's warning would have, after setting forth this solemn teaching of
revelation and of history, if he were to cry to the cities of to-
day, 'Except ye repent, ye shall all likewise perish'!

"Only after the vision of the fallen city comes the other
of the New Jerusalem descending from God out of heaven.
How significant this expression in our preacher's text!   The
ideal city does not rise up by evolution; it comes down by
revelation.   This is according to the divine way.   When the
race, in spite of all God's teaching, tended steadily downward,
redemption was effected only by 'the Son of man, *who came*

down from heaven.' When natural birth gendered only to sin and death, a great Teacher appeared, saying, ' Except a man be *born from above*, he cannot see the kingdom of God.' And when the history of great cities has repeated itself century after century, in luxury ending in corruption, and corruption ending in doom, God sets before us our only hope of municipal righteousness and holiness in a city *' coming down from God out of heaven.'*

" This teaching is not congenial, but it is convicting. Tell men the exact truth—that when God sent his only Son into the world he received a crucifixion instead of a coronation, and that therein is made manifest the last and most awful revelation of its depravity ; and the tendency of such faithful preaching will be to make men despair of human nature, and, as their only hope, lay hold of the divine nature. Tell men the literal fact of the repeated doom and decay of great cities under the weight of social depravity, and it may lead them to ' look for a city which hath foundations, whose builder and maker is God.' The hard, literal truth is not popular ; optimistic dreams are immensely so. Lord Chesterfield's maxim is universally true : ' If you would make men think well of you, make them think well of themselves.' But how constantly is it the mission of the faithful prophet to make men think meanly of themselves, that they may learn to think well of Christ !

" So far as the actual facts go, there is no evidence that the idyl of social evolution has any foundation. Within the sphere of conscious experience we may speak dogmatically. Saints are not evolved from sinners, except through the new birth ; and New Jerusalems are not evolved from municipal Babylons by improved drainage and sanitation. This is the undoubted fact, and on the whole we deem it more profitable to be occupied in ' truthing it in love' than in dreaming it in optimism."

No doubt it took courage to assert this view in those years,

when the idea of "progress" seemed absolutely to override
the age.   In later years the drift of opinion has been far away
from the speculative optimism formerly prevailing.   This
frame of mind, as Huxley remarked in almost his last message
to the world, "is met with more commonly at the tables of
the healthy and wealthy than in the congregations of the
wise." *   It was enough for Gordon that the New Testament
placed our hopes in something far greater than industrial reform or diffused education, in something more blessed than a
Utopia of production and distribution, where, under the happiest conditions, death would yet yearly slay its millions, and
disease waste and torture its tens of millions, and sin haunt
and trap and destroy.   A New Jerusalem with such citizens
would be the hatefulest of nightmares.   It adds much to our
interest to know that those best qualified to judge concur in
his belief that "our passion for progress is in great part the
product of an infatuation which consists in forgetting the goal
to be aimed at, and in absorbing itself in the pride and delight of each tiny step, one after another." †   The verdict of

* Sheldonian address, " Ethics and Evolution."   " The theory of evolution encourages no millennial anticipations.   If for millions of years our
globe has taken the upward road, yet some time the summit will be reached
and the downward road will be commenced.   The most daring imagination will hardly venture upon the suggestion that the power and intelligence of man can ever arrest the procession of the great year."

† Amiel, " Journal Intime," p. 169.

For example, Bryce says (" American Commonwealth," vol. ii., p. 733):
" In Europe, whose thinkers have seldom been in a less cheerful mood
than they are to-day, there are many who seem to have lost the old faith
in progress ; many who feel, when they recall the experiences of the long
pilgrimages of mankind, that the mountains which stand so beautiful in
the blue distance, touched here by flashes of sunlight and there by shadows
of the clouds, will, when one comes to traverse them, be no Delectable
Mountains, but scarred by storms and seamed by torrents, with wastes of
stone above and marshes stagnating in the valleys."

And Professor Seelye in like vein : " The creed which makes human history is, so far as it expresses itself on such matters, exceedingly dubious as to the way society is moving and as to the distance it has covered toward better things. Froude, Taine, Bryce, Carlyle, Sir Henry Maine, J. E. Thorold Rogers, Professor Seeley, and Mr. John Morley are but a few of those who seem to regard the conception of progress as a mirage. History ends, indeed, in a cul-de-sac from which there is no escape.

But it is just here, Dr. Gordon would say, that in the New Testament scheme despair is transmuted into hope, pessimism into optimism. The escape is from above. As man was redeemed individually by the first coming of Christ, so he is to be redeemed collectively and socially in the second coming. Jesus did not teach us to pray daily, " Thy kingdom come," only to mock us with such travesties on his kingdom as prevail wherever men have built cities and founded states. If it were so, there are not a few who, rather than face a future such as the past, would long to see Huxley's "kindly comet" efface with its hot, shriveling impact this suffering planet. But it is just because the King is coming in the power of his kingdom that we can patiently endure the present controlling democracy of lusts and crowding selfishnesses and shouldering vanities, with its " cries and counter-cries of feud and faction." Even the darkness has its message of cheer. " The shadows point to the dawn. As I wake in the twilight of the morning, I often

---

nature larger makes men at the same time capable of profounder sins ; admitted into a holier sanctuary, they are exposed to the temptation of a greater sacrilege ; awakened to the sense of new obligations, they sometimes lose their simple respect for the old ones ; saints that have resisted the subtlest temptations sometimes begin again, as it were, by yielding without a struggle to the coarsest ; hypocrisy has become tenfold more ingenious and better supplied with disguises ; in short, human nature has inevitably developed downward as well as upward, and if the Christian ages be compared with those of heathenism, they are found worse as well as better, and it is possible to make a question whether mankind has gained on the whole." (" Ecce Homo," p. 351.)

see the glimmer of the street-lamps falling upon the walls of my chamber; but in a little while the lamp-lighter passes by and turns out one after another, leaving the room in deeper darkness than it had been at any time during the whole night. Yet I know that he is only putting out the street-lamps because the sun is about to rise and flood all the heavens with his light. So the darkness heralds the dawn."

In the light of the church's present attitude on this subject, the question of Jesus, " Shall the Son of man, when he cometh, find faith on the earth? " seems prophetically suggestive. For, as the careless world repudiates Christ in his capacity of Saviour, so too, largely, the church denies him in his great and ever-imminent final mission to mankind. " The Syrian stars look down upon a grave from which Jesus never rose." This is the utterance of agnosticism. " The Syrian stars look out from distances through which Jesus shall never come again in person." This is the utterance of the dominant Christianity. If Christ is not risen our faith is vain. Yes, and if Christ is not coming our faith is doubly vain; for the risen Lord has then denied his promises and broken his plighted word. Without this hope we, who are disillusioned of the old watch-cry, " Progress," must indeed be " of all men most miserable."

" We need two motives, memory and hope, to keep the soul in equilibrium. Memory must constantly draw us back to the cross, and hope must constantly attract us forward to the crown, if our hearts are to be kept in even and balanced communion with God. As the waters of the sea are held between two mighty gravitations, the moon now drawing those waters toward itself, and the earth now drawing them back again, thus giving us the ebbing and flowing tide by which our earth is kept clean and healthful, so must the tides of the soul's affection move perpetually between the cross of Christ and the coming of Christ, influenced now by the power of memory, and now by the power of hope."

On this doctrine Gordon's voice was "to unawakened earth the trumpet of a prophecy." Hardly a sermon was preached without some allusion to "the glorious appearing." Never a day passed in which he did not prepare himself for it, in which its hastening was not sought for with prayer. "Yet a little while [how little! how little!], and he that shall come will come." * Those who know him will not soon forget the pathos and tenderness with which he used to introduce the untranslated words (ὅσον, ὅσον) into his reading of the passage. No Christian of the early church ever looked with more assurance for the manifestation of the Lord in the clouds. In his papers were found the following lines, which show what a reality the promise of Christ was to him personally, and how earnestly he cherished the hope of that coming which some day will purple the whole glad east.

(*Translated.*)

I

" Day-dawn and morning star,
    And upward call for me.
Ring out, ye bells of heaven, clear and far,
    When I my Lord shall see.

II

" Caught up to meet the Lord
    With sweep of angel wing,
No winding-sheet for me, or house of sod!
    O death, where is thy sting?

III

" Put out to sea no more;
    Drop anchor, furl the sail:
My storm-tossed bark at last has reached the shore;
    I'm moored within the veil."

* Heb. x. 37.

Advocacy of this doctrine cost him much. It seems to awaken suspicion and lead to estrangement—this great doctrine of hope. "It is not wanted," he used to say, "by a church with millionaire merchants and great universities. But, after all, it was for the assertion of this doctrine that Christ at the last was crucified.* The servant is not greater than his Lord, and should not complain of mere ostracism." Having the almost entire consensus of learned opinion with him as to New Testament teaching on the subject,† he was content to wait until the church should forsake allegorizing and spiritualizing interpretations, and turn back to the hope in its literalness. Meanwhile he always cautioned reasonableness and balance in the treatment of this as of other prophetic teaching.

"There has been more or less fanaticism in time past connected with this doctrine; and that may be a testimony to its truth. A Chinese proverb says, 'Towers are measured by their shadows, and great men by the detraction which follows them.' It is so of doctrines; those that are most compact with truth cast the deepest shadows of superstition. The eschatology of the new-departure theology will cast no shadow; it is so vague and general that the sunlight will easily shine through it. But those who hold the eschatology of the first century must guard it sacredly from all extravagance and excess. The best way is to be very certain about the fact of the Lord's return and very uncertain about the time; to profess no more than the Scriptures profess—that we know neither the day nor the hour when the Son of man cometh."

Nevertheless he believed that the New Testament gave significant intimations as to the occurrences which should pre-

---

* "Hereafter ye shall see the Son of man sitting on the right hand of power, and coming in the clouds of heaven." (Matt. xxvi. 64.)

† Godet, Christlieb, Pfleiderer, Alford, Ellicott, Harnack, Meyer, Oehler, Steir, etc.

cede and attend the second coming. In days when it is the custom to mutilate the gospel and to cast aside all that cannot be made to accord with preconceived opinions, the extent and importance of New Testament prophecy is generally overlooked. Those who dwell on the predictions in Isaiah, in Micah, and in the Psalms, the foregleams of Messiah's coming, will hear little of the passages in Matthew, Romans, Thessalonians, and the Apocalypse premonitory of his return. Eschatology is to most Christians an Ultima Thule, a faraway, acknowledged fact, yet of little interest in every-day life. Voyages thither are the most adventurous which men can make, and travelers returning thence are listened to with incredulous ears.

Yet why should it seem a strange thing that God should send a ray of light through history to guide the children of light? Surely he who lives beyond and above the time relation to which we are subject, and to whom past, present, and future are one, knows the last as perfectly as the first. May he not have sent from Patmos a message to us which those in the Spirit can interpret, just as he has sent from the remotest stars before the dawn of our history pencils of light whose story the spectroscope unseals and reads to us late-born? So Gordon thought. " Fossil sunlight," said he, " is what Herschel named anthracite coal. The vast stores of light poured out upon the globe during past geological ages were consolidated and packed away in the bowels of the earth because this busy nineteenth century, with its myriads of railways and ocean steamers and manufactories, would need them. Have you thought how large a proportion of both Testaments is prediction? And is it therefore of no use to the practical working church of to-day? Nay; the vast profusion of prophetic light, falling upon the minds of the prophets and treasured up in their inspired pages, may soon be needed. And those who are delving in the mines of eschatology, instead of being engaged in an aim-

less and profitless toil, may be providing the church with the
needed warmth for that predicted time when iniquity shall
abound and the love of many wax cold, and with light for the
day foretold by the watchman of Idumea: 'The morning
cometh, and also the night.'" *

The first of these intimations of the Lord's near approach
he found in the universal promulgation of the gospel which is
taking place in our day.   The witnessing churches which are
being planted world over announce the coming King as the
fire-beacons which flashed from hilltop to hilltop round the
whole arc of the Ægean coast proclaimed the fall of Troy and
the return of Agamemnon to Argos.   Here he found the final
and urgent motive for foreign missionary work.   If one believes that the renovation of the world is contingent on the
return of Christ, and that the time of his return will be determined, as far as the church is concerned, by a witnessing of
the gospel of the kingdom among all people, no expression of
doubt as to the preëminent value of missionary work among
the brutalized and pagan peoples of earth can deter one from
any self-sacr'fice which should hasten that consummation.
Now this was what Gordon believed: "We are literally the
people described by Paul as those upon whom the ends of

* He did not believe that the Book of Revelation was written by a
" Deus quidam deceptor " to befool us with strange symbology.   " Its
weird, mysterious pages contain," so he once wrote, "the whole map and
delineation of the church's career from the ascension to the return of the
Lord, but it was left for time to break the seals of this book and to discover its meaning.   It is like the sealed orders given to an admiral which
he is not to open till he is on the sea.   And as now, corresponding to this
chart, headland after headland of prophetic history has been descried, they
have been recognized by the students who have been searching what and
what manner of time the Spirit did signify in penning this prophecy.   And
though they have read no announcement of day or hour upon them, they
have found them displaying the same cautionary signal with which the
church started, ' Behold, I come as a thief.'"

the ages are come.* We are living at the terminal point of the old and the germinal point of the new, and happy shall we be if we know the time of our visitation."

Again, identifying as he did the papacy—"that stupendous spider-web which, reaching from Goa to Acapulco and from heaven to hell, o'ernets the souls and thoughts of men"—with the Antichrist of John, he naturally found in its loss of temporal rule and in its steady decadence suggestions of the approach of him who should destroy it altogether with the "brightness of his coming." † To many such an interpretation will seem fantastic and obsolete, the worn heritage of the wars of the Reformation. This is natural enough in our day when the papacy constitutes a comparatively unimportant figure, whose weakness is acknowledged in its policy of opportunism, and whose existence would be half forgotten were it not for its assiduous advertising by encyclicals. Those who deprecate this Puritan exegesis, however, forget the blackness and vastness of the shadow which this institution has cast, for a space of time covering nearly one fourth of the centuries, from the first dawn of human history. They forget its portentous crimes against light and the inexpressible savagery, lust, and deceit which have here incarnated themselves. No one who has read Gregorovius and Von Ranke, and who remembers the literal portraiture of history, can ever complain of this identification as harsh. Scientific history, with its Bertillon-like methods, has measured and photographed this old offender. So if it is true that the papacy is the only portent in Christian history wicked and forbidding enough to answer to the prophecy of Antichrist, it is conversely true that no theory can explain this grotesque satanophany, this incredible perversion of early Christianity, except that which considers it a predicted and mysteriously predestined device for turning the truth into a lie. Surely there are no naturalistic

* I Cor. x. II.   † 2 Thess. ii. 8.

grounds on which this bar sinister on the church of Christ can be accounted for.   There was nothing, surely, in the content of Christianity as preached by the apostles which could lead one to foresee any such abnormal development.

The movements in Israel, too, filled Gordon with anticipation.   To all thoughtful men the survival of the Jewish race must seem one of the most extraordinary facts in history. The shock of the barbarian invasions was so intense as to result in the complete evaporation of the Greek race; but the Jew has remained, as those preglacial plants and butterflies which still linger on our highest peaks, surviving the ages when ice covered whole continents and destroyed all other life. And what centuries of brutal persecution he has since undergone!   Greek orthodoxy and Roman Catholicism have been the ceaselessly turning millstones to bray and pulverize him. Yet he not merely survives, an indestructible residuum in the retort of history; his emergence into the place of leadership is one of the striking facts of present-day life.   The names of David Strauss, Mendelssohn, Heine, Marx, Neander, Gambetta, Halévy, Rothschild, De Hirsch, Liebknecht, Rubinstein, Disraeli, Bebel, Stendhal, Ricardo, Darmesteter, Franzos, Goldmark, Auerbach, Joseph Israels, Emin Bey, Bernard Weiss, Meyerbeer, Lasalle, Mendelijeff, Edersheim, the Saphirs, Palakof, Castelar, Blum Pasha, and a host of others, are suggestive of the power still latent in the race. For a Christian to doubt the extraordinary future in store for the people of the old covenant seems, in the light of the eleventh of Romans, wholly inexplicable.   For him to question it in these days of Jewish renaissance is wilful blindness.   To think that a race with such a past and of so great present vigor is to be forever condemned to play the humiliating rôle of pawnbroker and vender of old clothing to those of the outer court argues a mind singularly impervious to the significance of current events.   "Those who are opposed to millenarianism," wrote Gordon, "seem to consider Israel as a factor in God's providence utterly eliminated, nevermore to emerge. When they hear any discourse on the subject of the conversion or regathering of Israel, they consider it quite as absurd as it would be for one to suggest the revival of stage-coaches and hand-weaving after a half-century of railroads and looms. The gathering of immense wealth into the hands of the Jew, as though in preparation for some vast demand upon his resources soon to be made; the control which he has gained of the secular press in European countries; his rapid ascendancy in the sphere of politics and philosophy all over the world; his complicity in the revolutionary and antichristian movements which are now agitating and alarming the nations; and, lastly, his expulsion from the countries where he has dwelt and his visible regathering into the land of his ancient habitation— these are significant premonitions of a stupendous and long-predicted event: the removal of the veil from blinded Israel and the looking upon him whom they have pierced."

Gordon found, as he looked with straining eyes into the approaching years, a sort of historical barometer in the Jewish race. Their present rapid rise he felt to be indicative of a fair morning ahead. The organization of the Chovevi Zion, with its hundreds of thousands of members of all classes, from the Montefiores and Goldsmids to the poorest Polish and Rumanian schnorrers, and the expressed intention of its constituency of purchasing and repeopling Palestine, filled him with quivering interest. At various times he set apart in his church special days of prayer for the Jews. For the somewhat noisy "reformed" rabbis, who revile their own great past and frivolously throw aside the promises of future national restoration, he often expressed his repugnance. But to the poor enmeshed Talmudist he was ever ready to stretch out his hand. His interest in the race was not merely exegetical. Many refugees from eastern Europe—outcasts too frequently, with the unlovely traits of the "hungry Greekling" of the Lower Empire—he helped at his door or in their own poor homes.

The restitution of Israel and its grafting in again he looked for as one of the great events consequent upon Christ's coming.   But the advent day is also the day of the resurrection— "that blessed last of deaths, when death is dead."   Here, as before, his beliefs were those of the early church untainted by Hellenicisms.   Those two errors of an earthly theology, "that the world is the Christian's home and that the grave is the Christian's hope," were unqualifiedly rejected.   To an exposition of the last verse of the eleventh of Hebrews he adds this conclusion, which in its connection may seem somewhat mystical, but which is in its main teaching scriptural:

"Bodily perfection as well as spiritual perfection is included in the idea of complete sanctification.   As the earlier martyrs must wait for the later martyrs before they can receive their full consummation of blessedness, so must the renewed soul wait for the renewed body in order that it may be perfected. The radical error in our consideration of the subject has been that we have fixed our attention entirely upon the spiritual part of man, as though this alone were the 'I' in which his personality consists.   Because our eschatology has so generally overlooked this great fact and substituted the doctrine of the immortality of the soul for the scriptural doctrine of the resurrection of the man, the eye has been fixed on death as the object of hope.   And because our dying is held to release the soul from its gross environment of flesh, this event has been made the goal of the spirit's perfection.   But is death the great sanctifier?   No; it is only when the glorified soul is united to the glorified body that we shall awake satisfied in his likeness—an instantaneous photograph of Christ wrought in his members—the predestined purpose of redemp-tion, that we should be conformed to the image of his Son, consummated at last in a flash of advent glory.

" Those who have not watched the trend of opinion on this point have little idea of the extent to which even in orthodox ranks the Swedenborgian notion of elimination has supplanted the primitive doctrine of resurrection. Instead of holding that at the sound of the last trump God ' will quicken your mortal bodies by his Spirit that dwelleth in you,' it is becoming very common to maintain that at death a spiritual, incorporeal substance is released from the body. Thus one's death is his resurrection, since in that event an imprisoned spiritual body breaks its shell and comes forth like the butterfly from the chrysalis. It is not, therefore, the angel's trumpet calling the dead from the grave that ushers in the resurrection, but the sexton's bell tolling the dead to the grave. This notion seems to result largely from that ultra-spiritualism which would rule the body out of all recognition in the work of redemption. There is a kind of Manichean contempt for flesh and bones, and a feeling that it is gross materialism to assign them any place in the glorified life."

CHAPTER XXIV

IN LABORS ABUNDANT

Address before the Evangelical Alliance, 1890—Church unity—Personal experience of faith healing—Work in Chicago, 1890 and 1893—The World's Fair campaign—Rabinowitz

IN the winter of 1890 the Evangelical Alliance met in Boston. It fell to Dr. Gordon to give the address of welcome to the delegates. A portion of the address, illustrating his opinions on certain of the important questions with which the conference had to deal, we transcribe here.

After a few introductory sentences on the significance of these coöperative religious movements, he said:

"I have therefore few tears to shed with those who are weeping over 'the scandal of a divided Christendom,' as the phrase is. True, a church divided into manifold sects is not the ideal church; it is not the church which our Lord inaugurated in the beginning, and it is not the church for which he prayed in the end. But as the strength of Christ is made perfect in our weakness, so, I doubt not, the unity of Christ will finally be made perfect through our divisions. If a divided church meant a divided Christ, we might well lament and weep over the sects of Christendom; but if these sects hold the Head, this cannot be the case. As a handful of quicksilver flung to the earth breaks into a hundred separate globules reflecting a full-orbed sun, so, though by disruptions and revolutions and reformations the church has been broken into a hundred sects, each sect may hold in the bosom of its faith a full-orbed Christ.

"Therefore I beg you to reflect that for the last hundred years our ascended Lord has been showing what he can do through a divided church; thus bringing higher glory to himself out of what many regard as a most lamentable evil. 'Divide and conquer' is a maxim of skilful generalship. What if our great commander has said to his church, 'Be divided and conquer'? I cannot otherwise translate the providence of the nineteenth century.

"The door of every nation under heaven was to be opened during this hundred years; but the experience of all history proves that had the church been outwardly one, a conservative organic unity, holding all its parts together and moving them according to a uniform law of action, she would have been unequal to the task of entering these doors and conquering these nations.

"But look again. These sects have put into the field one hundred and forty-six foreign missionary societies, which are now operating along various lines and by divers methods for giving the gospel to the world. By the division of labor providentially arranged the Scriptures have been translated into two hundred and eighty dialects, the work of translation having progressed so rapidly that, as we close the ninth decade of this century, we find the Bible accessible to nine tenths of the entire human family.

"Observe, too, how the Christian forces have been deployed, as though an invisible commander had been arranging for his final campaign. There are forty missionary societies operating in India, thirty-three in China, thirty-four in Africa. Is there any likelihood that there would be a tenth of this number in the three fields, or a hundredth of the men whom they employ, if there were only one great and all-inclusive church to which the evangelization of the world was intrusted? Take the Dark Continent, for example. Thirty-three regiments of the Protestant army have completely invested it, as though all ready to move inward for its final conquest. ' The nineteenth century has made the African free,' says Victor Hugo; 'the twentieth is to make him a man.' But he cannot be a man except he is made acquainted with the divine Man, who alone can strike the fetters from his soul as he struck the chains from his body. ' Is Christ divided?' asked the apostle centuries ago. And from hundreds of missionary fields the answer comes to-day, ' Yes, divided only that he may be the more completely distributed to a starving world.' And over all we seem to see our risen Lord, holding in his pierced hands the fragments of his mystical body, the church, and saying to the hungry nations, ' *This is my body broken for you.*'

"But one may say, 'Yes; but think of the wreck of doctrine and the discord of faith which have been brought about by this disruption of the church. True; but what of the gains which have come out of this great loss? In the disintegration of the church a vast amount of free thinking and cheerless speculat on has been set free, even as the cold is liberated by the breaking up of a solid block of ice. But the question is, Has the ultimate temperature of Christianity been lowered or raised by the process? It is a magnificent answer which Professor Döllinger makes to those who point to the successive waves of deadly rationalism which have s vept over Germany in the last three hundred years, as a convincing proof of the criminal evil of that church disruption brought about by Luther and his fellow-reformers. Admitting the evil of the rationalism, Dr. Döllinger replies that, nevertheless, nine tenths of all the best exegesis and the best theology of Germany has been contributed by this Protestant church which Luther led out from Rome. Here is a confirmation of the same idea of disunity working out the highest unity. The full beauty of a ray of light never appears till it has been broken in the prism. So the harmony and glory of divine truth is destined to be made fully manifest only through the refraction which it has suffered in its sectarian divisions."

The address closed with the following appeal in behalf of the poor and of the oppressed:

"Upon the great questions that are now agitating society we find a characteristic temptation belonging to the olden age, one that was recorded concerning our Lord Jesus Christ— 'Command that these stones be made bread.' The great art of the adversary is to turn us Christians from soul-winners into bread-winners, to take the lower stratum of society and grind it up between the upper and nether millstone of power and capital, so that God may have to say again, 'Have all the workers of iniquity no knowledge? who eat up my people as they eat bread, and call not upon the Lord?' '*Command that these stones be made bread.*' Our Lord Jesus Christ speaks just the opposite word: 'God is able of these stones to raise up children unto Abraham.' Stones they are, rough and uncouth, but they can be turned into living stones, builded together for an habitation of God through the Spirit. Stones they are: but under the discipline of God's hand they can be made into corner-stones, polished after the similitude of a palace. Stones they are: but in the hands of the great Lapidary they may be made to adorn his breastplate and shine with nameless beauty—topaz and beryl and jacinth, each giving a different color to set forth the glory of the Lord."

In the fall of this year Dr. Gordon underwent certain personal experiences which were to him ever after as a divine imprimatur upon the doctrine of healing by faith which he advocated. These experiences were not indeed the first of their sort. Frequently in his letters references are made to relief from serious sicknesses obtained in this way.

"I had a sudden attack of the grippe," he writes during an

epidemic of that disease—"high fever, chills, sore throat, pain in bones, headache, all coming on at three in the morning, when I had retired perfectly well. But I determined that Satan should not get the advantage, committed the case to the great Physician, and determined, in spite of much advice, to preach on Sunday. So I did, and found no trouble. All the difficulty is gone, praise the Lord!"

And at another time:

"Many are sick among us of influenza. I was taken violently, but I called upon the Lord, and though there was a little time of waiting, when the cure came it swept the trouble away, so that not a trace remained behind. This is contrary to common experience with this disease. But my Physician made short work of the case."

In the case to which we now refer the sickness was of so radical a character and the cure so complete and effectual that the fact of divine intervention can hardly be doubted. For several years he had been subject to a severe and agonizing neuralgia of the solar plexus. The attacks, occasional at first, became, as time passed, more and more frequent and more and more distressing. Each one was followed by days of complete exhaustion. Medical applications, rest, in fact, everything suggested, were tried without any permanent relief. In the winter of 1890 Mr. Moody had arranged for an exchange of work with him, it being provided that he should lecture in the Chicago Training-school for one month. The neuralgic spasm, which was due now every second month, had been endured, and no further trouble was for the present expected. A few days, however, before the time appointed for starting another terrible and wholly unlooked-for attack completely prostrated the sufferer. A conference was held, and it was decided that the Chicago project must be abandoned. The physician present declared his conviction that the disease was now chronic, that the intervals between the seizures were likely to narrow, and that the continuance of life was but a question of time and of the natural resources of physique. At the earnest request of the patient appeal was now carried up to God himself. The sick man was anointed according to the commandment. His own prayers were accompanied by those of the few Christian friends about the bedside. Shortly after he rose up dressed, and went to his study in the room below. The pain had somewhat subsided, yet it still ran strong in undercurrent. As he stood in front of the mantel, leaning and resting on it, he was suddenly seized by an awful paroxysm—the most intense that he had ever experienced. It was as if the demon of sickness were tearing him grievously for the last time—for it was the last time. Never again did it enter the precincts of that body. The following week Gordon left for Chicago. For a whole month he lectured daily to the students, preparing the lectures as he proceeded, preaching twice or thrice each Sunday, conducting evening meetings during the week, and writing in the snatches of leisure his little book, "Faith—the First Thing in the World." Four more years passed before his death, years of extraordinary burden-bearing. Not the slightest intimation of the old chronic difficulty ever intruded. Never in all his life had he such a wealth of physical resource wherewith to perform the tasks laid on him, and accompanying physical healing there entered into him a new tide of spiritual life and blessing.

The summer of '93 found Dr. Gordon again in Chicago, lecturing to the students of the Bible Institute and preaching in the great meetings which Mr. Moody had organized in that city. These meetings were designed to reach the millions visiting the Exposition. Four theaters, five tents, and many churches were jammed every evening and several times on Sunday with strangers from all parts of the earth. Thirty-eight preachers, evangelists, and singers instructed the multitudes, while several hundred students in residence coöperated in an endless variety of house-to-house and highway-and-hedge effort. The Fair was finally closed on Sunday, after an exhibition on the part of the managers, upon the shamelessness of which there is no need to dilate here. The people refused to go in sufficient numbers to warrant Sunday opening. But the evangelistic services secured a Sabbath attendance of more than thirty-five thousand and an entire weekly attendance of not less than one hundred thousand. Even the great showman Forepaugh was obliged to capitulate to Mr. Moody. The circus tents, which had been opened for Sunday amusement, were handed over without charge and forthwith filled by ten thousand people.

For a whole month Gordon preached to hungry thousands, teaching all the while at the school on Institute Place. The influence of this work of Mr. Moody and his assistants was very far-reaching, and important in the life of thousands. The attention of the press and of the public was of course turned upon the " Parliament of Religions," with its cardinal's tea-gown, its shaven-pated bonzes, and its facile sub-truthful Calcutta babus. This to the novelty-seekers was the most important " religious " feature of that summer in Chicago. But of this heterogeneous assembly most men who know the East— the obscenities of Benares, the linga-worship of Muttra, the degraded beggary of Mandalay, to say nothing of present-day Islamism in Armenia—cherish convictions not flattering either to its promoters or to its participants. Gordon himself regarded the proceedings as thoroughly misleading in their appraisement of non-Christian systems, and as gratuitously disheartening to the representatives of our Lord among the heathen. The strangers whom he welcomed and with whom he consorted were of a very different type. None interested him more than a visitor from Bessarabia, Joseph Rabinowitz, whom Delitzsch considered the most remarkable Jewish convert since Saul of

Tarsus. In a few notes Gordon describes his conversations with this Israelite of the new covenant.

" Going to Chicago in July last for a month's service in connection with Mr. Moody's World's Fair evangelization campaign, we found ourselves at our lodgings placed in the next room to a Russian guest, whose name was not yet told us. Hearing in the evening the strains of subdued and fervent Hebrew chanting, we inquired who our neighbor might be, and learned that it was one Joseph Rabinowitz, of Russia. Thus, to our surprise, we found ourselves next neighbor to one whom we would have crossed the ocean to see, with only a sliding door now between us. Introduction followed, and then three weeks of study and communion together concerning the things of the kingdom, the memory of which will not soon depart.

" It seemed to us, as we talked day after day with this Israelite without guile and heard him pour out his soul in prayer, that we had never before witnessed such ardor of affection for Jesus and such absorbing devotion to his person and glory. We shall not soon forget the radiance that would come into his face as he expounded the Messianic psalms at our morning or evening worship, and how, as here and there he caught a glimpse of the suffering or glorified Christ, he would suddenly lift his hands and his eyes to heaven in a burst of admiration, exclaiming, with Thomas after he had seen the nail-prints, ' My Lord and my God.' So saturated was he with the letter as well as with the spirit of the Hebrew Scriptures that to hear him talk one might imagine it was Isaiah or some other prophet of the old dispensation. ' What is your view of inspiration? ' we once asked him, in order to draw him out concerning certain much-mooted questions of our time. ' My view is,' he said, holding up his Hebrew Bible, ' that this is the Word of God; the Spirit of God dwells in it. When I read

it I know that God is speaking to me, and when I preach it
I say to the people, "Be silent, and hear what Jehovah will
say to you." As for comparing the inspiration of Scripture
with that of Homer or of Shakespeare, it is not a question of
degree, but of kind. Electricity will pass through an iron bar,
but it will not go through a rod of glass, however beautiful
and transparent, because it has no affinity for it. So the Spirit
of God dwells in the Word of God, the Holy Scriptures, because these are his proper medium, but not in Homer or
Shakespeare, because he has no affinity with these writings.'

"'Do you know what questioning and controversies the
Jews have kept up over Zechariah xii. 10?' he asked one day.
'"They shall look upon me (ת א) whom they have pierced."
They will not admit that it is Jehovah whom they pierced.
Hence the dispute about the *whom;* but do you notice that this
word is simply the first and last letters of the Hebrew alphabet,
Aleph, Tav? Do you wonder, then, that I was filled with
awe and astonishment when I opened to Revelation i. 7, 8,
and read these words of Zechariah, now quoted by John,
"Behold, he cometh with clouds; and every eye shall see
him, and they also which pierced him;" and then heard the
glorified Lord saying, "I am Alpha and Omega"? Jesus
seemed to say to me, "Do you doubt who it is whom you
pierced? I am the Aleph Tav, the Alpha Omega, Jehovah,
the Almighty."'

"Nothing could be more thrilling and pathetic than to hear
this latter-day prophet of Israel dilate on the blessedness and
glory of his nation when it shall at last be brought back into
favor and fellowship with God. 'The Gentile nations cannot
come to their highest blessing till then, nor can our rejected
and crucified Messiah see of the travail of his soul and be
satisfied till his kinsmen according to the flesh shall own and
accept him.' Then, with a dramatic fervor and pathos impossible to describe, he made the following beautiful com-

ment: 'Jesus, the glorified head of the church, is making up his body now. Think you that my nation will have no place in that body? Yes; the last and most sacred place. When from India's and China's millions, and from the innumerable multitudes of Africa, and the islands of the sea the last Gentile shall have been brought in and Christ's body made complete, there will still be left a place for little Israel; she will fill up the hole in his side—that wound which can never be closed till the nation which made it is saved.' "

The deep affection which grew up between the two may be measured by the following brief note:

"Kishenev, March 11, 1895.

"DEAR MRS. GORDON: The most sad news in the paper, 'The Christian Herald,' about the death of your dear husband, my unforgotten friend, Dr. A. J. Gordon, reached me this morning. I was so overwhelmed with grief that for half an hour I could not keep back the tears. My wife and daughter, seeing me so broken-hearted, could not help shedding tears also, saying to each other, ' See how he loved him.'

"I assure you, dear Mrs. Gordon, that, far away over the ocean at Kishenev in South Russia, there is a heart deeply sympathizing with you in your bereavement, and lamenting with all those who personally knew dear Dr. Gordon and experienced his gentle Christian love. I shall never forget those happy moments we spent together in Chicago. I remember well with what joy he looked forward to the restoration of Israel, to Jesus' appearing in glory. . . . He is now in the bosom of Abraham enjoying the nearness of his Lord Jesus, whom he served so faithfully.

"JOSEPH RABINOWITZ."

CHAPTER XXV

FOR THE HEALING OF THE NATIONS

Work among the Jews—The Chinese mission at Clarendon Street—Incidents—The transition to a spiritual church life

DR. GORDON had, as has been suggested in the discussion of his theology, an especial interest in the future of Israel. Work among the Jews ever appealed to him, and was carried on with much vigor in his church. In the letters which follow we get a vivid impression of the character of this work. They are like leaves from that part of the Acts which describe the great apostle's experiences among the contentious, "stiffnecked" children of the synagogue in Derbe, in Lystra, and in Thessalonica.

"We had a great day yesterday—house filled to the doors both morning and evening. The special feature of the evening was the baptism of our second Hebrew convert. Fifty Jews at least were present, and at the close a large number came into the after-meeting. The Christian Hebrews bore witness for Christ; then the unconverted Hebrews began to get up. One vehemently declared that Christians hated the Jews and had always persecuted them. I tried in vain to show him that those who persecute are not Christian, but antichristian. B——was there, having just returned from Russia. As a Russian Jew, he put in some heavy shots in the disputation with these objectors. For a half-hour they contended out of the Scriptures whether this is Christ."

Again: " The Jewish work continues to be of great interest —one more confessed Christ last evening. The Hebrews of the North End are greatly excited over these accessions to Christ. Last Thursday night they assaulted Solomon as he was coming out of the hall. They called a meeting two weeks ago to see what could be done to resist the aggressions. The inclosed circular in Hebrew contains the call."

" I am just home from prayer-meeting and am moved to write a word. It was a wonderful meeting to-night, the subject being prayer for Israel. You would have believed the set time to favor Zion had come had you been there. One German Jew, a recent arrival from Europe, prayed powerfully in German. S—— followed in broken English. Then H—— S——, who is to unite with us next church meeting, spoke. He is a little fellow, born in Boston, but he spoke like a patriarch for wisdom and solidity. It was really wonderful how he set forth Christ and magnified his grace. Then a new man, quite prominent among the Hebrews, Niles tells me, rose to avow his determination to follow Christ. Perhaps the day of the Gentiles is drawing to a close. It really came to me very powerfully that it might be so, as I called in vain for confessors among our people, and then saw these rise so readily to own Jesus, for I know all that this involves. Persecution is breaking out bitterly. Several new-comers among us spoke of their surprise and delight at hearing us talk about the conversion of Israel, Dr. N——, Mr. McE——, and myself having taken up the subject. It is such a new and surprising thing to many. Alas, what do they lose who know nothing of this subject and connected truths! Had we not best begin to pray that the veil be removed from the faces of Gentile Christians, especially ministers of the gospel who know nothing of this theme? "

A long list of uncouth, monosyllabic names at the end of the church directory attests the patient interest which the Clarendon Street Church has taken in the Chinese of the city.

A school was organized many years ago for these strangers.
Its proportions grew rapidly. More than one hundred laundry-
men from all parts of Boston and from adjacent towns meet
each Sabbath. Of the twenty-five or more who were received
as members, Gordon once said: "They have proved superior
in most respects to any class of foreigners that has come
among us. Instead of being a burden to the church, it is their
disposition to take their place as burden-bearers with their
brethren in Christ. As they are exceedingly industrious and
thrifty in their business, so they are very hearty and generous
in their gifts for the work of the Lord. The first man who
was converted to Christ wrote out a statement of his conversion
and his views of the Christian doctrine. I have that document
in my possession. He wrote it without the aid of anybody.
In all the fifty years in which the church has been in existence,
we have never received an account of a conversion or a statement of the doctrines of Christianity so complete and explicit
and satisfactory as the one which this Chinaman wrote out on
entering the church."

For these Asiatics Dr. Gordon ever had a deep concern.
In his late years he frequently remarked that if he were to begin
life anew it would be as a missionary to the East. It was with
peculiar delight, therefore, that he brought these men into the
church of Christ. None will forget with what significant solemnity he used to repeat before his congregation of Americans,
when baptizing "these from the land of Sinim," the words of
the Lord, "And I say unto you, that many shall come from
the east and the west, and shall sit down with Abraham, and
Isaac, and Jacob, in the kingdom of heaven: but the sons of
the kingdom shall be cast forth into the outer darkness."

To all with whom he came in contact, no matter how ac-
cidentally, he ministered. "Returning one morning from an
errand," writes a correspondent in Waterville, Me., where
Gordon had held a ten days' conference during the summer

of '94, "he called at our house and said, 'I think that the Chinaman down here on the street is interested in religion, and I wish you would speak to him.' No amount of care and labor for the conference and for the whole world could drive from his mind and heart a sense of the need of the individual soul. He saw in the Celestial stranger laundryman 'my neighbor.'"

Many things have occurred which illustrate the fruitfulness of this branch of church work, and which conclusively refute the common assertion that these "stolid, tricky Asiatics" are beyond the reach of the gospel. One circumstance connected with the opening of the school is of special interest. Jure Sim, who, as first member of the church, gave such an intelligent exposition of doctrine, had been taught in the Scriptures by a lady before the Chinese Mission at Clarendon Street had been started. Soon after entering into membership he became convinced of the advantages which a Chinese school in the church would have. Without consulting any one, he set apart a week in which to pray that the Lord might establish such a school. Three times in the day he went by himself to press this request. Day after day followed without answer. On Friday noon, when he knelt down—so he explained afterward—something seemed to say to him, "Jure Sim, you must not pray for that any more. You have been answered." In the evening and on the following morning the same words were unaccountably impressed upon his mind. Shortly after he had begun work in his laundry Saturday morning, the mail-carrier stepped in and handed him a letter. On opening it he found a large red card, on which was printed, in English on one side and in Chinese upon the other, "A mission school for Chinese will be opened in the Clarendon Street Church, Sunday, March 4, 1887."

That conversion is much the same experience among all peoples can be clearly seen from the following:

Chin Tong came into the school a raw, uncouth, unresponsive Chinaman.   Unlike most of his fellows, he was in his person very unclean and unsavory.   The teacher to whom he was assigned worked with him month after month without making upon him the least apparent impression.   One Sunday the text, " If we confess our sins, he is faithful and just to forgive us our sins, and to cleanse us from all unrighteousness," was marked in his New Testament and assigned for the next lesson.   When he turned up the following Sabbath the verse was almost obliterated from the page by the incessant movement of his finger back and forth over the lines.   One word alone puzzled him, the word " cleanse."   However, this was easily explained to one whose daily work was over tubs and ironing-boards.   During the next week a young man called twice at the teacher's home, but would not leave his name.   When the hour for the Chinese school came round again the teacher took her seat in the accustomed place.   Presently a man in Occidental dress entered and sat down beside her.   It was Chin Tong, but so changed as not to be recognizable.   His cue was off, his hair shingled, his long finger-nails pared, his face clean as a new coin, his clothes new and well cared for.   The text had done its work.   " Jesus Christ make me clean inside and outside," he explained.   Heart, mind, and person had been transformed.

These Chinese Christians have organized a Y. M. C. A. among themselves, hiring a house near the church for its permanent quarters.   They have, too, a lot in Mount Hope Cemetery, where Christians can be buried apart without the usual concomitants of heathen funerals.   Some years ago one of their number died.   Through some misunderstanding the pastor of the church was absent, and the funeral exercises arranged for had to be omitted.   When they had gotten back to the Chinese Home they fell to talking about their dead friend.   Every one regretted that Lue Pen should have been laid away " as a dog " without a Christian service.   They determined, therefore, to hold a little meeting by themselves over the grave. Four of them accordingly went out the next day to the distant cemetery with an armful of flowers, and, gathering about the grave, read the account of the resurrection of Jesus, and of the walk to Emmaus, above the fresh mound. Then all knelt down, and in turn commended their friend and themselves to the Lord of the resurrection.

Yee Gow was one of the older men in the school, a slow, good, blundering fellow whom none could help liking and half pitying. One winter he fell sick and passed rapidly into consumption. He was carried to the hospital, but not much could be done for him. He was a Christian, and was frequently visited by his Chinese brethren. On the last day of his life he was found by Wong Tsin Chong, who had come to pray with the weak and disheartened sufferer. Wong did his best to cheer him with hopes of heaven. The old man did not respond with much eagerness at first. "I don't know whether I want to go there, after all," he reiterated. "I won't know anybody there; nobody will care for me." "Never mind, Yee Gow," was the reply; "I shall be there before long; and when I get there I will look first for the Lord Jesus, and when I find him I'll bring him to you." The old man was comforted and closed his eyes in peace.

"Wong Tsin Chong," writes Gordon, "whom we call 'our Chinese deacon,' so faithful is he in looking after his 'country-people' and fellow-Christians in the church, is a remarkable man. No Sunday passes without finding him preaching the gospel to his countrymen in the Chinese quarter. As he stands in the street speaking in his native tongue, crowds of English-speaking people will often gather. Then, changing his language, he will plead with these to be reconciled to Christ. 'What kind of Christian?' do you ask? Would that there were scores of such! His sole thought day and night is how to reach his 'country-people' at home and abroad. . . . For some years he has provided for the maintenance of a native missionary to preach to the people of his own village in China. Association with Christians is a delight to him. When he stood up to receive the right hand of fellowship on admission into the church, the pride and satisfaction with which he accepted such high honor were visible in his entire bearing. At the next communion, when other members were to be received, Wong innocently took his place in the line again. Though an unusual thing to repeat the ceremony, we did not pass him by. ' How I like this church! They shake hands every month.' said he. Certainly we ought to merit his encomium by more hearty and unfailing good fellowship with those who come among us.

" At the last four occasions of admitting members into the church a Chinaman was among the number each time. Noticing this with surprise and gratification, we said, ' Wong, isn't it remarkable that we have had a Chinaman on each of the last four Sundays?' With the most radiant look he replied, ' Not at all remarkable. I asked the Lord for ten this year; you have got four of them. Hold fast and you will get the other six before the year is over.' O Chinaman, I have not found so great faith, no, not among our American Christians!

" It is touching and cheering to hear them pray and sing and expound Scripture and exhort one another, all in such fervent and orderly manner, in their own weekly prayer-meetings. A few of these expositions will illustrate the sincerity and intelligence of their Christianity.

" Yeung, in a prayer-meeting talk on ' The Word of God is not Bound,' said : ' The Word of God binds ; it is not bound. We were astray, alienated from God. It bound us back to him. It binds our lives by its influence. Bind the Word of God? The Bible says it is a sword. Can you bind a sword? Will it not cut through the cords you attempt to bind it with ? Bind the Word of God? The Bible calls it light. Can you bind

light? Will it regard your cords and fetters? Can you keep it
in a room? Can you keep it from shining? It will penetrate
everywhere. The gospel will spread; man cannot prevent it.
Bind a sword, bind light; then may you bind the Word of
God.'

"Cheung Yule P'eng said: 'When a man and wife have been
married for eight or ten years without having any children, and
at last a child comes, they are full of joy. But if, after a while,
they find that the child is deaf or lame or blind or dumb, their
joy is turned to sorrow. So when I hear of baptisms now and
then—six or eight joining the church—I am rejoiced. But
alas! sometimes my joy is weakened and I am filled with
sorrow. Why? Some of these members are dumb or blind
or deaf or lame. How? Why, when a man becomes a
Christian and doesn't speak to others about Jesus he is dumb;
when a Christian doesn't read his Bible he is blind; when he
will not listen to advice and instruction, or when he sleeps in
church, he is deaf; when he neglects the meetings of the
brethren and fails to come to church on the Lord's days he is
lame. I rejoice to hear of baptisms, but how often converts
disappoint our hopes and turn out but blind or deaf or dumb
or lame children!'"

The local missions of the church included, in addition to the
work among Jews and Chinese, a mission for colored people,
which became in time self-sustaining; the work of the Industrial Home, administered largely by members of the Clarendon
Street Church; an important rescue work for women; the various evangelistic enterprises of the young people at the wharves,
car stables, and hospitals; and the evangelistic work of the
deacons in weak churches. To the participation in foreign
work reference has already been made. In addition to the
support tendered the missions of the denomination, an independent mission in Corea was organized by a member of the
church, with five workers in the field. This number is to be

increased shortly.   On the walls of the vestry, where the
prayer-meetings are held, are inscribed the names of missionaries and evangelists connected with the church.   The number
varies from time to time, averaging anywhere from ten to
twenty.

Thus was the church transformed, until the formal, self-
contained congregation had become "a little kingdom of God
in itself," unobtrusive, but none the less aggressive in its multifarious religious agencies.   It had now been brought into a
condition of spiritual equipment and organization; new motives
had replaced the old.   The saving of souls had taken the pre-
eminent place.   The birth of this new ideal had been with
much labor and toil, but its development was the salvation
of the church.   For twenty-five years this purpose was emphasized week after week.   In an address at Minneapolis,
in 1887, Dr. Gordon drew a contrast, which is strikingly suggestive to one who reads between the lines, of the life of old
and new Clarendon Street: "Ask social scientists concerning
the perils which threaten our republic, and among these they
will mention the out-populating power of the foreign races.
They tell us that negro and Celt are multiplying so rapidly that
there is danger that our native stock may be swallowed up by
them.   And as the counterpart to this, they admonish us that
the Americans, as they grow rich and aristocratic, evade the
responsibilities of child-bearing, and so put the Saxon and
Puritan stock to a constant disadvantage in the competition of
races.   I mention this only that I may dwell upon the analogous
spiritual fact.   As soon as Zion travailed she brought forth
children.   It is the law of God that renewed souls should come
forth through the birth-pangs of prayer and faith in the church
of Christ.   But the tendency is for the church, as soon as it
becomes wealthy and aristocratic, to shirk the responsibilities
of child-bearing, preferring the luxuries of worship, the music,
the oratory, and the architecture of an elegant sanctuary, to

the bringing forth and nursing of children. Fashionable religion frowns on prayer-meeting exhortations as sanctified baby talk, and on simple gospel preaching as weak pulpit milk, and on lifting the hand and rising for prayers as nursery exercises in which cultivated Christians do not care to engage. But the church that knows its calling as the mother and nurse of souls will use all these things because God has enjoined milk for babes, and the rudiments of faith for children. All honor to the church that accepts the function of child-bearing and nursing; but no honor to that church which prefers barrenness to maternity in order that she may be at ease in Zion. May God save us from this temptation, which culture and social position are constantly forcing upon us. It is the certain precursor of doctrinal unsoundness as well as of spiritual blight. I can look out upon scores of churches in my own city, planted in orthodoxy but now fallen from the faith, and I find that their history for the most part verifies this maxim. Their doctrinal looseness began in spiritual laziness; it was when they ceased to bring forth children that they began to bring forth heresies."

" Christianity is both a cement and a solvent," says Vinet. The preaching of spiritual truths and the insistence on spiritual methods had a sifting effect, the results of which were twofold. The restless, the worldly, the unfriendly, gradually dropped off and went elsewhere. This was in some ways a great relief to the pastor. Indeed, during a period of friction he prayed earnestly a whole summer long for the departure of a leading member whose presence he felt to be fatal to the church's best interests. In the autumn this man left in a most unexpected way without trouble or irritation. On the other hand, there gathered around the church a large clientele of earnest, devout souls, whose views of church life corresponded with those set forth from the pulpit. Hundreds were converted, too, bringing with them the vigor which goes with fresh and powerful religious experiences. For this was no church built up by attracting the comfortable and well dressed from other churches with oratory and subtle, dexterous rhetoric. There was here no flinching from the hard realities, no avoidance of uncomfortable truths and unpopular causes, no magnanimous (though sophistical) tolerance of all parties and all beliefs however opposed they might be. Into these walls were built all manner of rejected material—the drunkard, the outcast, the vagabond, the opium-slave. As the sun distils and draws to itself from the vilest tarn the fleeciest clouds, so the Spirit of God carried on his redeeming work in Clarendon Street Church. The impulses gained vitalized, too, the Baptist churches of eastern Massachusetts. For years Clarendon Street stood as a religious clearing-house between the city and surrounding towns. Young people from the country and from the Provinces would spend five or ten years here, and then, when married, go to establish homes about suburban churches—stanch, reliable men and women with the stamp of the city church upon them.

Let us go into the church of the nineties. Here is no longer a select congregation of pewholders. No longer do the humming-birds of fashion flit up the aisles. No longer does the usher distribute strangers with furtive glances at the numberless gaps in the congregation. Now the rich and the poor meet together; the Lord is the Maker of them all. We are upborn by the weighty sense which a great concourse of people gives, especially of people of like interests and motives, of a unanimity of life and spirit. A noble type of Christianity is regnant in these hearts. What cordiality, what affection, what mutual forbearance and assistance among the members! John Stuart Mill remarked cynically that it could hardly be said now, as it was said by those of pagan Rome, "Behold how these Christians love one another." Yet this could be claimed without exaggeration of the people whom Gordon left behind him in the church of his training. For

CLARENDON STREET CHURCH.

had he not explained to them the source of unity and love?
" ' If two of you shall agree on earth as touching anything that
they shall ask,' " said he, quoting our Lord's own words, " ' it
shall be done for them.'   That word 'agree' is a beautiful
one in the original, meaning to be in symphony or musical
accord.   But it is not possible for two to be in holy agreement
among themselves unless each is attuned to a third, the Holy
Comforter.   The harp strings must be keyed to a common
pitch in order to chord with each other."

How were these deep and comprehensive changes effected?
Not with struggling, but in quietness and peace.   Reforms
were waited for in prayerful patience when opposition arose.
Conferences were held for the deepening of the spiritual life.
Week after week, year after year, the most spiritual truths were
presented to the people.   The steel was turned and wrought
and tempered.   Like the Japanese sword-smith who spends
a lifetime on a daimio's single blade, Gordon worked at his
church for twenty-five long years.   No wonder it became an
effective instrument.   He loved his people.   When at home
he bound them to him by the tenderest ministries, at the side
of the sick, comforting the bereaved, burying the dead.   When
away he wrote frequently to them.

"I am resting powerfully, and have much time for communion and quiet talking with the Lord," he writes.   "I feel
that my busy and hurried life in Boston robs me too much of
this.   How much we need the times of refreshing to fit us for
toil, lest we become mere superficial and routine servants! . . .
I have written to many in the parish, having time now to think
of all their wants and sorrows, and all I wish to say to them
by way of exhortation.   So that I have written long letters
and am going to write scores more."

And again: "I am using great diligence in the midst of
my country work in writing letters to such as need a word of
comfort or counsel.   Yet I begin to feel quite anxious to get

back again to my parish, and to all the interests and labors that are so dear to me. I cannot entirely cast off the burden of it, even while so far away, but am constantly sending back my desires and longings toward those whom God has given me to watch over and care for. I really desire, above all things, to go back to a more devoted ministry for the good of souls."

In the fragment of spiritual autobiography published after his death Gordon describes this metamorphosis, this passage of his church from pupa to imago.

"'Why not withdraw from the church which has become thus secularized and desecrated?' it is asked. To which we reply emphatically, ' Until the Holy Spirit withdraws we are not called upon to do so.' And he is infinitely patient, abiding still in his house so long as there are two or three who gather in Christ's name to constitute a *templum in templo*, a sanctuary within a sanctuary, where he may find a home.

"What the lungs are to the air the church is to the Holy Spirit ; and each individual believer is like a cell in those lungs. If every cell is open and unobstructed the whole body is full of light; but if, through a sudden cold, congestion sets in, so that the larger number of these cells are closed, then the entire burden of breathing is thrown upon the few which remain unobstructed. With redoubled activity these now inhale and exhale the air till convalescence shall return. So we strongly believe that a few Spirit-filled disciples are sufficient to save a church ; that the Holy Ghost, acting through these, can and does bring back recovery and health to the entire body.

"Woe then to those who judge before the time ; who depart from their brethren and slam that door behind them before which Jesus is gently knocking ; who spue the church out of their mouths while he, though rebuking it, still loves it and owns it and invites it to sup with him.

"'For the law of the Spirit of life in Christ Jesus hath made me free from the law of sin and death,' writes the apostle. This is the method of the Lord's present work—death overcome by life. 'I cannot sweep the darkness out, but I can shine it out,' said John Newton. We cannot scourge dead works out of the church, but we can live them out. If we accuse the church of having the pneumonia, let us who are individual air-cells in that church breathe deeply and wait patiently and pray believingly, and one after another of the obstructed cells will open to the Spirit, till convalescence is reëstablished in every part.

"With the deepest humility the writer here sets his seal of verifying experience. When the truth of the inresidence of the Spirit and of his presiding in the church of God became a living conviction, then began a constant magnifying of him in his offices. Several sermons were preached yearly, setting forth the privileges and duties of Christians under his administration ; special seasons of daily prayer were set apart, extending sometimes over several weeks, during which continual intercession was made for the power of the Holy Ghost. It was not so much prayer for particular blessings as an effort to get into fellowship with the Spirit and to be brought into unreserved surrender to his life and acting. The circle of those thus praying was constantly enlarged. Then gradually the result appeared in the whole church ; the incoming tide began to fill the bays and inlets, and as it did so the driftwood was dislodged and floated away. Ecclesiastical amusements dropped off, not so much by the denunciation of the pulpit as by the displacement of the deepening life. The service of song was quietly surrendered back to the congregation, and instead of the select choir, the church, who constitute the true Levites as well as the appointed priesthood of the new dispensation, took up the sacrifice of praise anew and filled the house with their song. Later came the abolition of pew-rentals and the disuse of church sales for raising money for missions and other charities. The prayer-meeting soon passed beyond the necessity of being 'sustained,' and became the most helpful nourisher and sustainer of the church. The pulpit, too, acquired a liberty hitherto unknown ; the outward hampering being removed, the inward help became more and more apparent, and the preacher felt himself constantly drawn out instead of being perpetually repressed, as in the olden time. So noiselessly and irresistibly as the ascending sap displaces the dead leaves which have clung all winter long to the trees, so quietly did the incoming Spirit seem to crowd off the traditional usages which had hindered our liberty."

CHAPTER XXVI

A SOWER WENT FORTH TO SOW

Convention work in American cities—The convention of premillennial
Baptists in Brooklyn—Dr. Gordon's address—Teaching on the Holy
Spirit

THE convention work which Gordon undertook increased
yearly during the last half-decade of his life. We find
notices of conferences in which he participated in Buffalo,
Cincinnati, Brooklyn, Philadelphia, Chicago, New York,
Springfield, Providence, Boston, Lawrence, Rochester, Detroit,
the Canadian cities, and scores of minor points.

" ' I laid me down and slept; I awaked; for the Lord sustained me,' " he writes on a postal from a " sleeper." " Am
I not getting to be a traveling evangelist, an itinerant preacher,
a peripatetic lecturer? It is all so contrary to my inclination,
who would like so much better to settle down and to keep so.
Well, the Lord would stir up my home-fixedness and beget in
me the spirit of go-ye-forthedness. I trust I may do good to
souls."

Most of these conferences were organized in behalf of foreign
missions. One of the more unique was the one called in
Brooklyn by one hundred and fifty Baptist pastors, together
with many more laymen, as a demonstration in behalf of the
doctrine of the Lord's reappearing. Many of the leading men
in the denomination took part, among others Professors Stifler

and Gilmore and Messrs. Haldeman, Needham, and A. C. Dixon. This important meeting was hardly noticed by the denominational press. Of Gordon's address at the conference the New York " Independent " said:

" The church could hardly contain the crowds when Dr. Gordon spoke on the last night on the relation of Baptists to the doctrine of the Lord's second coming. He aimed to show that the doctrine of the premillennial advent has been the faith of the Baptists from the beginning, the cogent testimony of Professor Harnack and of Professor Briggs being cited as to the views of the Anabaptists and of the later English Baptists, further proof being adduced from the declarations of the Baptist confessions and Baptist confessors of several generations. That it was a convention of remarkable power is conceded by all in attendance. Are the large Baptist company who originated and conducted it innovators or renovators? is a question for our Baptist brethren to settle."

The question was settled once for all and in classical form by this address. The unbroken chain of traditional Baptist interpretation was traced from the records of the nameless, faithful Anabaptists of the Reformation to its representatives to-day. The three propositions which follow were defended with copious and convincing references to the history of the church.

" 1. That premillennialism was the orthodox faith of the church in the primitive and purest ages; that it only began to be seriously discredited when the church passed under the shadow of the Roman apostasy, which threw all of the most vital truths of the gospel into eclipse; that it was only partially revived at the Reformation, but for the last half-century has been reasserting itself with such power that it may be safely affirmed that nine tenths of the best European biblical scholarship now stands solidly for its defense.

" 2, That the Baptists, because devoted to primitive Christianity, and holding to the literal interpretation of the Scriptures, have been from the beginning more constantly and pronouncedly identified with this doctrine than any of the reformed sects; embodying it more or less distinctly in several of their historical confessions, and proclaiming it by the mouth of many of their most eminent preachers and theologians.

"3. These propositions being true, the Baptists would seem to be committed to the acceptance of the premillennial interpretation by precisely the same threefold consideration on which they defend their faith and practice as to the mode and subjects of baptism, viz., *the voice of primitive Christianity, the principle of literal interpretation of Scripture, and the wellnigh unanimous consensus of critical scholarship.*

"After noting the gradual disappearance of chiliasm before the advancing corruptions of the Roman Catholic Church, and after referring to the hidden stream of doctrine in which this primitive faith still flowed on, Professor Harnack explores this stream, and in doing so strikes at once 'the pure evangelical forces of the Anabaptists,' many of whom, he declares, 'need not shun comparison with the Christians of the apostolic and post-apostolic ages.' At the Reformation Luther and his coadjutors failed fully to revive this doctrine, for which the theologian Martensen expresses regret. But Harnack, referring to this fact, adds: 'Millenarianism, nevertheless, found its way with the help of the apocalyptic mysticism and Anabaptist influences into the churches of the Reformation.' 'Anabaptist influences'—let the candid reader trace these and see how our ecclesiastical ancestors are haunted by the shadow of this premillennial faith, so odious to many of their sons. We have not room for detailed history, but we follow this shadow for a little.

"Professor Briggs, of the Union Theological Seminary, with no evident liking for this doctrine, but with evident desire to rule it out of the Presbyterian camp, says: 'The confession of faith of the seven Baptist churches issued in 1645–46 gave expression to premillenarianism, and *it became the especial doctrine of the English Baptists and Fifth Monarchy Men.*' ('Whither?' p. 214.) One of our editors vehemently denies the exasperating imputation, as though it were a slander upon our ecclesiastical forefathers to connect them with this doctrine. But if the allegation is false, why has so competent an historian as Dr. William R. Williams made such an eloquent defense of the early Baptists on this point, not denying the charge, but justifying them under it? ('Lectures on Baptist History,' pp. 157–159.) Then let us turn to the famous Confession of 1660, to which more than twenty thousand English Baptists gave their assent. By writers of the highest authority on the question we find this document constantly quoted as chiliastic, one eminent author speaking of it as embodying '*the purest early patristic millenarian doctrine.*' A single sentence from the confession will show how little its framers anticipated the triumph of the church before Christ's return in glory, and how steadfastly they looked for his coming to usher in that triumph. In Article XXII. we read :

"'That the same Lord Jesus who showed himself alive after his passion by many infallible proofs, and who was carried up into heaven, shall so come in like manner as he was seen to go into heaven. And when Christ, who is our life, shall appear, we shall appear with him in glory. . . . Though now, alas! many men be scarce content that the saints should have so much as a being among them, *but when Christ shall appear then shall be their day, then shall be given unto them power over the nations to rule them with a rod of iron. Then shall they receive a crown of life which no man shall take from them, nor shall they by any means be turned or overturned from it, for the oppressor shall be broken to pieces.*'

"If we turn from the confession to the confessors, the early faith of our co-religionists comes out even more strongly. John

Bunyan's millenarianism is well known and generally conceded. He maintained the early patristic view that the seventh millenniad will be the Sabbath of the world, to be ushered in by the advent of Christ. (Works, vol. v., p. 286 ; vol. vi., p. 301.) One of Bunyan's contemporaries—Benjamin Keach, an illustrious predecessor of Spurgeon in the pastorate—has left a very full confession of his views on this point. He was brought to trial October 8, 1664, on the two charges of Anabaptism and millenarianism. As he stood before Lord Chief Justice Hyde, the representative of the state church, he was summoned first to answer for his 'damnable doctrine' concerning baptism ; which being disposed of, the second article of indictment was taken up, viz., that he held that '*the saints shall reign with Christ a thousand years*.' The judge pronounced this 'an old heresy which was cast out of the church a thousand years ago, and was likewise condemned by the Council of Constance five hundred years after, and hath lain dead ever since, till now this rascal hath revived it.' Nevertheless the stalwart Baptist preacher firmly defended his view, bringing out clearly the doctrine of the first resurrection, followed by the millennium and the reign of the saints with Christ, and as the result he was condemned and sent to the pillory, where, standing all day with his accusation written over his head, he bade the spectators 'take notice that it is not for any wickedness I stand here, but for writing and publishing the truths which the Spirit of God hath revealed in the Holy Scriptures.'

" Dr. John Gill, the commentator and theologian, has drawn out the premillennial scheme more fully and set forth the scriptural arguments for it more cogently, perhaps, than any other Baptist writer who has treated the subject. For a full statement of his views we must refer the reader to his 'Body of Divinity' and his 'Commentary on Revelation.' Couple his testimony with that of Charles H. Spurgeon, who said, in a recent sermon, that there can be no millennium without the presence of the visible Christ, 'any more than there can be summer without the sun. *He must come first, and then will the golden age begin.*' Thus we have an illustrious trio of Baptist witnesses in a single pastoral succession—Keach, Gill, and Spurgeon. The teachings of these three great confessors would seem to shake the integrity of the assertion above quoted, that 'premillenarianism is no more an article of Baptist faith than is second probation.'

"Perhaps this statement was intended to apply to American Baptists; well, we have to say that just as clearly as those founders of New England, the Mathers and the Davenports and the Walleys, were millenarians, so clearly were our Baptist fathers who were contemporary with them.

"Hear Roger Williams's unequivocal utterance on the personal and imminent advent of our Lord. 'It is the counsel of God,' he says, 'that Jesus Christ shall shortly appear, a most glorious Judge and Revenger against all his enemies, while the heavens and the earth shall flee before his most glorious presence.' But what did Roger Williams believe as to the condition of things on earth at Christ's appearing? Did he hold to that 'from time immemorial' Baptist doctrine, the conversion of the world previous to the second advent? Listen to him again. 'The Lord will come when an evil world is ripe in sin and antichristianism; will come suddenly, and then will he melt the earth with fire and make it new. Till then I wait and hope, and bear the dragon's wrath.' ('Bloudy Tenet,' 1644, pp. 32, 72, 73, 361.) Roger Williams, we need not remind our hearers, was driven into the wilderness before the face of the state church dragon.

"His co-religionist, John Clarke of Newport, was condemned to pay twenty-five pounds or be well whipped for his Baptist faith and practice, but escaped the penalty through the intervention of his friends. That Clarke was of those who 'come behind in no gift, waiting for the coming of the Lord,' is evident from his testimony, recorded in his confession of faith and delivered to the magistrates of Boston, 1651. In this confession he speaks of 'the anointed King who is gone unto his Father for his glorious kingdom, and shall ere long return again'; and identifies himself with those who 'wait for his coming the second time in the form of a Lord and King, with his glorious kingdom, according to promise.' (Backus, 'History of New England,' 1871, vol. i., pp. 182, 183.)

"Obadiah Holmes, who was scourged in Boston for his Baptist teaching and practice, receiving thirty lashes with a three-corded whip, drew up a confession of his faith in 1675 for the information of friends in England who had misjudged him. . The doctrines of the coming of Christ, the conversion of Israel, and the millennial reign are stated as clearly by Holmes Martyr in the seventeenth century as by Justin Martyr in the second. I quote from his confession:

"'33. I believe the promise of the Father concerning the return of Israel and Judah, and the coming of the Lord to raise up the dead in Christ, and to change them that are alive, that they may reign with him a thousand years.

"'34. I believe in the resurrection of the wicked to receive their just judgment.

"'35. As I believe in eternal judgment to the wicked, so I believe the glorious declaration of the Lord, "Come, ye blessed of my Father, enter into the joy of your Lord;" which joy eye hath not seen, ear hath not heard, neither can it enter into the heart of man to conceive the glory that God hath prepared for them that do love him and wait for his appearance; *wherefore come, Lord Jesus, come quickly.* In this faith and profession I stand, and have sealed the same with my blood, in Boston, in New England.'

"I think we must conclude from these quotations that millenarianism was the martyr faith of our denomination, even though it may not be the modern faith. The fact is

that this primitive doctrine of the church has always tended
to reappear with a fresh planting of the gospel and in a revival
of spiritual religion.   It is just as true that when the church has
entered upon a career of worldly prosperity the tendency has
been to repudiate this apostolic faith as antiquated, pessimistic, and out of joint with the times.   This sentence, in which
the church historian, Kurtz, accounts for the decline of the
early doctrine of the Lord's coming and his reign, is very significant.   He says : 'As the church saw herself now entering
upon an extended career of worldly prosperity, her early millennial hopes passed into oblivion.'   Possibly we to-day may
be unconsciously repeating that early experience.   Think of
Holmes whipped in Boston and Williams banished into the
wilderness for avowing the Baptist faith ; and then come down
two centuries to find the once despised Baptist sect grown to
be the largest Protestant body in Boston, and the second largest in the Union, with its three million communicants, its great
universities, its large endowments, and its millionaire merchants, some of whom stand ready to be as munificent patrons
to it as Constantine was to the church of his age!   What
wonder that he seems to strike a discordant note in the Te
Deum of our prosperity who intrusively takes up the words of
the apostle, 'Here we have no continuing city.'   'For our
citizenship is in heaven ; from whence we also look for the Saviour, the Lord Jesus Christ.'"

In his advocacy of Jesus' teaching on this point, Dr. Gordon was much opposed, especially by the ministry.   In the
memorable Canadian missionary tour many came to him and
urged him to refrain from references to the second coming of
Christ, that offense might not be given.   Upon this fact he
adverts in a letter from one of the Canadian cities in which
he was speaking :

"While standing at a street corner last evening," he says,
"waiting for a car, a Salvation Army band came along, and

then a poor redeemed man took off his hat and spoke to the crowd. It was so pathetic, so true, so correct in its gospel preaching, that it won all our hearts. I think I could not have resisted it had I been unconverted. Thank God for the Salvation Army. . . . I am stopping with a lovely family of Scotch people, full of interest in missions and clear in the truth, wanting me so much to go and give a message on the Lord's coming; and yet the ministers are opposed to it. Is it not humiliating that in so many cases the flock has to lead the shepherds? "

While emphasizing powerfully these much-neglected doctrines, he dwelt equally upon the fact that the Spirit abides here in this dispensation, the source of energy for all Christian ministrations.

His interest in this theme was not altogether new. There is much about it in " The Twofold Life," a book to which the president of a leading New England college has expressed his profound indebtedness, and which, on the other hand, of all the volumes in the library of the Vermont State Prison, was, some years ago, the favorite among the convicts, being read and re-read until it fell apart and disappeared. It was in Dr. Gordon's last years, however, that he dwelt upon the doctrine with especial stress. He realized how slightly informed Christians were on the subject. His own views were maturing and deepening. He was, too, experiencing personally the presence of the Spirit as he climbed steadily to the table-lands of the higher life. From the nebula of convention addresses, sermons and articles was developed gradually a system in which " The Ministry of the Spirit " holds a central place, " The Holy Spirit in Missions " and " How Christ Came to Church " being dependent and tributary to it. The first and last of these books were published posthumously. Many think that in them Gordon did for his day what John Owen, the Puritan, in the " Discourse Concerning the Spirit," did for his. " He brought up," says a competent authority,* " from the debris of the past the apostolic doctrine of the Holy Spirit's personality, deity, and actual presidency in the assembly of the saints, and gave it increased emphasis for a decade of years."

Insistence on the importance of the Spirit's ministry has been the glory of Quakerism and the unquestionable reason for its preëminence in every form of good works. The distortion of the doctrine, in the contention that " the Spirit which bloweth where it listeth " is confined to certain ecclesiastical channels, has proved the vigorous tap-root of an immoral clericalism.† The neglect into which the teaching has fallen explains the languor and debility so common in Protestant churches. " Of the Holy Ghost as a divine person, resident in the church, to be honored and invoked and obeyed and implicitly trusted, many Christians know nothing. Is it conceivable that there could be any deep spiritual life or any real sanctified energy for service in a community of such? "‡

The Spirit he believed to be a definite personality, whose coming was announced by Jesus as distinctly as the latter's advent was foretold by prophets and angels. The upper room was his cradle, as the manger at Bethlehem was the cradle of the Son of God. His time ministry, " distinct from all that went before, and introductory to all that is to come after, a ministry with a definite beginning and a definite termination," §

---

* Rev. Arthur T. Pierson, D.D.

† " In the doctrine of tactual succession there is not only a kind of cheapness and pettiness, but especially a foreshortening of the Spirit's arm as though the consecrating touch depended on the intervention of some visible ecclesiastic. On the contrary, the hands of the Paraclete have often stretched across a century or generation and set apart an apostle by foreordination long before any bishop or presbyter has moved to set him apart by ordination."

‡ " The Ministry of the Spirit," p. 73.

§ *Ibid.*, p. 15.

he thought as susceptible of biographic treatment as the earthly life of Jesus.

"The work of the Spirit is preëminently to communicate and apply the work of Christ to human hearts. . . . The Son glorifies the Father; the Spirit glorifies the Son. . . . In the church two processes are in operation, one of life, the other of death. If either is interrupted disorder results. To effect this twofold operation, the daily death of the church in fulfilment of the crucified life of her Head, and her daily living in manifestation of his glorified life, the Spirit dwells evermore with us." * His is the Real Presence.

The specific method of the Spirit's work of vivification is indicated by three terms used in Scripture—sealing, filling, anointing. Each of these is connected with some special divine endowment; the seal with assurance, the filling with power, and the anointing with knowledge. "The contrast between working in the power of the Spirit and in the energy of the flesh is easily discernible. Even more so is the contrast between the tuition of learning and the intuition of the Spirit in knowledge and teaching." †

"It costs much," said Dr. Gordon in one of these convention addresses, "to obtain this power. It costs self-surrender and humiliation and the yielding up of our most precious things to God. It costs the perseverance of long waiting and the faith of strong trust. But when we are really in that power, we shall find this difference: that, whereas before it was hard for us to do the easiest things, now it is easy for us to do the hardest."

And again: "As we become deeply instructed in this matter, we shall learn to pray less about the details of duty and more about the fullness of power. The manufacturer is chiefly

* "The Ministry of the Spirit," pp. 63, 64.
† *Ibid.*, p. 90.

anxious to secure an ample head of water for his mills; and, this being found, he knows that his ten thousand spindles will keep in motion without particular attention to each one. It is, in like manner, the sources of our power for which we should be most solicitous, and not the results."

This doctrine of the baptism of the Spirit, it will be readily seen, articulates itself to his whole theory of man's status before God. The implanted life of God alone can save man from moral decomposition. The expected return of Christ to earth is the one hope in the struggle for social redemption. The presence of the Spirit in the heart is the condition precedent to an acceptable witness for Christ by the regenerate until the day of that appearing. Everywhere does the New Testament declare the impotence of man and the sovereign sufficiency of God.

CHAPTER XXVII

TILL THE DAY DAWN

Twenty-fifth anniversary of pastorate—Closing days—Sickness and death
—The cries of bereavement—Funeral addresses

ON the 27th of December, 1894, Gordon completed the twenty-fifth year of his pastorate in the Clarendon Street Church. The anniversary was observed by his people with appropriate exercises, a reception, and a tea, followed by addresses from his colleagues in the ministry of the city. The eulogy which ordinarily characterizes such occasions was rebutted by him in a brief speech, half humorous, half serious. He distributed the praise heaped on himself to his people and to his "splendid cabinet of deacons," contending that the growth of a tree is due, not to its own excellences, but to the excellence of the soil at its roots, and that his only merit consisted in his staying so long where God had placed him and where conditions were so favorable. He reminded his hearers, on the other hand, of the danger which lay hid in all eulogy of one whose record was not closed, and of the possibility which shadowed himself as well as the great apostle of becoming a castaway on the dark seas of unfaithfulness.

In the evening, while sitting with his wife at home, he took down the "Life of Andrew Bonar," which he had been reading, and, after commenting on the events of the day, opened to these words, saying, "Here is something which just expresses my feelings":

" ' Last night's jubilee passed over very pleasantly in one way, but was to me at the same time very solemn and humbling. I see in the retrospect so much that was altogether imperfect and so much that was left undone. But it was a great gathering and most hearty on the part of all the friends who came. May the Lord save me from the danger that lurks under praise and laudation of friends. I had no idea that I had so many friends in so many parts, and that the Lord had been pleased to use me in so many ways. . . . The anniversary was carried through in a way that interested the people, but as for myself, when I returned home and sat in the evening alone I felt deep and bitter regret at the thought of my past. I think I felt what is meant by being ashamed before God, as Ezra expresses it. And all this was aggravated by the thought of all the immense kindness of the Lord to me and to mine. I have been thinking to-night that perhaps my next undertaking may be this, appearing at the judgment-seat of Christ when I give an account of my trading with my talents. I wish to hide in the shadow of the Plant of Renown, and be found there when the Voice says, " Where art thou ? " ' "

It was a singular suggestion, a strange premonition, as if he had caught a glimpse of the dark cloud on the distant horizon. Yet all the world was bathed in sunshine still. Children and grandchildren were gathered about his breakfast-table the next morning. With him, too, was his close friend, Dr. A. T. Pierson, whose presence ever was as flint to steel. What raillery, what wit, what flow of anecdote that morning! Retort and repartee coruscated and sparkled. Twenty-seven admirable stories were jotted down afterward by an interested listener, just as birds are picked up by the game-dogs after an unusual shot. The following Sunday he preached as usual. The new year opened, with its round of engagements. Everything looked as if he were entering upon another cycle of usefulness, even larger and more fruitful than the one just closed.

There were, however, indications of a coming break, as of a straining beam upon which additional pressure is being constantly placed. His work during the month of January was continuous and intense. One might almost have believed that he was trying to illustrate the proverb, " The more light a torch gives, the less time it burns." An idea of his ceaseless activity can be obtained from a mere catalogue of his engagements for the brief two weeks of the sickness which followed. He was to give addresses at Philadelphia, at Newark, at the midwinter convention of Dr. Cullis's church, at the conference of the Christian Alliance, Boston, at Mount Holyoke College, and two addresses at Rochester, N. Y. This in addition to his church cares at home. " I must get out from under these burdens for a little," he would say. Yet when suggestions were offered and plans perfected for rest he could never be induced to stop. His system was thus depleted and prepared for the entrance of the disease which was to prove fatal.

Monday, January 21st, was his last day of service. In the evening he attended the annual meeting of the Industrial Home, and went thence to address the Young Men's Baptist Union on the subject of missions. Never did he speak with more delicate humor, with more captivating grace, with greater earnestness ; but the lines were deep on his face, as if the graver overwork had been more active than ever, and those who sat near could clearly see that he was far from well. The next day he was unable to leave his bed. The physician was called and the disease pronounced to be grippe, with tendencies to bronchitis. Then for days did he struggle on as in a blinding storm. The fever became violent and was accompanied with intermittent delirium. Night after night he lay in the agonies of a prolonged insomnia. He complained of " the ceaseless storm, the incessant noise as of great raindrops on a windowpane," though all the while the air outside was as still as an Indian summer. He would groan at " the sudden bursts of blackness " which overwhelmed him " as if he were felled with a club to the ground." Often in those night hours could we hear him whispering John Angelus' hymn :

> " Jesus, Jesus, visit me ;
> How my soul longs after thee!
> When, my best, my dearest friend,
> Shall our separation end? "

For with all the intense physical suffering there went along a sense of isolation and of desertion. On the Wednesday night before his death this feeling seemed to be overpowering. He asked that every one might leave the room that he might be alone and face to face with Jesus. Then followed such a heartrending confession of unworthiness, such an appeal for the presence and companionship of the Saviour, such promises, with strong crying and tears, of renewed consecration, of greater diligence and devotion in God's service, as are rarely heard. It was as if the Gethsemane prayer were again ascending.

Conscious of his condition and with a presentiment of the approaching end he called his wife to his side and said, " If anything *should* happen, do not have a quartet choir ; I have selected four hymns I want *sung by the people.* Write them down : ' Abide with me,' ' The sands of time are sinking,' ' Lord, if he sleep he shall do well,' ' My Jesus, I love thee.' " This was done, to his apparent relief.

The next morning it was clear that he was worse. The long period of sleeplessness was fast wearing him out. Toward evening the doctor, coming in, said in a cheery voice, to rouse him from his lethargy, " Dr. Gordon, have you a good word for us to-night?" With a clear, full voice he answered, " Victory!" It was as if, after the typhoon-like sickness, he had passed the last range of breakers and had been given a glimpse of the Eternal City gleaming beyond.

This was his last audible utterance. Between nine and ten in the evening the nurse motioned to his wife that she was wanted. As she bent over him he whispered, "Maria, pray." She led in prayer; he scarce followed sentence by sentence, trying at the close to utter a petition for himself; but his strength was not sufficient for articulation.

Five minutes after midnight on the morning of February 2d he fell asleep in Jesus. In a few minutes the solemn tolling from the belfry of the church apprised his people that their pastor and friend was gone. The stars in the dark sky looked down calmly as ever. The crunching of the snow outside under an occasionally passing team alone broke the silence as the chamber door was closed upon the still form, tenantless now "until the morning breaks and the shadows flee away."

That night the wires carried to thousands the message of bereavement. With the morning the returning replies of a sorrowing sympathy began to pour in. First came scores of yellow envelops—brief, heart-wrung exclamations from those who could not wait to write; then a flood of letters from near points, widening out as the days passed, until every State and Territory was represented. With the mails from beyond the sea came the same words—from England, from France, from Cape Colony, from Brazil, from the West Indies, from India, from Japan. "All the religious papers from Sweden," wrote a Kansas Swede, "have dwelt upon our loss." Finally, weeks after, messages of sorrow arrived from the lonely mission stations far up the river-ways of Africa and from the extreme western provinces of China. "We have been holding a memorial service here in Yachow [Szechuen] for him," wrote a missionary. It was only one among many such.

What a revelation of love this vast pile of letters constituted! What utterances of grief, what acknowledgments of indebtedness, it contained! "Oh, how we loved him!" "How I honored and revered him!" "He was Great-heart to us

poor pilgrims." "The loss is paralyzing." "We are dazed
with sorrow." "O my friend!"* "The loss is almost irrep-
arable." "We are heartbroken." "The loss to the world is
past telling." "My dear benefactor is gone." "'Help, Lord;
for the godly man ceaseth; for the faithful fail from among the
children of men.'" "I loved him as I did no other man."
"His influence for good has been incalculable." "Dear,
dear Gordon! I loved him dearly, and always have. Faith
is hardly equal to this. How can he be spared!" "I never
knew one more transparent and more lovable." "He was the
whole world's good friend." "He was a living conscience to
the city." "There are many of us who owe to him more than
we can ever tell." "All that was truly dear to me in Boston
seems gone. We sorrow most of all that we shall see his dear
face no more." "I never met him but I learned to love him."
"I bless God that I ever knew him." "I thank God for that
perfect life, that simple, childlike, pure spirit which has strengthened me in the most holy faith." "I have never seen him, but
for twenty years I have been indebted to him as to no other
minister." "O man greatly beloved!" "'O my father, my
father! the chariot of Israel, and the horsemen thereof.'"
"Would God I had been more worthy of his companionship.
I must try now to be more like him." "I am almost prostrated, for I can never forget his kindness to us in affliction."
"No other departure of any man or any ten men, save of my
own sons, could have stirred me so to the depths." "I cannot put language into form that would describe the stricken
sense under which we suffer here at the news." "The greatest and truest saint it has been my privilege to know!" "I
never spoke to him but once; yet I think of him as a brother."
"Express to the children my sense of thankfulness for a share
of their dear father's love, of grief at his removal, of determi-

---

* A single exclamation on a sheet of paper sent from some train flying
through the night far away in the West.

nation to follow with them in his footsteps." " I can scarcely realize that I shall not look again on that noble countenance." " God help us! No human being can! What are we to do without him?" " How we loved him! He was the Apostle John of our day." " He loved the drunkard as well as the moralist." * " So great is the loss that I have been wishing I could have accepted the 'enemy's' summons if thereby he could have been spared." " We shall not be able to get along through life without him." † " His genius, his simplicity, his modesty, his bravery, his evangelical fervor, his firm adhesion to the gospel of Christ, his unity of life, have given him an incomparable place in our hearts." " He was the rarest and most Christ-like spirit I have ever known." " I went to bed last night and remained awake a long time weeping before the Lord. I truly loved him." " When I received word of his death I immediately left my office, went to my home ; then had prayers with my wife. After which we spake of the loss to God's Zion. *I am homesick for heaven.*"

The funeral occurred on the following Tuesday. All through that winter morning a great concourse passed tearfully and slowly by the casket. Men were sobbing convulsively like children. Strange faces in great numbers of the poor and of the meanly clad there were—a significant reminder of much that the right hand had hid from the left. A group of Chinese members were observed weeping in a corner of the vestry. One of them, a poor laundryman, when told that flowers were refused, laid three dollars upon the coffin for the preaching of the gospel of the resurrection among his countrymen. " Dr. Gordon would have wished it," he said. The suggestion was taken up, and a large sum was immediately subscribed by the young people of the church for a memorial missionary fund.

* From a reformed man.

† From a misspelled letter evidently from some humble one whom he had helped.

At one o'clock the casket was brought upstairs and placed in the spot where monthly for twenty-five years the dead pastor had poured wine and broken bread to his flock in the communion feast.   The church was filled to its utmost capacity and hundreds regretfully turned homeward from the closed doors.   Outside the wind cut like a sand-blast and the snow wraiths tore circling through the streets; for it was the coldest day of winter.

A deep sense of awe and of subdued triumph seemed to have taken the place of outpouring grief.   The crowding memories of his life were to the multitudes, as his living presence in the death-chamber had so often been, "a cup of strength in the great agony."   The towering floods of anguish were held back as by the very hand of Jehovah, so that we passed through that afternoon dry-shod.   It was not "the dark day of nothingness."   The heavens had opened and a vision of victory had been vouchsafed.   Never was faith more convinced; never were "those mighty hopes that make us men" more potent.   On that day all in the vast gathering realized with more than intuition that the dead had reached the blessed goal, that Christ had reached him out the shining hand.

The singing was pervaded with a solemn power.   Grief and triumph had here their common outlet, flowing commingled in an unhindered tide.   Every soul in the house seemed to be singing, and the sound was as the noise of many waters.   What a vindication of congregational music!   How spectral the singing of the conventional quartet would have seemed after those mighty billows of sound thundering along with the inspired words of Samuel Rutherford! *

Four of the dead man's comrades spoke for him that day. Dr. Henry C. Mabie represented the missionary interests for which he toiled; President Andrews, of Brown University, recalled the old days and the alma mater he had served in

* "The sands of time are sinking," etc.

later years; Joseph Cook, his unswerving fidelity to Christian truth and his unfaltering championship of struggling causes; and Dr. Pierson the labors at Northfield and the many campaigns through which they went together.

The addresses were in part as follows:

" It has been deemed fitting that one of the representatives of the American Baptist Missionary Union, associated with Dr. Gordon in a far-reaching form of foreign mission enterprise, should say a few words in connection with this service— that he should speak a word concerning Dr. Gordon's relation to missions. If I were to express it in one word, I should say that Dr. Gordon's interest in missions was *integral;* it entered into his very spiritual personality; it was but the natural breathing and outcome of his being; it was no form of service that was put on as a garment, no perfunctory performance, no line of duty taken up because he had been elected to fill some official position. Missions with him, as with the God who instituted them and with Jesus Christ his Son, who by his atonement made them possible, were constitutional. He could no more think of missions as geographically limiting his thoughts, his heart, his life, his enterprise, than you could think of there being limits to the sympathies of our Lord Jesus Christ.

" He was naturalized to all Christ's work. To him that work was a circle, not an arc. It was globed. Hence he was as much at home in alien cities as in his own Boston, at the World's Missionary Conference in London as some of us saw him—easily king of missionaries as he was imperial among pleaders for missions, the one man without whom no single session was thought complete till they had heard his voice. Hence it was that in Edinburgh and Glasgow and throughout Scotland he was welcomed everywhere, and fitted into the relations and voiced the missionary interest of these people just as naturally as if he were addressing his own prayer-meeting

here in Clarendon Street Church.   So their testimony was,
'He fed us with the finest of the wheat.'   He enlarged their
horizon in respect to the world and gave them a relish for its
conquest.   Hence it was that in Paris, with the McAll Mission workers, he was not only welcomed, but eagerly sought
for, cabled for; they must have him, and for them he crossed
the seas again and again.   Hence it was that in our own land
he was sought on all platforms where missions were to have a
peculiar and effective advocacy.   Hence it was that the student volunteer movement, the great conferences at Northfield
and Ocean Grove and elsewhere, regarded his presence and
his addresses as indispensable.   Hence his favor for the Salvation Army movement, which he commended and cheered
when almost all men set it at naught.   Hence it was that in
the stables of street-car drivers, on the wharves along the
shore in Boston, or in refuges of the lost, he was everywhere
welcomed as the supporter, advocate, and brother, vitally
linked with all these organizations of any and every name.

"But who shall tell what our beloved brother was to the
American Baptist Missionary Union—our counselor, our inspiration, our pride; none so meek as he.   I may be allowed
to say, without disparagement to any one, that all through his
official relations to that body, through so many weary years
in our committee-rooms in this city, he often surrendered opinions of his own respecting ways and means in deference to his
brethren, whom he was always ready to think of as more to
be considered than himself.   He was always ready to take the
field for us, and was the bulwark of that organization.   How
this noble church has stood by him and followed him, till at
length they only wanted to know his thought and they would
anticipate it!   There was with him no pulling of people's door-
bells to extract from them unwilling offerings; no passing
around nervously, hat in hand, to beg for Peter's pence; but
rather a quiet exaltation of the lofty privilege of giving and a

reminder of the blood mortgage on all men to redeem the world. . . .

"History in its ongoings, as Dr. Gordon viewed it, was missionary history. He was not a man sailing over a track-less deep without chart or compass, with no desired haven in view. History was not to him a confused mass of incidents, as it is to the materialistic thinker of our day—an insoluble riddle, a hopeless tangle. The history of the world, as he viewed it, started from a beginning, and went on through the middle to the end in an orderly way, and the end was a glori-ous and divine consummation. The one last word that es-caped his lips was 'Victory!' He believed that this was as-sured in history. His faith swept the entire perspective, and hence it was that he saw great mountain-peaks in that won-drous landscape where some of us, perhaps, see only hillocks, if we see even these. His view of history was simply the suc-cessive stages of the plan of human redemption, with its glori-ous culmination.

"If some thought at times that his view of proper mission work was superficial or pessimistic, I bid them think again. If some think that he emphasized unduly what he regarded as the great and immediate duty of the church in this present age, viz., to preach the gospel 'for a *witness*,' let them think how long, how ardently, how profoundly he pondered the words of the Lord, for his words they are: 'This gospel of the kingdom shall be preached in all the world for a witness unto all nations, and then shall the end come.' What Dr. Gordon meant by the 'witnessing' is not that superficial post-boy, flash-light method of Christian enterprise which some imagine. What it is let his own tremendously earnest and concentrated efforts, which burned out the fires of this life, testify. He meant all that Jesus Christ meant when he said, 'To this end was I born, and for this cause came I into the world, that I should bear witness unto the truth.' Christ's personal ministry, from the manger to the throne, he believed to be but a witness; the beginnings of things, not the consummation of them; the foundations only of the eternal kingdom that God was to rear. He meant all that the Apostle Paul meant when he spoke of his consummate privilege 'to testify the gospel of the grace of God.'"

"Dear Friends: I do not consider it profitable that I should say much on a solemn occasion like this, for I stand here in an official relation. Were I to speak personally, detailing the knowledge I had of this good man, it would take more time than I have any right to occupy. Dr. Gordon was a graduate of Brown University. He graduated in the class of 1860, and he was a light in that class. He was very dearly beloved by his classmates. Quite early in his ministry to this congregation he was chosen to be a member of the governing board of Brown University, and I cannot tell you how faithful he has always been in that relation. He not only attended the meetings whenever possible—and the occasions when it was not possible were very few—but he entered warmly into all matters brought before the board. He always showed an uncommon grasp of the college's business matters, keeping them in mind from one year's session to another. I felt very proud of Dr. Gordon on this account. He was mainly engaged in spiritual work, but he was never so lost in it that he was not able to take up any necessary temporal details. I believe that the men most immersed in business also respected him on account of this quality. Not to speak further upon this, I wish to mention a line of Dr. Gordon's activity of which very few even in this church, even those very intimate with him, have been aware. He was accustomed to tear himself away from his toils here and run down to Brown University for a single day or more to assist in our services. Two or three times on these occasions it was absolutely indis-

pensable that he should at night come back to Boston for some
duty.   He would then fly to Providence again and resume
work.   It is not every man—not even every good or every
able man—who can touch the hearts of students.   In all my
acquaintance I have never met many—never more than two
or three—who began to have the power in this sort of work
that Dr. Gordon had.   He never came to us without bringing
a blessing, a large blessing, never without leaving behind him
a permanent blessing.   Never did he speak a word in our
student body without so impressing many a student heart that
the impress of that lesson must abide forever.   It was my
privilege during such visits within the last four or five years to
become acquainted with Dr. Gordon personally as I was never
acquainted with him before.   I had often listened to his preaching, sometimes in this church, sometimes elsewhere, always
with great delight; and I had on a few occasions drawn near
him to seek personal counsel.   What multitudes could say the
same!   Still, till the times to which I refer when he came to
our college to address the students, I felt that I had not much
personal acquaintance with him.   Till then I never knew the
immeasurable depth and breadth of his religious life; but these
visits revealed it.   After the meetings were over and before he
could take the train—sometimes, indeed, before the meetings
—he would come to my house, where I had the privilege of
conversing with him.   I enjoyed a precious opportunity of
this kind the very last time he came to us, in November, 1894.
He preached to a large number of students, and personally
prayed with some; then he came to my house and we talked
about many, many things.   It would be impossible, even if
we took this whole afternoon, to-night, to-morrow, and all the
month, to go over all that you, the other friends of Dr. Gordon, know about the immensity and grandeur of his religious
life. . . .

" I wish to lay emphasis also upon the amazing catholicity

of this good brother in thinking of those who differed from him. I suppose that the man does not live—I suppose the man has never lived—who ever heard from Dr. Gordon's lips the first bitter or even reproachful word about any who did not agree with him. He went his way, he saw the light, he heard the call of our Lord Jesus Christ in the road before him. He followed, and he followed with absolute fearlessness."

"If I were at this moment on my death-bed, there is no preacher of my acquaintance with whom I should more gladly consult, were he alive, than that one who has been snatched from us so recently, and who now knows what light is while we sit in the shadow. Were I a student beginning a course of theological study, there is no one to whom I should look for safer advice in comparing Scripture with Scripture than to that servant of God who in this city lived a biblical life and preached an unadulterated gospel. If I were commencing a career of advocacy of moral or social, industrial or even political reforms, I do not know where I could find one who would be a more judicious guide than he would have been who was a warrior in his best days for many a noble reform, and who now lies dead on his shield on the field of battle. . . .

"These three tests of a public career are the severest we can apply: Would we ask this man to give us advice when we take our leap into that unseen holy region into which all men haste? Would we follow him in our study of God's Word? Would we take him as an adviser in conflict with the evils of our day? I do unreservedly pray God that the mantle of this servant of his may fall on young theological students, may fall on young reformers, may fall on all who are preaching God's Word, may fall on all who knew him on either side the sea, may fall on the missions which he befriended to the very ends of the earth. Let us sorrow only for ourselves. All the mysteries of his providence God himself understands, and this ought to be enough for our peace. There are no broken columns in cathedrals that God builds—no unfinished arches.

" It is as a reformer that some of us look to Dr. Gordon as one who could not be spared. We do not see his successor in the pulpit ; at least, not precisely his parallel. It would be hard to find a man who had such a grasp upon the confidence of the Christians of the United States, and who was as pronounced as he in advocating strong doctrines on the subject of the temperance reform. As a preacher he was first, midst, last, biblical. It would have amazed his audiences if he had often quoted the secular poets or illustrated his courses of thought by anecdotes of adventure of a secular kind, or if he had been in any way sensational in the bad meaning of that word. He was pungent. He was spiritually incisive. He held the sword of the Spirit, and was able to thrust it through and through the fabric of error, through and through even hard hearts. But if he quoted at all in his discourses, it was usually from the Puritan divines ; it was from the deepest students of the inner life ; it was from the biographies of those saints of the modern and of the medieval and of the apostolic church who are canonized by the universal consent of Christendom. And you feel that in their presence he was in company fit for his own soul, and that his own was fit for this company. The astonishing thing to me in Dr. Gordon, when I heard him, was that he seemed to be one with Savonarola and with Wesley and with the Friends, who have spoken most effectively from the impulse of the inner voice. He was one with St. John and with St. Paul in his doctrine, and it seemed natural for him to compare Scripture with Scripture and bring out meanings not often emphasized.

" He made a geodetic survey of his life along the loftiest summits, and found the trend of those heights pointing definitely in certain directions. This, as I suppose, is one of

the most safe and searching tests any man can apply to his
own career: In his highest moments, what is said to him?
What do those highest moments mean if, when placed in line,
they all trend in a given direction? Dr. Gordon believed,
not that he had special illuminations, but that he was in the
way of duty; for year after year his efforts along the lines of
an apostolic ministry were prospered; year after year his devotions, his study of the Bible, his watchful analysis of current
providences, gave him more and more confidence that God
was encouraging him. . . .

" Read Dr. Gordon in full. Read all his many books;
several of them are religious classics. It is a remarkable fact
that, in this city of Boston, three books have been written that
are worthy to lie on the table by any dying couch, side by
side with Thomas à Kempis's ' Imitatio Christi' and Jeremy
Taylor's ' Holy Living and Dying.' These three were among
our brother's volumes, and entitled ' In Christ,' ' The Twofold
Life,' and ' The Ministry of the Spirit,' the last coming from
the press within a few hours of our bereavement. They are
fit to be placed among the religious classics approved after
long experience by Christians of every name. I believe they
will live as such, and in this opinion I am not singular. It is
held by men of far better judgment than myself, who are,
many of them, here to-day. I believe it will be indorsed by
the churches as the years roll on. Mr. Spurgeon and a dozen
other critics I could mention have spoken of Dr. Gordon's
books in terms which one might think fulsome, if personal acquaintance with their value had not shown the merits of those
writings so powerful, so quiet, so filled with the Spirit. I read
Dr. Gordon's volumes from end to end. The Scotch said,
when Dr. Pierson and Dr. Gordon made a tour as lecturers
after the great World's Missionary Convention in London in
1888, ' Dr. Pierson inspired us; Dr. Gordon fed us.' Several
times the cover had been worn off and replaced on his copy

of the Greek New Testament. Dr. Gordon was the superior of most of us in spiritual insight. He was born with wonderful natural capacities in the direction of religious thought, emotion, and intuition. He was a thinker, he was a philosopher, and he was a mystic also. He had a great head, a great heart. He was able to get a bucket down very deeply into the wells of spiritual truth. I advise you to notice what crystalline waters he brought up, and to drink often from those fountains.

"Two facts concerning Judson Gordon I am very sure history will remember: first, that he was polygonal; next, that every side of him was biblical. He was distinguished as preacher, pastor, evangelist, reformer, editor. He was the scholar's assistant toward the narrow and strait way. One of the most difficult things he ever did, I think, was to bring the holy awe of self-consecration to the somewhat thoughtless, always rather impetuous, circles of students in many colleges. He was a traveler; he faced strange audiences abroad, and fed them; he was in his family a priest. He was known here in the attics and cellars as one who could imitate the Saviour in going from house to house doing good. He built this church on the pattern shown to him by the Holy Spirit in Scripture and life. These are only a few sides of his work; but every side was scriptural. I revere exceedingly this comprehensiveness in his religious outlook and culture and activity. He was not one of those who *tried* to master so many things as not to be an authority on any one of them. In all these departments of his activity he was looked upon by many of us, I am sure, as a leader."

"My brother, against the day of thy burying have I kept this alabaster flask, and I come now beforehand to anoint thy body for the burial.

"There are some things that ought not to be spoken of a yet living man; but our lips may perhaps be unsealed when

God has taken him. I dare not speak—and it would not be proper nor delicate—of what this loss is to me personally. He was a great man. I never knew a man who lived on the bosom of God as he did. I never expect to see his like; I never knew his like; he has no successor. When God made him, he broke the mould. As I look upon this life which I have studied intensely for years and from the inner circle of friendship, there seems to be in it a strangely rounded symmetry. He was so heavenly in character. Did you ever see such a countenance as his was? When I sat here on the platform at his late anniversary, and looked at him, I went away from the place with just one verse of Scripture prominent in my mind, which has remained so ever since: 'And all that sat in the council, looking steadfastly on him, saw his face as it had been the face of an angel.' He was a ripe fruit, and the Husbandman simply bent down and plucked it at its ripeness; he wanted a closer taste of it at his own banquet board. You could not expect to keep him longer, for the light on his brow was the light of anticipated transfiguration. But then his lifework, like his character, was singularly complete. Just look at the twenty-five years of work in this church! Think of the manliness and the boldness of his testimony to the whole rounded gospel. Look at the way in which he administered this church, which by the grace of God he led by a gradual process into such illumination as to the mind of God and such elimination of worldly elements that it was a fitting place for the Holy Ghost to preside; and the Holy Ghost did preside here as I venture to say he presides in, perhaps, no other one church in the United States. That church is itself a living epistle. . . .

"There is something beautiful to me in God's taking him away right in his prime, in the fullness of his beauty; for we remember men as they make their last impress upon us. We shall always remember Adoniram Judson Gordon as the full-grown man in his prime of intellect, in his prime of Christian achievement, in the midst of the glory of the work that has grown to this point and now never could decline under his hand, for his hand is no more upon it. Is not that better than for him to have grown old, to have decayed in intellectual power, to have declined in social influence, to have dimmed the majesty of his imperial scepter?

" He will be remembered as the full-statured man, whose power was full-orbed and whose sunset was without a cloud. He is forever beyond the possibility of marring his own life-work even by imprudence or incaution, and no one else can impair its symmetry. When his character and career reached their nearest approximation to the ideal, God suddenly crystallized the vision into permanence, and so it will forever stand for men to contemplate and imitate."

On a warm day in the following spring, when the frost had left the ground and the trees stood clothed in living green, the casket was taken from the vault and laid in its final resting-place in Forest Hill Cemetery. It had been the first impulse of the dead man's friends to put him in the uplands of his old home, where his grave should face the solemn arc of snow-tipped mountains which circle half the horizon. " A man's birthplace may well be his burial-place," said Joseph Cook, when he heard of it, " but I think his battle-field may better be. For one, I wish we might have the privilege of often standing at the tomb of this warrior. I could have wished that he might have remained with us here at the edge of the great deep."

The suggestion was pressed by others. It was recalled how eagerly Gordon himself had sought out the graves of Eliot, of Brainerd, of Edwards, and how much inspiration their simple headstones had been to him. In the hope, therefore, that in days to come his memory might quicken those who should stand above his grave, he was buried hard by the city where his lifework was wrought out. Over him was placed a massive boulder with this inscription:

PASTOR A. J. GORDON

1836–1895

"UNTIL HE COME"

Not to him had it been given to be "caught up to meet the Lord in the air," as he had hoped and prayed. Rather will it be his to return with the Lord and with those tarrying within the veil, when the trump of the archangel shall enswathe the whole earth. To this return, to "the glorious appearing of the great God and of our Saviour Jesus Christ," his grave alone among the thousands in the great cemetery bears written and explicit testimony.

TITLES in THIS SERIES

geles, 1925), *AROUND THE WORLD BY FAITH, WITH SIX WEEKS IN THE HOLY LAND* (Los Angeles, n. d.), *TWO YEARS MISSION WORK IN EUROPE JUST BEFORE THE WORLD WAR, 1912-14* (Los Angeles, [1926])

6. Boardman, W. E., *THE HIGHER CHRISTIAN LIFE* (Boston, 1858)

7. Girvin, E. A., *PHINEAS F. BRESEE: A PRINCE IN ISRAEL* (Kansas City, Mo., [1916])

8. Brooks, John P., *THE DIVINE CHURCH* (Columbia, Mo., 1891)

9. RUSSELL KELSO CARTER ON "FAITH HEALING." R. Kelso Carter, *THE ATONEMENT FOR SIN AND SICKNESS* (Boston, 1884) *"FAITH HEALING" REVIEWED AFTER TWENTY YEARS* (Boston, 1897)

10. Daniels, W. H., *DR. CULLIS AND HIS WORK* (Boston, [1885])

11. HOLINESS TRACTS DEFENDING THE MINISTRY OF WOMEN. Luther Lee, *"WOMAN'S RIGHT TO PREACH THE GOSPEL; A SERMON, AT THE ORDINATION OF REV. MISS ANTOINETTE L. BROWN, AT SOUTH BUTLER, WAYNE COUNTY, N. Y., SEPT. 15, 1853"* (Syracuse, 1853) *bound with* B. T. Roberts, *ORDAINING WOMEN* (Rochester, 1891) *bound with* Catherine (Mumford) Booth, *"FEMALE MINISTRY; OR, WOMAN'S RIGHT TO PREACH THE GOSPEL . . ."* (London, n. d.) *bound with* Fannie (McDowell) Hunter, *WOMEN PREACHERS* (Dallas, 1905)

12. LATE NINETEENTH CENTURY REVIVALIST TEACHINGS ON THE HOLY SPIRIT. D. L. Moody, *SECRET POWER OR THE SECRET OF SUCCESS IN CHRISTIAN LIFE AND*

WORK (New York, [1881]) *bound with* J. Wilbur Chapman, RECEIVED YE THE HOLY GHOST? (New York, [1894]) *bound with* R. A. Torrey, THE BAPTISM WITH THE HOLY SPIRIT (New York, 1895 & 1897)

13. SEVEN "JESUS ONLY" TRACTS. Andrew D. Urshan, THE DOCTRINE OF THE NEW BIRTH, OR, THE PERFECT WAY TO ETERNAL LIFE (Cochrane, Wis., 1921) *bound with* Andrew Urshan, THE ALMIGHTY GOD IN THE LORD JESUS CHRIST (Los Angeles, 1919) *bound with* Frank J. Ewart, THE REVELATION OF JESUS CHRIST (St. Louis, n. d.) *bound with* G. T. Haywood, THE BIRTH OF THE SPIRIT IN THE DAYS OF THE APOSTLES (Indianapolis, n. d.) DIVINE NAMES AND TITLES OF JEHOVAH (Indianapolis, n. d.) THE FINEST OF THE WHEAT (Indianapolis, n. d.) THE VICTIM OF THE FLAMING SWORD (Indianapolis, n. d.)

14. THREE EARLY PENTECOSTAL TRACTS. D. Wesley Myland, THE LATTER RAIN COVENANT AND PENTECOSTAL POWER (Chicago, 1910) *bound with* G. F. Taylor, THE SPIRIT AND THE BRIDE (n. p., [1907?]) *bound with* B. F. Laurence, THE APOSTOLIC FAITH RESTORED (St. Louis, 1916)

15. Fairchild, James H., OBERLIN: THE COLONY AND THE COLLEGE, *1833-1883* (Oberlin, 1883)

16. Figgis, John B., KESWICK FROM WITHIN (London, [1914])

17. Finney, Charles G., LECTURES TO PROFESSING CHRISTIANS (New York, 1837)

18. Fleisch, Paul, DIE MODERNE GEMEINSCHAFTS-BEWEGUNG IN DEUTSCHLAND (Leipzig, 1912)

19. SIX TRACTS BY W. B. GODBEY. *SPIRITUAL GIFTS AND GRACES* (Cincinnati, [1895]) *THE RETURN OF JESUS* (Cincinnati, [1899?]) *WORK OF THE HOLY SPIRIT* (Louisville, [1902]) *CHURCH—BRIDE—KINGDOM* (Cincinnati, [1905]) *DIVINE HEALING* (Greensboro, [1909]) *TONGUE MOVEMENT, SATANIC* (Zarephath, N. J., 1918)

20. Gordon, Earnest B., *ADONIRAM JUDSON GORDON* (New York, [1896])

21. Hills, A. M., *HOLINESS AND POWER FOR THE CHURCH AND THE MINISTRY* (Cincinnati, [1897])

22. Horner, Ralph C., *FROM THE ALTAR TO THE UPPER ROOM* (Toronto, [1891])

23. McDonald, William and John E. Searles, *THE LIFE OF REV. JOHN S. INSKIP* (Boston, [1885])

24. LaBerge, Agnes N. O., *WHAT GOD HATH WROUGHT* (Chicago, n. d.)

25. Lee, Luther, *AUTOBIOGRAPHY OF THE REV. LUTHER LEE* (New York, 1882)

26. McLean, A. and J. W. Easton, *PENUEL; OR, FACE TO FACE WITH GOD* (New York, 1869)

27. McPherson, Aimee Semple, *THIS IS THAT: PERSONAL EXPERIENCES SERMONS AND WRITINGS* (Los Angeles, [1919])

28. Mahan, Asa, *OUT OF DARKNESS INTO LIGHT* (London, 1877)

29. THE LIFE AND TEACHING OF CARRIE JUDD MONTGOMERY Carrie Judd Montgomery, *"UNDER HIS WINGS": THE STORY OF MY LIFE* (Oakland,

[1936]) Carrie F. Judd, *THE PRAYER OF FAITH* (New York, 1880)

30. THE DEVOTIONAL WRITINGS OF PHOEBE PALMER
Phoebe Palmer, *THE WAY OF HOLINESS* (52nd ed., New York, 1867) *FAITH AND ITS EFFECTS* (27th ed., New York, n. d., orig. pub. 1854)

31. Wheatley, Richard, *THE LIFE AND LETTERS OF MRS. PHOEBE PALMER* (New York, 1881)

32. Palmer, Phoebe, ed., *PIONEER EXPERIENCES* (New York, 1868)

33. Palmer, Phoebe, *THE PROMISE OF THE FATHER* (Boston, 1859)

34. Pardington, G. P., *TWENTY-FIVE WONDERFUL YEARS, 1889-1914: A POPULAR SKETCH OF THE CHRISTIAN AND MISSIONARY ALLIANCE* (New York, [1914])

35. Parham, Sarah E., *THE LIFE OF CHARLES F. PARHAM, FOUNDER OF THE APOSTOLIC FAITH MOVEMENT* (Joplin, [1930])

36. THE SERMONS OF CHARLES F. PARHAM. Charles F. Parham, *A VOICE CRYING IN THE WILDERNESS* (4th ed., Baxter Springs, Kan., 1944, orig. pub. 1902) *THE EVERLASTING GOSPEL* (n.p., n.d., orig. pub. 1911)

37. Pierson, Arthur Tappan, *FORWARD MOVEMENTS OF THE LAST HALF CENTURY* (New York, 1905)

38. *PROCEEDINGS OF HOLINESS CONFERENCES, HELD AT CINCINNATI, NOVEMBER 26TH, 1877, AND AT NEW YORK, DECEMBER 17TH, 1877* (Philadelphia, 1878)

39. *RECORD OF THE CONVENTION FOR THE PROMOTION OF*

SCRIPTURAL HOLINESS HELD AT BRIGHTON, MAY 29TH, TO JUNE 7TH, 1875 (Brighton, [1896?])

40. Rees, Seth Cook, *MIRACLES IN THE SLUMS* (Chicago, [1905?])

41. Roberts, B. T., *WHY ANOTHER SECT* (Rochester, 1879)

42. Shaw, S. B., ed., *ECHOES OF THE GENERAL HOLINESS ASSEMBLY* (Chicago, [1901])

43. THE DEVOTIONAL WRITINGS OF ROBERT PEARSALL SMITH AND HANNAH WHITALL SMITH. [R]obert [P]earsall [S]mith, *HOLINESS THROUGH FAITH: LIGHT ON THE WAY OF HOLINESS* (New York, [1870]) [H]annah [W]hitall [S]mith, *THE CHRISTIAN'S SECRET OF A HAPPY LIFE,* (Boston and Chicago, [1885])

44. [S]mith, [H]annah [W]hitall, *THE UNSELFISHNESS OF GOD AND HOW I DISCOVERED IT* (New York, [1903])

45. Steele, Daniel, *A SUBSTITUTE FOR HOLINESS; OR, ANTINOMIANISM REVIVED* (Chicago and Boston, [1899])

46. Tomlinson, A. J., *THE LAST GREAT CONFLICT* (Cleveland, 1913)

47. Upham, Thomas C., *THE LIFE OF FAITH* (Boston, 1845)

48. Washburn, Josephine M., *HISTORY AND REMINISCENCES OF THE HOLINESS CHURCH WORK IN SOUTHERN CALIFORNIA AND ARIZONA* (South Pasadena, [1912?])